THE 365

MOST IMPORTANT

BIBLE PASSAGES

FOR MOTHERS

THE 365
MOST IMPORTANT
BIBLE PASSAGES
FOR MOTHERS

*Daily Readings and Meditations
on Experiencing
the Lifelong Blessing of Being a Mom*

Faith
Words

FaithWords
Hachette Book Group
237 Park Avenue
New York, NY 10017

Visit our website at www.faithwords.com.

Printed in the United States of America

First Edition: April 2012

10 9 8 7 6 5 4 3 2 1

FaithWords is a division of Hachette Book Group, Inc.
The FaithWords name and logo are trademarks of Hachette Book Group, Inc.

Library of Congress Cataloging-in-Publication Data

ISBN 978-0-446-57501-0

Editor: Diane Stortz

Manuscript: Debbie Goodwin, Debbie Webb, and Vicki J. Kuyper in association with Snapdragon Group℠, Tulsa, OK; Sheila Cornea

Design: Whisner Design Group

The LORD gives wisdom,
and from his mouth
come knowledge
and understanding.

—Proverbs 2:6 NIV

Do not worry about anything, but pray and ask God
for everything you need, always giving thanks.
And God's peace, which is so great we
cannot understand it, will keep your
hearts and minds in Christ Jesus.

—Philippians 4:6–7 NCV

Contents

CONTENTS, CONTINUED

CONTENTS, CONTINUED

CONTENTS, CONTINUED

Faith

Contents, continued

Contents, continued

Change

CONTENTS, CONTINUED

Hope & Peace

CONTENTS, CONTINUED

Influence & Love

CONTENTS, CONTINUED

Commit yourselves wholeheartedly to these commands that I am giving you today. Repeat them again and again to your children. Talk about them when you are at home and when you are on the road, when you are going to bed and when you are getting up.

—Deuteronomy 6:6–7 NLT

INTRODUCTION

Motherhood is the greatest privilege and most sobering responsibility of any woman. Mothers come in many varieties: adoptive mothers, birth mothers, stepmothers, foster mothers, grandmothers, mothers-in-law, and mothers-of-influence. All women were birthed by only one mother but may have several mothers whom they grow to cherish. Many women have never given birth to children naturally, yet their motherly influence has changed the lives and legacies of the next generation.

A woman's choice to embrace, nurture, mentor, and teach the children God has placed in her path is, in fact, motherhood. The age of the child, the maturity of the mother, and the nature of the relationship are less important than the love between them. The responsibility and privilege of motherhood can be summed up in the most important commandments that were given: love God first with all your heart; then love others around you as you also love yourself.

Watch what God does, and then you do it, like children who learn proper behavior from their parents. Mostly what God does is love you. Keep company with him and learn a life of love. Observe how Christ loved us. His love was not cautious but extravagant. He didn't love in order to get something from us but to give everything of himself to us. Love like that.

Ephesians 5:1–2 MSG

Purpose

Is it possible that you have a purpose beyond being a spectacular mom? So much is said about discovering your purpose, but finding yourself can be disillusioning when you spend your day changing diapers or chauffeuring children. Don't confuse your daily, maybe even mundane, routine with your purpose! God tells you very plainly what he requires of you. Your purpose should be others centered. "Others" begins with your family but doesn't stop there. Figure out how you would most enjoy serving God and others, and you'll know your purpose!

O people, the LORD has told you what is good, and this is what he requires of you: to do what is right, to love mercy, and to walk humbly with your God.

Micah 6:8 NLT

PLAN A IS ALWAYS IN PLACE

God was kind and decided that Christ would choose us to be God's own adopted children. God was very kind to us because of the Son he dearly loves, and so we should praise God.

Christ sacrificed his life's blood to set us free, which means that our sins are now forgiven. Christ did this because God was so kind to us. God has great wisdom and understanding, and by what Christ has done, God has shown us his own mysterious ways. Then when the time is right, God will do all that he has planned, and Christ will bring together everything in heaven and on earth.

God always does what he plans, and that's why he appointed Christ to choose us. He did this so we Jews would bring honor to him and be the first ones to have hope because of him.

Ephesians 1:5–12 CEV

A treasure is hidden within the words of these verses. First of all, the concept that you have been adopted is comforting. God wanted to make a permanent investment in his relationship with you—no trial basis but immediate adoption. Then, the idea that God always has a plan and will always see that it is accomplished is certainly encouraging. If that isn't enough, you can be inspired to know that God is willing to show you his great mysteries.

Family is created in a variety of ways. You may have birthed your children naturally, adopted them, fostered them, or you may have welcomed them as a stepmother. No matter how your family was formed, it created an eternal connection among you. God appointed you as his surrogate here on earth. You have an awesome opportunity to make a lifelong impression on each child under your care. When you awaken your children each morning, remind yourself that God has chosen you to be mother to each of your children specifically. Remind them too that God placed them as important parts of your family to work together to fulfill his plan for one another.

It's about the Attitude

Show me your ways, O Lord, teach me your paths; guide me in your truth and teach me, for you are God my Savior, and my hope is in you all day long. Remember, O Lord, your great mercy and love, for they are from of old. Remember not the sins of my youth and my rebellious ways; according to your love remember me, for you are good, O Lord.

Good and upright is the Lord; therefore he instructs sinners in his ways. He guides the humble in what is right and teaches them his way. All the ways of the Lord are loving and faithful for those who keep the demands of his covenant.

Psalm 25:4–10 NIV

The psalmist is interested in how we fulfill our purpose, but the focus of the psalmist is more on how God wants us to conduct ourselves than on what he specifically wants us to accomplish. It is interesting that the how or "way" comes before the where or what of purpose in this Scripture, because as mothers we are often asking God what we should *do* about situations rather than how we should feel about them or react to them. When you ask God to show you his ways, expect him to show you not just a next step but a full understanding of his purpose.

The truth is that you can teach your children to travel along the right path and to do many good things, but it is more important for them to have the manner of God as they go about accomplishing good things on the right path. Just as you most likely teach your children about the importance of attitude, it is the same with you and God. If you allow God to teach you the *how* first, the *what* and *when* of your purpose will naturally follow.

THREE PILLARS OF PURPOSE

"Remember your journey from Acacia Grove to Gilgal, when I, the LORD, did everything I could to teach you about my faithfulness."

What can we bring to the LORD? What kind of offerings should we give him? Should we bow before God with offerings of yearling calves? Should we offer him thousands of rams and ten thousand rivers of olive oil? Should we sacrifice our firstborn children to pay for our sins?

No, O people, the LORD has told you what is good, and this is what he requires of you: to do what is right, to love mercy, and to walk humbly with your God.

Micah 6:5–8 NLT

Oh, if parenting could just be as simple as 1-2-3, right? Well, things that are simple are not always easy, but the prophet Micah shared a simple three-point strategy to help you fulfill your purpose as a mom and as an individual. God's requirements are simple: do right, love mercy, and walk humbly with him.

"Do right" refers to God's way of handling situations and relationships. "Love mercy" means that you eagerly offer restoration, whether someone has been wronged or is the one at fault. Finally, "walk humbly" simply means living with an attitude of reliance and trust in God.

These simple strategies aren't always easy. Even though you love your children unconditionally, their choices may lead to difficult consequences. A mother never expects to deal with an unexpected teen pregnancy or criminal misbehavior, but real challenges occur in good families. There are times when you as a mother must extend mercy because it is the godly reaction to have; then you must rely on God to provide a positive outcome to the situation.

God wants us to relate to him and to people as Jesus did! Not always easy, but as simple as 1-2-3.

PRIMARY PURPOSE

"Long after Abraham, Isaac, and Jacob had died, God said, 'I am the God of Abraham, the God of Isaac, and the God of Jacob.' So he is the God of the living, not the dead."

When the crowds heard [Jesus], they were astounded at his teaching.

But when the Pharisees heard that he had silenced the Sadducees with his reply, they met together to question him again. One of them, an expert in religious law, tried to trap him with this question: "Teacher, which is the most important commandment in the law of Moses?"

Jesus replied, "'You must love the LORD your God with all your heart, all your soul, and all your mind.' This is the first and greatest commandment. A second is equally important: 'Love your neighbor as yourself.' The entire law and all the demands of the prophets are based on these two commandments."

Matthew 22:31–40 NLT

Isn't it great that the most important rule in life is simply love? Everything in life comes down to loving God and loving people. This teaching of Jesus even tells us how to love God—with our whole selves—and how to love people—with the same concern we have for ourselves.

These two commandments are great cornerstones for your family's house rules. Everything that you are trying to teach your children likely falls into the category of loving God or loving others. It doesn't matter how old your children are; these rules will work. For younger children, the family rule might be to use kind words toward others; for teens the expectation might be to display a respectful attitude to parents as instructed by God in the Ten Commandments.

Discuss your house rules with your family in comparison to these two principles of love. Read the Bible together and make revisions to your rules if needed. Your children may even want to add some rules of their own. What better way to disciple your children than to have everything in your home center around the greatest of all the commandments?

By Grace, through Faith, for Good Works

Because of his great love for us, God, who is rich in mercy, made us alive with Christ even when we were dead in transgressions—it is by grace you have been saved. And God raised us up with Christ and seated us with him in the heavenly realms in Christ Jesus, in order that in the coming ages he might show the incomparable riches of his grace, expressed in his kindness to us in Christ Jesus. For it is by grace you have been saved, through faith—and this not from yourselves, it is the gift of God—not by works, so that no one can boast. For we are God's workmanship, created in Christ Jesus to do good works, which God prepared in advance for us to do.

Ephesians 2:4–10 NIV

Paul wanted the Ephesian Christians to understand that their old way of life needed to give way to a lifestyle characterized by doing good. But they also needed to grasp that good works would not save them—only God's grace, his forgiving love, could do that. For busy moms, the truth that we are saved by grace through faith is such a comfort. We don't have to try to earn God's approval. Whether you are a stay-at-home mom or have a job outside the home, every mom is a working mom. Sometimes the days seem full of work, work, and more work. The lure of accomplishment can be tempting at times.

God positioned you as a mom and set his plan in place ahead of you. He has great things for you to accomplish. The work itself is not the goal but provides opportunities for you to serve others. Don't stress over the undone things in your life. God made advance preparations to enable you to accomplish all that he needs from you. Just focus on returning love to him in your daily routine as a hardworking mom.

PICK ME, PICK ME!

I have told you this so that my joy may be in you and that your joy may be complete. My command is this: Love each other as I have loved you. Greater love has no one than this, that he lay down his life for his friends. You are my friends if you do what I command. I no longer call you servants, because a servant does not know his master's business. Instead, I have called you friends, for everything that I learned from my Father I have made known to you. You did not choose me, but I chose you and appointed you to go and bear fruit—fruit that will last. Then the Father will give you whatever you ask in my name. This is my command: Love each other.

John 15:11–17 NIV

One of the biggest heartbreaks for children is not being the one picked. You might even have flashbacks to your own childhood as your youngster tearfully recites how he was the last one chosen for a team at recess, or how all of the seats were saved for someone else at lunch, or that she wasn't invited to a birthday party. And the flattery of being one picked—perhaps for girls' night out or a day at the mall—can be as exciting for us moms as it is for our children.

How much more thrilling it is to realize, and to help your child realize, that even if you aren't chosen by people, you have been chosen by God! He himself picked you as his friend and as his representative of love to others who might be feeling sad or lonely too.

If you have a child who is feeling left out, talk to your child's teacher to determine if there might be some social skills that you can practice. Your child may be very outgoing at home but shy at school. It might be good to partner with your child's teacher for help.

TIME TO GET BUSY

It will happen suddenly, quicker than the blink of an eye. At the sound of the last trumpet the dead will be raised. We will all be changed, so that we will never die again. Our dead and decaying bodies will be changed into bodies that won't die or decay. The bodies we now have are weak and can die. But they will be changed into bodies that are eternal. Then the Scriptures will come true, "Death has lost the battle! Where is its victory? Where is its sting?"

Sin is what gives death its sting, and the Law is the power behind sin. But thank God for letting our Lord Jesus Christ give us the victory!

My dear friends, stand firm and don't be shaken. Always keep busy working for the Lord. You know that everything you do for him is worthwhile.

1 Corinthians 15:52–58 CEV

A popular country song says, "Everybody wants to go to heaven, but nobody wants to go now." As a believer you most assuredly want to be in the presence of Jesus. But as a mother you understand your purpose and importance in raising your children to be able to make the same decision in their lives. Although most of us like to think about heaven, few of us really want to ponder death, especially our own. But this passage, even though focused on this undesirable subject, is still encouraging. It assures us that we have an appointed time to live and fulfill our purpose. We are to keep at our purpose until it is fulfilled.

The time is now to take advantage of every opportunity possible. Watch for, arrange, and grasp the teachable moments. Teach math in the grocery store. Rehearse Bible songs with your toddlers during car rides. Discuss modesty or dating as you browse magazines with your teens. Everyday situations offer occasions to teach everything from the alphabet to the Ten Commandments to relationships to self-respect. Moms, you have so much to teach!

MUTUAL RESPONSIBILITY

Be filled with the Spirit by reciting psalms, hymns, and spiritual songs for your own good. Sing and make music to the Lord with your hearts. Always thank God the Father for everything in the name of our Lord Jesus Christ.

Place yourselves under each other's authority out of respect for Christ.

Wives, place yourselves under your husbands' authority as you have placed yourselves under the Lord's authority. The husband is the head of his wife as Christ is the head of the church. It is his body, and he is its Savior. As the church is under Christ's authority, so wives are under their husbands' authority in everything.

Husbands, love your wives as Christ loved the church and gave his life for it. He did this to make the church holy by cleansing it, washing it using water along with spoken words.

Ephesians 5:18–26
GOD'S WORD

Mothers often find themselves playing the lead role in many areas of their lives: career, social networks, running the household, parenting. Accepting the supporting role in marriage, then, can require finesse. Do you have to give up your individuality to be a godly wife? No. Understanding the meaning of the Greek word translated as *authority* allows moms to fully embrace the power within it.

Authority in this case refers to a wife cooperating with or assuming responsibility with her husband—voluntarily. A wife positions herself by choice in this supporting role of cooperation; it is not forced upon her. Think of volunteer soldiers in a military troop following their commanding officer by taking their place in formation.

Balancing being a submissive wife with being an in-charge mom can be challenging at times. It can be especially interesting if you and your husband have different ideas about discipline. But when all in the family voluntarily align themselves in proper formation, the mutual respect and responsibility actually create an interdependence that allows everyone to flourish. Following the advice of the apostle Paul in this important passage is an essential way for moms to fulfill their purpose.

UNIQUELY YOU

God's strong foundation continues to stand. These words are written on the seal: "The Lord knows those who belong to him," and "Everyone who wants to belong to the Lord must stop doing wrong."

In a large house there are not only things made of gold and silver, but also things made of wood and clay. Some things are used for special purposes, and others are made for ordinary jobs. All who make themselves clean from evil will be used for special purposes. They will be made holy, useful to the Master, ready to do any good work.

But run away from the evil desires of youth. Try hard to live right and to have faith, love, and peace, together with those who trust in the Lord from pure hearts.

2 Timothy 2:19–22 NCV

There is no such thing as being "just a mom." Being a mom is one of the most important assignments in life. Even if you feel there is nothing particularly special about your ability to be a mom, God picked *you* to raise the children he has given you. Every mother has been given the special qualities that her children will need to be nurtured and taught in the way that is best for them.

Think about how many different "vessels" are available for use in your kitchen. How specifically each one fills its purpose! Look at spoons, for example. There are sugar spoons, grapefruit spoons, slotted spoons, ladling spoons, serving spoons—the list goes on. All are spoons, but each one has its own distinction, and purpose.

God assigned your personality and skills specifically to meet the needs of your family. You have your own attributes that set you apart from all of the other mothers in the world. God gives each mom the unique potential to accomplish whatever he has established for her to do. As long as you focus on pursuing God's purposes for you as a parent, you'll fulfill your potential.

Rise Up!

Mordecai told [the messenger] to reply to Esther, "Don't think that you will escape the fate of all the Jews because you are in the king's palace. If you keep silent at this time, liberation and deliverance will come to the Jewish people from another place, but you and your father's house will be destroyed. Who knows, perhaps you have come to the kingdom for such a time as this."

Esther sent this reply to Mordecai: "Go and assemble all the Jews who can be found in Susa and fast for me. Don't eat or drink for three days, night and day. I and my female servants will also fast in the same way. After that, I will go to the king even if it is against the law. If I perish, I perish."

Esther 4:13–16 HCSB

Thankfully, most moms today are not faced with life-or-death situations when they are trying to defend their families. But we do face situations with teachers, coaches, and other parents that require confrontation.

Esther's husband, the king of Persia, was unaware of Esther's Jewish heritage. Influenced by a court official angry at Esther's cousin Mordecai, the king issued a proclamation allowing his people to destroy the Jews in Persia on an upcoming specified day. Persian law forbade Queen Esther to present herself to the king without an invitation, and he had not called for her for an entire month.

Esther's bold resolution to confront the king with her request sprung out of her obligation and love for her people and her sense that this mission was from God. But she didn't go to the king unarmed. Esther knew that for such a bold move, she needed support from other believers.

The next time you have to face another mom, a teacher, or a coach on behalf of your child, prepare yourself fully first. Then rise up with boldness and go armed with prayer support for wisdom and favor.

PERSONAL TUTORING

God had special plans for me and set me apart for his work even before I was born. He called me through his grace and showed his son to me so that I might tell the Good News about him to those who are not Jewish. When God called me, I did not get advice or help from any person. I did not go to Jerusalem to see those who were apostles before I was. But, without waiting, I went away to Arabia and later went back to Damascus.

After three years I went to Jerusalem to meet Peter and stayed with him for fifteen days. I met no other apostles, except James, the brother of the Lord. God knows that these things I write are not lies. Later, I went to the areas of Syria and Cilicia.

Galatians 1:15–21 NCV

A mommy manual with definitive answers to every question moms ask would be a best seller. However, there isn't one. So what is a mother to do with all of those questions? It begins the first week home with a new baby—Why is she crying in the middle of the night? How can I get some rest? It doesn't end when children grow older— How can I help her find a job? Should I help him out financially?

After Paul had a miraculous transformation in his life when he encountered God, he most likely had many questions too. Throughout his life he utilized many sources of help. He relied on the Scriptures, he traveled with other believers like Barnabas, and as he noted in this passage, he spent time in prayer with God.

When you are inundated with questions as a mom, there are many resources that can help you, including friends, your own mother, your pediatrician, and great books by experts. But don't forget the most essential source of wisdom for a mother—God. Go straight to him daily for direction and answers to all your questions as a mom.

Straighten Up!

Don't all parents correct their children? God corrects all of his children, and if he doesn't correct you, then you don't really belong to him. Our earthly fathers correct us, and we still respect them. Isn't it even better to be given true life by letting our spiritual Father correct us?

Our human fathers correct us for a short time, and they do it as they think best. But God corrects us for our own good, because he wants us to be holy, as he is. It is never fun to be corrected. In fact, at the time it is always painful. But if we learn to obey by being corrected, we will do right and live at peace.

Now stand up straight! Stop your knees from shaking and walk a straight path. Then lame people will be healed, instead of getting worse.

Hebrews 12:7–13 CEV

Creative moms use all kinds of disciplinary tactics. You may have tried redirecting, encouraging, think time, lost privileges, and of course time-out. Let's be honest—most of us have even tried the less effective coaxing, begging, and bribing too. But whatever our strategy, the goal is the same: a change from undesirable to desirable behavior.

Have you ever wondered if God has *you* in time-out? When things seemingly are not going the way that he (or you) designed, you might be quick to think that you are not fulfilling your responsibilities to your family well. Oftentimes, though, God might just be allowing you time for reconsideration, restoration, or maybe even repentance.

Even though we are moms, we also are children—God's children—and subject to his correction. So if you feel like you are in a time-out, use your time wisely. Straighten up your thoughts and ways. We don't need to be afraid of God's discipline. Like the wise Father that he is, God wants to refine you and make you more like Jesus, more useful to others and more able to be the mother he created you to be.

You've Graduated—So Get to Work

I want you woven into a tapestry of love, in touch with everything there is to know of God. Then you will have minds confident and at rest, focused on Christ, God's great mystery. All the richest treasures of wisdom and knowledge are embedded in that mystery and nowhere else. And we've been shown the mystery! I'm telling you this because I don't want anyone leading you off on some wild-goose chase, after other so-called mysteries, or "the Secret." . . .

My counsel for you is simple and straightforward: Just go ahead with what you've been given. You received Christ Jesus, the Master; now *live* him. You're deeply rooted in him. You're well constructed upon him. You know your way around the faith. Now do what you've been taught. School's out; quit studying the subject and start *living* it! And let your living spill over into thanksgiving.

Colossians 2:2–4, 6–7 MSG

Feeling like an expert as a mom doesn't happen overnight. In fact, the feeling can be quite elusive to both new and experienced moms. But you don't have to have a degree in psychology or theology to have wisdom and expertise to fulfill your purpose as a mother.

The most vital information that a mom can teach her children are those things with an eternal impact. Stories from the Bible, the mysteries of heaven and earth, and the secret things of God are all treasures that a mother can discover along with her children. As God teaches you, you then can teach your children his virtues.

Consider beginning a thematic Bible study with your children to discover the treasures of Scripture together. If your son likes dinosaurs, study Creation. If your daughter is into princesses, learn about Queen Esther. Maybe your teen would rather investigate love or friendship; there are hidden treasures in store for you there too. Children cherish time with mom! Why not combine that time with biblical treasure hunting too? You will see the impact quickly, and the results can last a lifetime.

Speak Up

This is a trustworthy saying that deserves full acceptance (and for this we labor and strive), that we have put our hope in the living God, who is the Savior of all men, and especially of those who believe.

Command and teach these things. Don't let anyone look down on you because you are young, but set an example for the believers in speech, in life, in love, in faith and in purity. Until I come, devote yourself to the public reading of Scripture, to preaching and to teaching. Do not neglect your gift, which was given you through a prophetic message when the body of elders laid their hands on you.

Be diligent in these matters; give yourself wholly to them, so that everyone may see your progress. Watch your life and doctrine closely. Persevere in them, because if you do, you will save both yourself and your hearers.

1 Timothy 4:9–16 NIV

No matter how old we get, there always seems to be someone wiser and more mature than us. It can be intimidating to think of teaching someone twice your age who has more life experience. But that shouldn't stop you—you might have insight or knowledge that she's been searching for.

Evidently, people were already watching and listening to Timothy, a young minister. But Timothy must have been a little reticent in sharing his knowledge and gifts to prompt the encouraging words in this passage. The apostle Paul, being more experienced, recognized that youth doesn't disqualify anyone from service.

Don't let your age or inexperience stop you. Think about what you can do to make another mom's daily life easier. You might be able to teach another mother something as simple as handling coupons or household budgets to make her family life more enjoyable. Or you might be just the right person to offer fresh new ideas to the older, more experienced church nursery director. Pursue your purpose and use your gifts that can help others. You never know; they might be praying and waiting for your help or expertise.

BE READY FOR THE REQUEST

I took up the wine and gave it to the king. Now I had not been sad in his presence. So the king said to me, "Why is your face sad though you are not sick? This is nothing but sadness of heart." Then I was very much afraid. I said to the king, "Let the king live forever. Why should my face not be sad when the city, the place of my fathers' tombs, lies desolate and its gates have been consumed by fire?" Then the king said to me, "What would you request?" So I prayed to the God of heaven. I said to the king, "If it please the king, and if your servant has found favor before you, send me to Judah, to the city of my fathers' tombs, that I may rebuild it."

Nehemiah 2:1–5 NASB

Nehemiah had the heart to help the Jewish people advance the rebuilding of their city wall after they had returned from Babylonian captivity. Nehemiah was certainly no weak man, and he was not afraid to be in the king's presence, as that was part of his daily job as the king's cupbearer. But when the king asked Nehemiah a provoking question, his immediate reaction was fear. Yet Nehemiah did not respond impulsively to the king. He had already spent time in prayer about the need of his people. But as he considered his response to the king, he prayed once more before giving his answer. He knew that this opportunity was to fulfill God's purpose.

We mothers tend to want to fix situations immediately for our children, no matter what their age. When you see that your child has a need, follow Nehemiah's example. Wait. Pray. Then react to the need after you have instruction from God. Waiting is important because God might show you a better way of handling the situation than what you would do on your own. He might even show your child how to resolve the matter for himself.

It's Up to Him

As soon as I pray, you answer me; you encourage me by giving me strength.

Every king in all the earth will thank you, Lord, for all of them will hear your words. Yes, they will sing about the Lord's ways, for the glory of the Lord is very great. Though the Lord is great, he cares for the humble, but he keeps his distance from the proud.

Though I am surrounded by troubles, you will protect me from the anger of my enemies. You reach out your hand, and the power of your right hand saves me. The Lord will work out his plans for my life—for your faithful love, O Lord, endures forever.

Psalm 138:3–8 NLT

David encouraged himself with this prayerful psalm. Here he reminded himself, even as he spoke to God, of God's authority and faithfulness in his life. He understood that his life had a plan and a planner. God, the faithful planner of David's life, is your life planner also. He has a purpose in everything he creates or allows in your life.

Sometimes purpose is exposed through the challenging seasons of motherhood. Purpose arises in simple times when you find yourself once again consoling a crying child in the middle of the night, and your eagerness to comfort outweighs your desperate need for a good night's sleep. You may also find purpose in more solitary times like entering your empty nest to find yourself with an unfamiliar fear of insignificance, yet with a yearning to remain an influence in the lives of others in a way that matters.

Look back at God's faithfulness in your life during other times of difficulty. You can see his direction and guidance. He will accomplish his plan for you. Look to God for strength and purpose in every experience, whether it is one of ease or hardship.

Unfathomable Ways

I don't think the way you think. The way you work isn't the way I work. For as the sky soars high above earth, so the way I work surpasses the way you work, and the way I think is beyond the way you think. Just as rain and snow descend from the skies and don't go back until they've watered the earth, doing their work of making things grow and blossom, producing seed for farmers and food for the hungry, so will the words that come out of my mouth not come back empty-handed. They'll do the work I sent them to do, they'll complete the assignment I gave them.

So you'll go out in joy, you'll be led into a whole and complete life.

Isaiah 55:8–12 MSG

You never thought that you would resort to using your parents' phrase "Because I said so," did you! But one day it seems to escape from your mouth too. Then you realize that some things a mother just cannot explain to a child. Even if there are very good reasons for your answer, sometimes your child doesn't have the requisite experience or maturity to understand it.

Consider how many times God must have to say, "Because I said so" to us too when we inundate him with the whys of life. We just cannot understand his reasons or ways sometimes. It is hard to understand why he would say no to what seems like a godly request or make us wait for answers in the midst of a challenge. But just as we know what is best for our children, he knows what is best for us.

We try to encourage our children by saying, "Trust me." God asks us to do the same with him. We must trust that he will accomplish his purpose in and through us. Sometimes we might not understand the method, but we can trust his motive.

PERSONAL EFFECTS

[Jesus said,] "The hour has come that the Son of Man should be glorified. Most assuredly, I say to you, unless a grain of wheat falls into the ground and dies, it remains alone; but if it dies, it produces much grain. He who loves his life will lose it, and he who hates his life in this world will keep it for eternal life. If anyone serves Me, let him follow Me; and where I am, there My servant will be also. If anyone serves Me, him My Father will honor.

"Now My soul is troubled, and what shall I say? 'Father, save Me from this hour'? But for this purpose I came to this hour. Father, glorify Your name."

Then a voice came from heaven, saying, "I have both glorified it and will glorify it again."

John 12:23–28 NKJV

In this passage John gives us some of Jesus' words during his last week on earth, between the triumphal parade into Jerusalem and his death on the cross. Jesus knew how his mission would end, but he did not let that distract him from his purpose.

As mothers we tend to have life planned out. You probably have definite ideas about what your children's life plans should be. You observe their temperaments, gifts, and interests, and your mission includes strategies to help them develop their strengths and talents. But the journey of life often offers bumps and unexpected curves. Sometimes our circumstances appear to be contrary to our plans. But looks can be deceiving.

Don't let today's situation detour you. Even if your soul is troubled and you see impending pain or challenge coming your way, embrace your mission. Living a purposeful life will influence your children to do the same. You may have many goals and passions as a mom. But remember that when you fulfill your mission of teaching your children to glorify God in their own lives, you will have accomplished the most important purpose assigned to you.

CUSTOM-CRAFTED

Are you going to object, "So how can God blame us for anything since he's in charge of everything? If the big decisions are already made, what say do we have in it?"

Who in the world do you think you are to second-guess God? Do you for one moment suppose any of us knows enough to call God into question? Clay doesn't talk back to the fingers that mold it, saying, "Why did you shape me like this?" Isn't it obvious that a potter has a perfect right to shape one lump of clay into a vase for holding flowers and another into a pot for cooking beans? If God needs one style of pottery especially designed to show his angry displeasure and another style carefully crafted to show his glorious goodness, isn't that all right?

Romans 9:19–23 MSG

Paul addressed the remarks in this passage to Jewish Christians who weren't sure that God should have extended his saving love to anyone but the Jews. Like those Jewish believers, we moms tend to compare ourselves to other mothers to mark our own journey toward success. But we must be careful not to allow those comparisons to create envy in us. The illustration of the potter and clay in this passage makes envy plain for us to see.

You might see another mom who is wonderful as the classroom mom at school, but you know that you just aren't crafty enough to do as well. Instead of envying her purpose, recognize and fulfill your own. You might be surprised to find that another mom would love to be a great soccer coach like you are.

You don't need to question how God created you. You can fully embrace your own purpose only when you have no desire for someone else's. Don't compare your purpose to someone else's and think that you are less important. God knows how many vases and how many pots he needs to accomplish his purpose on the earth.

TRY A LITTLE OF THIS AND THAT

Send your bread on the surface of the waters, for after many days you may find it. Give a portion to seven or even to eight, for you don't know what disaster may happen on earth. . . . One who watches the wind will not sow, and the one who looks at the clouds will not reap. Just as you don't know the path of the wind, or how bones [develop] in the womb of a pregnant woman, so you don't know the work of God who makes everything. In the morning sow your seed, and at evening do not let your hand rest, because you don't know which will succeed, whether one or the other, or if both of them will be equally good.

Ecclesiastes 11:1–2, 4–6 HCSB

The old cliché "Don't put all your eggs in one basket" provides a simple understanding of this passage, which was most likely written by King Solomon as he reflected on his life. Both the cliché and the king caution us that risk is a part of every investment.

All of our resources are tools for investment, whether our time, talent, or treasure. We can't depend on a sure return for our outlay of expertise or emotion in professional or personal relationships, but our investments retain their value nevertheless.

Don't let risk stop you from investing. Instead, we're encouraged to invest in more than one place at a time because we do not know what is going to be most profitable. For moms, this is a key concept. Your children and family are a great investment, worth your time and attention. But there are other areas that may return a great benefit from your investment too. Consider relationships and projects that reap a mutual benefit from your investment of time, talent, or treasure. Maybe it's time for you to get involved in a charity event, encourage a younger mom, or rekindle a friendship.

THERE IS A REASON

The Spirit of the Lord GOD is upon me, because the LORD has anointed me to bring good news to the afflicted; He has sent me to bind up the brokenhearted, to proclaim liberty to captives and freedom to prisoners; to proclaim the favorable year of the LORD and the day of vengeance of our God; to comfort all who mourn, to grant those who mourn in Zion, giving them a garland instead of ashes, the oil of gladness instead of mourning, the mantle of praise instead of a spirit of fainting so they will be called oaks of righteousness, the planting of the LORD, that He may be glorified.

Isaiah 61:1–3 NASB

In a synagogue in his hometown, Jesus read aloud a portion of this prophecy about his purpose and ended by stating that the prophecy was being fulfilled at that moment. One interesting point is the reaction of those who heard Jesus that day. They were all amazed because the young man they knew as Joseph's son was so gracious yet so bold in his reading. Jesus recognized his purpose and embraced it in a way that others noticed.

God has a purpose for all of the intellect, compassion, expertise, and zeal he has developed in you. He has also gifted your children with qualities that will help them accomplish their purposes. Imagine that your children could express their hopes and dreams for the future with great conviction and intention—what would they say? As you recognize your own purpose, nurture the dreams of your children and help them identify their purposes too. The Bible will help you. As you read it, ask God to reveal his purpose for creating you and each of your children. Then as you begin to recognize it, embrace it, so that you can impact others just as Jesus did.

FULLY EQUIPPED

Obey your leaders and submit to them, for they are keeping watch over your souls, as those who will have to give an account. Let them do this with joy and not with groaning, for that would be of no advantage to you.

Pray for us, for we are sure that we have a clear conscience, desiring to act honorably in all things. I urge you the more earnestly to do this in order that I may be restored to you the sooner.

Now may the God of peace who brought again from the dead our Lord Jesus, the great shepherd of the sheep, by the blood of the eternal covenant, equip you with everything good that you may do his will, working in us that which is pleasing in his sight, through Jesus Christ, to whom be glory forever and ever.

Hebrews 13:17–21 ESV

Mom's in charge—except when she's not. Being a leader and following a leader at the same time challenges moms who dictate their day according to its purpose. How does a woman lead her children, lead herself, and follow her own leaders simultaneously? These verses assure you of success when you do what they outline. Whether your leader is your husband, your boss, or your committee chair, your responsibility is to have a submissive spirit with a joyful attitude when you are in the role of follower.

Even if you are torn between roles, switching gears from time to time, this Scripture reminds you that you are equipped to handle each day's purpose. You can help prepare your children to accomplish their purpose whether they are the leader or a follower. Let your children take turns being the leader with their siblings. The older child will benefit from learning how to follow, and the younger will learn by leading for a change.

The same God who raised Jesus from the dead and remains the model Shepherd equips you with the power, passion, and purpose you need to lead—and to follow—every day.

PURPOSEFUL CONFRONTATIONS

The LORD said to Moses, "Get up early in the morning, confront Pharaoh and say to him, 'This is what the LORD, the God of the Hebrews, says: Let my people go, so that they may worship me, or this time I will send the full force of my plagues against you and against your officials and your people, so you may know that there is no one like me in all the earth. For by now I could have stretched out my hand and struck you and your people with a plague that would have wiped you off the earth. But I have raised you up for this very purpose, that I might show you my power and that my name might be proclaimed in all the earth.'"

Exodus 9:13–16 NIV

Most moms don't like confrontation. But when the stakes are high enough, we are more willing to confront matters of importance. For Moses, it was freedom for a nation. For you, it might be a sassy response from a teenager.

Some important aspects of confrontation are revealed in this Scripture. First of all, God provoked Moses, not anger. If you go back earlier in the story, at the very beginning of the confrontation, you find that Moses' initial response was, "If the Israelites will not listen to me, why would Pharaoh listen to me, since I speak with faltering lips?" (Exod. 6:12 NIV). His first thought was his own inadequacy, not revenge. Secondly, this confrontation was on behalf of others, not self-focused. Finally, part of the purpose of this confrontation was to help Pharaoh fulfill his own purpose in glorifying God.

The next time you want to confront a matter, take the Pharaoh test with these simple questions: Did God initiate this desire? Is this self-serving or others-serving? Will this help the other person better align with his or her purpose? The answers to the test will reveal to you whether you should proceed.

WHAT'S YOUR GRACE?

Of this gospel I was made a minister according to the gift of God's grace, which was given me by the working of his power. To me, though I am the very least of all the saints, this grace was given, to preach to the Gentiles the unsearchable riches of Christ, and to bring to light for everyone what is the plan of the mystery hidden for ages in God who created all things, so that through the church the manifold wisdom of God might now be made known to the rulers and authorities in the heavenly places. This was according to the eternal purpose that he has realized in Christ Jesus our Lord, in whom we have boldness and access with confidence through our faith in him. So I ask you not to lose heart over what I am suffering for you, which is your glory.

Ephesians 3:7–13 ESV

Imagine a box wrapped in gorgeous paper, gilded with a flowing ribbon and a card that says, "Just for you, because I love you." How long would you wait before tearing into the beautiful package to find the treasure inside?

Have you ever thought of your abilities as perfectly wrapped treasures? In this passage, Paul calls his ability to preach a gift of grace from God.

Maybe you are a great baker, singer, nurturer, or organizer. What are you going to do with that ability? Recognize how you use your gifts every day with your children. If you love to bake, encourage them to create new recipes with you and tap into their own love for math, art, or imagination in your baking. If you are a great organizer, put your gift to good use by teaching your children how to organize their study time and space.

Most moms have an emergency gift drawer for unexpected occasions. Often it contains "re-gifts" too—you know, the gifts given to you that someone else would love to enjoy. Think of your gifts from God as a grace re-gift that someone is waiting to receive from you.

There's Proof in the Plan

O Lord, I will honor and praise your name, for you are my God. You do such wonderful things! You planned them long ago, and now you have accomplished them. . . .

Therefore, strong nations will declare your glory; ruthless nations will fear you. But you are a tower of refuge to the poor, O Lord, a tower of refuge to the needy in distress. You are a refuge from the storm and a shelter from the heat. For the oppressive acts of ruthless people are like a storm beating against a wall, or like the relentless heat of the desert. But you silence the roar of foreign nations.

Isaiah 25:1, 3–5 NLT

Isaiah declares that God is an accomplisher of what he plans. He praises God not only because of the wonderful things he does, although he was thankful for them. Rather, in this passage Isaiah praises God because he is his own God—One whom he values and loves.

If you pause and give Isaiah's thoughts some reflection, you realize that his insight takes a little pressure off you as a mother. You are not responsible to accomplish everything on your own. Your first purpose is to love and glorify God. You are responsible for that primarily. He then enables you to accomplish everything else that he has planned for you.

You may still have to fold mountains of laundry each week, along with all of your other chores. But if the laundry stays in a pile a day longer than usual, it is OK! You will find your refuge and fulfill your purpose by loving him.

The wonderful things that you see happen in your everyday life are because of God's planning and purpose for you. You are accomplishing great things because he is the great accomplisher through you.

ONE MORE CHANCE

This is what the LORD says: When Babylon's 70 years are over, I will come to you. I will keep my promise to you and bring you back to this place. I know the plans that I have for you, declares the LORD. They are plans for peace and not disaster, plans to give you a future filled with hope. Then you will call to me. You will come and pray to me, and I will hear you. When you look for me, you will find me. When you wholeheartedly seek me, I will let you find me, declares the LORD. I will bring you back from captivity. I will gather you from all the nations and places where I've scattered you, declares the LORD. I will bring you back from the place where you are being held captive.

Jeremiah 29:10–14
GOD'S WORD

Did you notice that this popular Scripture doesn't begin, "To all of you who always follow my every instruction without fail"? No, this passage was directed to the Israelites in Babylon, exiled because of their disobedience to God time after time, even though God had warned and forgiven and rescued and provided numerous opportunities to begin again. Yet this passage tells us God still had great plans for his people.

Just as a child might not always follow all your instructions or meet all your expectations, there will most likely be times when you do not accomplish all that you hope for your family. Even if you miss reading your child his favorite book at bedtime because you worked overtime this week, God can still accomplish his plans for your family.

God is the giver of new beginnings. Don't beat yourself up if you haven't lived up to your own expectations for the mom you always wanted to be. Whatever your mistakes, just do what God asks: pray, request his help, mean it with your whole heart, and obey him. Then he will answer you with his promise of a very good future indeed.

STRONG-WILLED OR GOD-WILLED?

He who comes to Me shall never hunger, and he who believes in Me shall never thirst. But I said to you that you have seen Me and yet do not believe. All that the Father gives Me will come to Me, and the one who comes to Me I will by no means cast out. For I have come down from heaven, not to do My own will, but the will of Him who sent Me. This is the will of the Father who sent Me, that of all He has given Me I should lose nothing, but should raise it up at the last day. And this is the will of Him who sent Me, that everyone who sees the Son and believes in Him may have everlasting life; and I will raise him up at the last day.

John 6:35–40 NKJV

A determined young mom was facing off with her strong-willed, two-year-old son. He had refused to obey his mom's request, so she sent him to the time-out chair. The little boy was determined to keep getting out of that chair, but his mom was equally determined to put him there again. After she spent a full thirty minutes chasing her zooming toddler and placing him time and again in the chair, she finally prevailed. The little boy succumbed to the will of his mom.

Have you ever been that mom? Have you been like her strong-willed child, zooming around, determined to have your own way? As tenacious as the mom was to teach her son to do right, God is as caring for you to do his will.

Jesus did not always have an easy, enjoyable life. He was betrayed, misunderstood, and mocked. Yet he always surrendered to the will of his Father. Follow Jesus' example and yield to God's will. Think about what God as a caring Father wants you to enjoy in your life. You can trust that he always has the best in mind for you.

It's a Sure Thing

Can you compare me to anyone? No one is equal to me or like me. . . .

Remember what happened long ago. Remember that I am God, and there is no other God. I am God, and there is no one like me. From the beginning I told you what would happen in the end. A long time ago I told you things that have not yet happened. When I plan something, it happens. What I want to do, I will do. I am calling a man from the east to carry out my plan; he will come like a hawk from a country far away. I will make what I have said come true; I will do what I have planned.

Isaiah 46:5, 9–11 NCV

As much as we mothers try to be strong and committed to our purpose, there are times when doubt creeps in. When your teenager declares that she detests your rules because you will not allow her to wear the outfit she would like, you may feel like an unsuccessful mom. Though we may doubt our purpose or our ability to achieve it, we never need to doubt God. His declarations in this passage help us conquer double mindedness and doubt.

Every mom needs two things to sustain her during the challenging times and seasons of motherhood: a clear vision of God's plan for her life and the assurance that God will help her accomplish the purpose he planned for her. These are not simply nice ideas you can think about if you want them to offer you strength and support—you must grip them and rely on them until you see them being fulfilled.

Write down God's purpose in your life. What do you feel is your number one reason for existence? Write down a verse from this key passage too. When you start to doubt your purpose, read both of these together: your purpose and God's promises.

IT ALL COMES TOGETHER

In the same way the Spirit also helps our weakness; for we do not know how to pray as we should, but the Spirit Himself intercedes for us with groanings too deep for words; and He who searches the hearts knows what the mind of the Spirit is, because He intercedes for the saints according to the will of God.

And we know that God causes all things to work together for good to those who love God, to those who are called according to His purpose. For those whom He foreknew, He also predestined to become conformed to the image of His Son, so that He would be the firstborn among many brethren; and these whom He predestined, He also called; and these whom He called, He also justified; and these whom He justified, He also glorified.

Romans 8:26–30 NASB

We need encouragement that everything will work out all right only when circumstances say that it might not. Maybe that is the reason Romans 8:28 has long been a favorite of moms. When we take a closer look at the surrounding verses, this passage becomes even more heartening.

Many times you know exactly how to pray for your children and your family. The will of God in some situations is easily discernible. But difficult situations that are not so easily understood sometimes challenge you even to know how to pray; all possible answers seem to have risks. Even if all possible answers seem impossible, be encouraged to know that the Holy Spirit himself is praying for you! He is praying God's will for you and your family.

Mothers face many decisions in a day. Some days hold big decisions: In which school should we enroll him? Who is the best doctor to provide treatment? Which part-time job should I accept, if any? When you have tough decisions facing you, don't focus on the issue at hand. Instead, pray and ask God to do his perfect will to fulfill his purposes for your family.

HE CAN EXPLAIN IT ALL

It is written: "No eye has seen, no ear has heard, no mind has conceived what God has prepared for those who love him"—but God has revealed it to us by his Spirit.

The Spirit searches all things, even the deep things of God. For who among men knows the thoughts of a man except the man's spirit within him? In the same way no one knows the thoughts of God except the Spirit of God. We have not received the spirit of the world but the Spirit who is from God, that we may understand what God has freely given us. . . .

The man without the Spirit does not accept the things that come from the Spirit of God, for they are foolishness to him, and he cannot understand them, because they are spiritually discerned.

1 Corinthians 2:9–12, 14 NIV

In the movie *Return to Me*, the main character is a young woman who receives a heart transplant after many years of waiting on the donor list. A very spiritual woman, she deals with mixed emotions about receiving a new heart, feeling as if she is benefiting from someone else's grief. When she learns that her donor is her new boyfriend's former wife, her tearful response is, "What was God thinking?"

Sometimes we just cannot know what God is thinking. When we look at situations, we see the surface one-, two-, or maybe three-dimensional version. But God looks at situations from angles and dimensions we cannot. He navigates in ways we cannot understand, but he has a purpose. An unexpected pregnancy just when you felt your family was getting settled, a job loss right after a move, or an illness might not make sense to you. But God has purpose even in his timing and surprises in your life.

When you must deal with situations that just don't make sense, search for spiritual understanding. Ask God to reveal his purpose to you. Seek to understand, but even if you cannot, trust God's perspective and his process.

SPA FOR THE SOUL

We know that the one who brought the Lord Jesus back to life will also bring us back to life through Jesus. He will present us to God together with you.

All this is for your sake so that, as God's kindness overflows in the lives of many people, it will produce even more thanksgiving to the glory of God. That is why we are not discouraged. Though outwardly we are wearing out, inwardly we are renewed day by day. Our suffering is light and temporary and is producing for us an eternal glory that is greater than anything we can imagine. We don't look for things that can be seen but for things that can't be seen. Things that can be seen are only temporary. But things that can't be seen last forever.

2 Corinthians 4:14–18
GOD'S WORD

Human nature is to fight any appearance of physical or economic distress. We are tempted to keep it together and look like we have it together. But the truth is that all families go through difficulties. Paul faced many challenges and confrontations that not only affected him but also impacted the Corinthian church to whom he wrote this passage. When you or your spouse, individually or as a couple, go through difficulties, your whole family is affected. Yet however significant family problems might be, they are only temporary concerns that should be overshadowed by eternal purpose.

Especially during times of difficulty, it's vital to spend time in prayer without distractions. You must be able to pour out your innermost thoughts to God and hear his response to you as well. You might have to offer to exchange child care with a friend for a couple of hours, but arrange to spend time alone with God, your Bible, and your journal, to renew your focus on the future. When difficulty hits, take some time for yourself to contemplate God's eternal purpose for your life and how you can partner with him to accomplish it.

Teamwork Is All You Need

"All this he made clear to me in writing from the hand of the Lord, all the work to be done according to the plan."

Then David said to Solomon his son, "Be strong and courageous and do it. Do not be afraid and do not be dismayed, for the Lord God, even my God, is with you. He will not leave you or forsake you, until all the work for the service of the house of the Lord is finished. And behold the divisions of the priests and the Levites for all the service of the house of God; and with you in all the work will be every willing man who has skill for any kind of service; also the officers and all the people will be wholly at your command."

1 Chronicles 28:19–21 ESV

King David's words to his son Solomon in this passage were spoken immediately after David charged Solomon with building the temple in Jerusalem—a huge undertaking. No wonder David had to remind Solomon to be strong and courageous! David had hoped to take on this task himself. He had created detailed plans—everything from design to materials to the teams of builders and artisans that would be needed. God did not allow David to proceed, however, and David understood that some things could be delegated and purpose could still be fulfilled. He focused on preparation, not execution, and then gave the responsibility and authority over to his son to complete it.

Most mothers have sensed the overwhelming responsibility of creating a well-established home as well as instilling in their children all they will need for a successful life. Control is sometimes hard to relinquish for moms who want the very best for their families. But delegating responsibilities can be a great method of teaching too. Are there some tasks, whether simple or significant, that you should delegate to your children? Sometimes a mother's purpose is to develop potential in the next generation and nurture it to fruition.

THE POWER OF WORDS

His father, Zechariah, was filled with the Holy Spirit and gave this prophecy: "Praise the Lord, the God of Israel, because he has visited and redeemed his people. . . . And you, my little son, will be called the prophet of the Most High, because you will prepare the way for the Lord. You will tell his people how to find salvation through forgiveness of their sins. Because of God's tender mercy, the morning light from heaven is about to break upon us, to give light to those who sit in darkness and in the shadow of death, and to guide us to the path of peace."

John grew up and became strong in spirit. And he lived in the wilderness until he began his public ministry to Israel.

Luke 1:67–68, 76–80 NLT

Zechariah's words of blessing to his son John began at an early age. He understood the importance of helping his son create a vision—God's vision—for his life. John would need strong conviction about his purpose as the "announcer" that the Messiah had come and people should get ready—because not everyone wanted to hear his message.

When you bless your children (to *bless* is to speak positively about someone's future), you are building their confidence to accomplish the purposes for which they were created. At times like birthdays, weddings, and other landmark occasions, you can formally bless your children, but you can also affirm them every day. Mornings for most mothers can be hectic, but you can still begin each day with a blessing. When you awaken your children, or during your drive to school, remind them of the qualities that God has given them. If your son can make others laugh, tell him so and encourage him to spread joy through his humor.

Speak words of blessings to your children as Zechariah did to John. Let them hear promise, potential, and purpose in your positive words toward them.

READY, GET SET . . .

"Be like servants waiting to open the door at their master's knock when he returns from a wedding. Blessed are those servants whom the master finds awake when he comes. . . . They will be blessed if he comes in the middle of the night or toward morning and finds them awake.

"Of course, you realize that if the homeowner had known at what hour the thief was coming, he would not have let him break into his house. Be ready, because the Son of Man will return when you least expect him.". . .

The Lord asked, "Who, then, is the faithful, skilled manager that the master will put in charge of giving the other servants their share of food at the right time? That servant will be blessed if his master finds him doing this job when he comes."

Luke 12:36–40, 42–43
GOD'S WORD

Getting the whole family ready on time for church on Sunday mornings can be stressful, if not chaotic, for a family with many children. Maybe you have gone through the routine of asking each child, "Are you ready to go?" and hearing a resounding "Yes!" from each one, only to find one child missing shoes, one missing hair ribbons, and the other with unbrushed teeth. Your response? "I thought you were ready!"

Ready means to be in fit condition for immediate action. This passage gives both positive and negative scenarios to show us our need for readiness. As a mother you have to be ready for anything, from an unexpected visitor to a burst of tears over a scraped knee. Your life is much like a car with the engine idling.

Notice that we are not encouraged to be busy—just to be *ready*. What will it take for you to be in fit condition for immediate action? Maybe more rest would prepare you, or eating more healthily, or more time for prayer, or feeling better organized in your home or life? Give some thought to what God desires from you; are you ready yet?

WHAT AN EYE~OPENER!

The Lord also said, "I will protect you from the Jews and from the Gentiles that I am sending you to. I want you to open their eyes, so that they will turn from darkness to light and from the power of Satan to God. Then their sins will be forgiven, and by faith in me they will become part of God's holy people."

King Agrippa, I obeyed this vision from heaven. First I preached to the people in Da-mascus, and then I went to Jerusalem and all over Judea. Finally, I went to the Gentiles and said, "Stop sinning and turn to God! Then prove what you have done by the way you live." . . .

But all this time God has helped me, and I have preached both to the rich and to the poor.

Acts 26:17–20, 22 CEV

When you read this passage, do you tend to focus on Paul's statement of accomplishment rather than his assignment? Mothers often take on full responsibility for situations inside and outside their homes. We feel accountable not only for the initiative but the process and the results too. Yes, Paul obeyed the vision God gave him. But see the simplicity of what God asked of Paul—"open their eyes."

The people that Paul would speak to needed to turn to God. They needed God's truth to invade their darkness like lights going on. Paul's assignment, however, was not to assure that every person responded positively. He simply had to be an eye-opener.

As you look at the assignment of motherhood that God has given you, focus on what he has asked you to do—simply to raise your children to know and love him. You will have to release them to make their own decisions one day, and that brings a great sense of responsibility for any mother. Don't get burdened by this but focus on opening their eyes to the great love God has for them as the only sound foundation for their future.

ABSOLUTE RESOLUTE

The Sovereign LORD has given me his words of wisdom, so that I know how to comfort the weary. Morning by morning he wakens me and opens my understanding to his will. The Sovereign LORD has spoken to me, and I have listened. I have not rebelled or turned away.

I offered my back to those who beat me and my cheeks to those who pulled out my beard. I did not hide my face from mockery and spitting.

Because the Sovereign LORD helps me, I will not be disgraced. Therefore, I have set my face like a stone, determined to do his will.

Isaiah 50:4–7 NLT

The book of Isaiah is full of words that encouraged the people of his day as well as us today. This portion of Scripture is actually a foretelling about what Jesus would experience and how he would react to it. His purpose was set in place before his birth on the earth, just as yours was. He experienced both emotional and physical harm, but he did not let it distract him from his purpose.

We mothers often know what future situations will hold for our children because we have gained discernment that comes from God through previous experiences, prayer, or counsel. You may predict an impending breakup for your son with his first girlfriend long before he does. Not every situation will be enjoyable for your child to experience or for you to watch, but your purpose to glorify God with your children through the unpleasantness must remain steadfast.

As God reveals his will to you, you must decide what to do with it. Like Jesus, set your face like stone, staring at the day ahead, feet well grounded, arms ready for work, eyes focused on fulfilling his purpose and will for you.

PLANNERS AND JOURNALS

You made my whole being; you formed me in my mother's body. I praise you because you made me in an amazing and wonderful way. What you have done is wonderful. I know this very well. You saw my bones being formed as I took shape in my mother's body. When I was put together there, you saw my body as it was formed. All the days planned for me were written in your book before I was one day old.

God, your thoughts are precious to me. They are so many! If I could count them, they would be more than all the grains of sand. When I wake up, I am still with you.

Psalm 139:13–18 NCV

How exciting to see the first sonogram during your pregnancy! With each succeeding sonogram you see your child in more and more detail—eyes, nose, fingers, every part formed with exactness and intricacy. So exciting are these visits to the doctor that many new moms return home to journal about the growth of their baby and the maternal feelings of nurture growing along with the child.

Just as we watch, mark, and embrace the growth of our children even while still in the womb, God not only notes their progress too but he is the very one forming each part. And he did the same for each of us as we grew within our mothers. He has planned out each season of our lives to fulfill his purpose through us.

Our little ones cannot fathom how often we think of them, their choices, their future, and we cannot imagine God's constant thought and care for us, but the words of this psalm of David picture it for us. Spend time reflecting on the seasons of life as a mother. As you remember, journal all the ways God has nurtured your growth and trust in him.

CONFIDENCE

In the seasons of motherhood, confidence comes and goes with each new endeavor. Whether you are facing your first night at home with your newborn infant or your first night alone after seeing your young adult off to college, new situations can cause uneasiness, even doubt. Feeling confident in the transition to new motherhood, going back to work after a baby, leaving a job you love to be a stay-at-home mom, or becoming an empty nester requires reliance on more than just the decision to do it. God gives us great comfort in his reminder that we do not have to be confident in our *own* abilities.

Look! God is my Savior. I am confident and un-afraid, because the LORD is my strength and my song. He is my Savior.

Isaiah 12:2 GOD'S WORD

My Mind's Made Up

I will not fail you or abandon you.

Be strong and courageous, for you are the one who will lead these people to possess all the land I swore to their ancestors I would give them. Be strong and very courageous. Be careful to obey all the instructions Moses gave you. Do not deviate from them, turning either to the right or to the left. Then you will be successful in everything you do. Study this Book of Instruction continually. Meditate on it day and night so you will be sure to obey everything written in it. Only then will you prosper and succeed in all you do. This is my command—be strong and courageous! Do not be afraid or discouraged. For the LORD your God is with you wherever you go.

Joshua 1:5–9 NLT

Joshua was the man to follow Moses, a great leader of thousands. It is no wonder that God had to remind him to have confidence. Can you imagine being the one to follow Moses, the man to whom God gave the Ten Commandments? But God didn't simply tell Joshua to be confident; he also told him where he could find the confidence he needed—in the "Book of Instruction." Joshua would not gain his confidence through becoming most popular. He wouldn't get strength by fighting battles. Instead, making good decisions based on Scripture was the way for him to become strong and courageous.

Moms can follow the same advice and get the same result as Joshua. The more knowledge of God we have from the Bible, the better equipped we'll be to make good decisions, whether for ourselves or for the children we're teaching and leading. Relationships, parenting, finances, and more—it's all in the Book.

Your decisions might not always be popular. In fact, most times the right decisions are the unpopular ones. But when you are basing your decisions on the Bible, you can be confident that you have the right answer.

SHOUT IT OUT

Oh, clap your hands, all you peoples! Shout to God with the voice of triumph! For the LORD Most High is awesome; He is a great King over all the earth. He will subdue the peoples under us, and the nations under our feet. He will choose our inheritance for us, the excellence of Jacob whom He loves.

God has gone up with a shout, the LORD with the sound of a trumpet. Sing praises to God, sing praises! Sing praises to our King, sing praises! For God is the King of all the earth; sing praises with understanding.

God reigns over the nations; God sits on His holy throne.

Psalm 47:1–8 NKJV

This early psalm shows you how to encourage yourself by reminding yourself who is in control of your life—no, not you, but God! When life seems uncertain, how easily we begin questioning ourselves and our decisions. Self-doubt leads quickly to withered confidence too, but that is a fallacy in human thinking.

You are not expected to be confident in your own abilities. God is the source of your talents, skills, and aptitudes. You are to be confident in God as your sustaining resource. So when you begin to wonder whether you are a good mother, or capable, or well organized, the question to ask is whether God is able to make you those things. You will always find the same answer: Yes! God is able to create the confidence and strength in you that you need to accomplish whatever task he has assigned.

There are times for quiet reflection, but a shout is a symbol of victory. The psalmist could shout with confidence because he understood that God was his source for everything in life. Moms who know God have reason to shout!

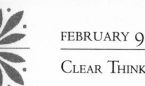

CLEAR THINKING

Keep your minds on whatever is true, pure, right, holy, friendly, and proper. Don't ever stop thinking about what is truly worthwhile and worthy of praise. You know the teachings I gave you, and you know what you heard me say and saw me do. So follow my example. And God, who gives peace, will be with you. . . .

I have learned to be satisfied with whatever I have. I know what it is to be poor or to have plenty, and I have lived under all kinds of conditions. I know what it means to be full or to be hungry, to have too much or too little. Christ gives me the strength to face anything.

It was good of you to help me when I was having such a hard time.

Philippians 4:8–9, 11–14 CEV

Think about the content of all the noise that fills your home and your mind daily—TV, radio, video games, the Internet. How much of what you and your children hear throughout the day is what this passage calls worthwhile? Log how much of your child's day is spent with music, television, or video playing; then note how much of that has a positive message that encourages the right things in life. Are your children receiving messages that instill godly confidence?

By harnessing the distractions, or noise, in our lives, we can focus more readily on maintaining a positive perspective. Your children might not enjoy restrictions on entertainment, but the change can provoke a good lesson in contentment.

The challenge of a new environment can teach us to be joyful under any circumstances. If you want to give an extreme lesson in contentment, you might even consider having a missionary meal by preparing an unusual food or minimal portion of rice that one might eat in another country. The activity can prompt a lively discussion about how missionaries can maintain confident faith, even when they may be lacking necessities or luxuries in life.

Who's Listening?

Here's how you test for the genuine Spirit of God. Everyone who confesses openly his faith in Jesus Christ—the Son of God, who came as an actual flesh-and-blood person—comes from God and belongs to God. And everyone who refuses to confess faith in Jesus has nothing in common with God. . . .

You come from God and belong to God. You have already won a big victory over those false teachers, for the Spirit in you is far stronger than anything in the world. . . . We come from God and belong to God. Anyone who knows God understands us and listens. The person who has nothing to do with God will, of course, not listen to us. This is another test for telling the Spirit of Truth from the spirit of deception.

1 John 4:2–4, 6 MSG

As your children become tweens and teens and begin spending time away from home, it becomes even more important for you to know their friends and their friends' families.

You have spent all of their elementary school years trying to nurture faith in them. Now your role is to help them continue to develop into confident Christians. The peers they associate with at school, sports, and church impact that development. In this passage we are not given a checklist of what others should do or not do to present themselves as people who love God. It is simple—they openly talk about their faith in Christ.

One way to monitor your children's confidence in their faith is by the way they answer questions about church, prayer, the Bible, and faith in front of friends and strangers. If a once-bold child becomes timid, it might be a sign that he needs some spiritual encouragement.

Listen to your children describe their friends' experiences in faith. Ask your children if their friends are Christians. If they seem unsure in their response, then you have an opportunity to determine if these are friendships that will strengthen your child's faith.

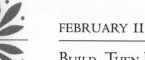

BUILD, THEN BEHOLD

Make yourself an ark of gopherwood; make rooms in the ark, and cover it inside and outside with pitch. And this is how you shall make it: The length of the ark shall be three hundred cubits, its width fifty cubits, and its height thirty cubits. You shall make a window for the ark, and you shall finish it to a cubit from above; and set the door of the ark in its side. You shall make it with lower, second, and third decks. And behold, I Myself am bringing floodwaters on the earth, to destroy from under heaven all flesh in which is the breath of life; everything that is on the earth shall die. But I will establish My covenant with you; and you shall go into the ark—you, your sons, your wife, and your sons' wives with you.

Genesis 6:14–18 NKJV

If your child has spent any time at all in children's church, you have most likely heard the song that begins, "The Lord told Noah to go and build an ark-y, ark-y. . . ." A memorable tune, and a memorable story! Most children can recite the simple version of the story, but it is worth taking another look at as an adult too.

When God told Noah there would be a flood, Noah didn't really know what that would be like—Noah had never seen rain. Noah's response shows that Noah was confident that the notion to build the ark came from God, and that if God said it would occur, it would indeed occur. Another thing to notice in this story is the details. God not only told Noah to build a boat, but he told him the exact measurements, materials, and methods to use.

Many mothers have become entrepreneurs with a simple combination of confidence and creativity. If God gives you what seems to others to be an unusual idea, he can also provide you with everything you need to make an innovation successful, whether it improves only your family or your entire community.

Brave Heart

The LORD is my light and my salvation; whom shall I fear? The LORD is the strength of my life; of whom shall I be afraid? . . . Though an army may encamp against me, my heart shall not fear; . . . in this I will be confident.

One thing I have desired of the LORD, that will I seek: that I may dwell in the house of the LORD all the days of my life, to behold the beauty of the LORD, and to inquire in His temple.

For in the time of trouble He shall hide me in His pavilion; in the secret place of His tabernacle He shall hide me; He shall set me high upon a rock.

Psalm 27:1, 3–5 NKJV

One night as a mom chided her son gently that he didn't have to be afraid of the dark, he responded, "I'm not afraid *of* the dark. I'm afraid of what's *in* the dark." Even though we are mothers instead of children, we can be afraid of what is lurking in the unknown too. Sometimes it's hard to remain confident—when you go through a divorce, lose your job, or have a child leave home before you think she is ready. But like our children running to our beds during a storm, we also have a safe place to run. God is our safe place.

We don't have to reserve our safe place only for times we are afraid. We can make it our desire, as this passage states, to "dwell" with the Lord. To dwell means "to live as a resident," or "to keep attention directed upon."

When we stay focused on living in God's presence, especially when we pray and remember Bible verses throughout the day, the direct result is peace. When we live confidently with God, darkness becomes a place for the light of God's love to shine.

Now and Then

When Jesus saw that [the rich man] became very sorrowful, He said, "How hard it is for those who have riches to enter the kingdom of God! For it is easier for a camel to go through the eye of a needle than for a rich man to enter the kingdom of God."

And those who heard it said, "Who then can be saved?"

But He said, "The things which are impossible with men are possible with God."

Then Peter said, "See, we have left all and followed You."

So He said to them, "Assuredly, I say to you, there is no one who has left house or parents or brothers or wife or children, for the sake of the kingdom of God, who shall not receive many times more in this present time, and in the age to come eternal life."

Luke 18:24–30 NKJV

A rich man seemed eager to follow Jesus, but when he realized he would have to make faith his main priority, his zeal dwindled. He wasn't willing to give Jesus more importance than his wealth. But not only money can lure our focus away from faith. Anything that consumes our attention more than our love for God needs to be put in its proper place.

You might not be able to read the Bible and pray longer than you work in a day. Thankfully, we are not expected to keep a time log! What matters is that we stay focused on our relationship with God consistently. Yes, that will include prayer and Bible study, but it also includes serving others in his name. Jesus surely understands that a mother's family relationships easily become a priority in her life. But strong personal faith gives you the confidence to be the right influence on your children.

Jesus' response to Peter wasn't telling the disciples to abandon the most important people in their lives. He was reassuring them that if they kept their faith in God their main concern, they would be rewarded in their relationships.

INFINITY AND BEYOND!

I ask the Father in his great glory to give you the power to be strong inwardly through his Spirit. I pray that Christ will live in your hearts by faith and that your life will be strong in love and be built on love. And I pray that you and all God's holy people will have the power to understand the greatness of Christ's love—how wide and how long and how high and how deep that love is. Christ's love is greater than anyone can ever know, but I pray that you will be able to know that love. Then you can be filled with the fullness of God.

With God's power working in us, God can do much, much more than anything we can ask or imagine.

Ephesians 3:16–20 NCV

Whether toys that come to life, cars that talk, or news reporters who change clothes in a phone booth, superhuman powers intrigue parents as well as children. If you could be Supermom for a day, what would you most want to accomplish?

Sure, you might want to clean the entire house in seconds or become invisible whenever you need a few minutes to yourself. But give it further thought: What are the things that you just cannot manage without superhuman strength? What do you really want to accomplish with extreme greatness for your children, in your family, in your home?

Every great superhero has a quotable legacy, whether it is a modern "To infinity and beyond!" by Buzz Lightyear or "Up, up and away!" by the classic Superman. Think about what your Supermom mantra would be and what you would want to accomplish. The next time you feel weak or insecure as a mom, don't just pray vaguely for help—pray specifically that God will reveal his expansive love to you. Realizing the depth of God's love for you can quickly strengthen your confidence to become a supermom!

FALSE CONFIDENCE AT FAULT

At first everyone spoke the same language, but after some of them moved from the east and settled in Babylonia, they said: Let's build a city with a tower that reaches to the sky! We'll use hard bricks and tar instead of stone and mortar. We'll become famous, and we won't be scattered all over the world.

But when the LORD came down to look at the city and the tower, he said:

These people are working together because they all speak the same language. This is just the beginning. Soon they will be able to do anything they want. Come on! Let's go down and confuse them by making them speak different languages—then they won't be able to understand each other.

So the people had to stop building the city, because the LORD confused their language and scattered them all over the earth.

Genesis 11:1–8 CEV

This account of the Tower of Babel tells what happens when we put confidence in the wrong things. These people had become so confident in their own talents and skills that they did not think they needed God any longer. Self-reliance can trick us into feeling that we have no need of others or of God.

We do need to teach our children independence—making their own beds, tying their own shoes, and other personal tasks. You most likely have also heard, "I can do it myself!"—whether from a four-year-old trying to bathe himself or a sixteen-year-old wanting to drive alone the first day she has her license.

It is somewhat easy to identify the balance of self-confidence and self-reliance in your children, but what about in your own life? Is there something you have been struggling to accomplish on your own that leaves you feeling confused and defeated? God wants to help you. He wants you to place your confidence in him. Reach out to God for help. You can be confident in his ability to help you.

Relentless Wells

You will say in that day, "I thank you, God. You were angry but your anger wasn't forever. You withdrew your anger and moved in and comforted me.

"Yes, indeed—God is my salvation. I trust, I won't be afraid. God—yes God!—is my strength and song, best of all, my salvation!"

Joyfully you'll pull up buckets of water from the wells of salvation. And as you do it, you'll say, "Give thanks to God. Call out his name. Ask him anything! Shout to the nations, tell them what he's done, spread the news of his great reputation!

"Sing praise-songs to God. He's done it all! Let the whole earth know what he's done!"

Isaiah 12:1–5 msg

So you messed up. You lost focus yesterday, maybe even lost your temper. But every day is a new day. You don't have to worry that God carries grudges; he doesn't. His judgment is wrapped in love for you. Just as you don't withhold love from your children even though you have to discipline them, God doesn't either.

This poetic passage tells us we can't use up God's grace. This song is an expression of praise for redemption from difficult times. Just as those who spent time in captivity embraced the mercy of God, you can enjoy his blessings too.

We will never be perfect in this life. It is impossible to meet everyone's expectations all the time. It might be even harder for you to meet your own expectations of being a great mom. Instead of striving for perfection, strive to do your best—whatever that may be at this moment. If yesterday was a day full of mistakes or disappointments, leave those behind. When you awaken in the morning, begin your day by expressing your gratitude for a new beginning full of mercy. Enjoy a fresh start every day.

LIFELINE

I love the LORD, because he listens to my prayers for help. He paid attention to me, so I will call to him for help as long as I live. The ropes of death bound me, and the fear of the grave took hold of me. I was troubled and sad. Then I called out the name of the LORD. I said, "Please, LORD, save me!"

The LORD is kind and does what is right; our God is merciful. The LORD watches over the foolish; when I was helpless, he saved me. I said to myself, "Relax, because the LORD takes care of you." LORD, you saved me from death.

Psalm 116:1–8 NCV

Did you buy training flippers and floaties to cautiously coax your children a little farther out of the shallow end to learn to swim? Some parents toss the children into the deep end and let them learn by need! Whatever your approach might be, you build trust with your children by being near enough to grab them if they begin to sink. They become more brave when you are their safety net.

God uses many different approaches to teach us. David learned through many experiences in his life. He learned how to provide care through shepherding, he built his courage and strength in battles with bears and a giant, and he learned regret and reform through the loss of a child. Sometimes we feel that we've been thrown into a battle before we are ready to fight. When this happens, think back to everyone God rescued in the Bible and all the times he has rescued you. If you feel afraid of new experiences, put your confidence in his ability and desire to keep you safe. He might be teaching you to swim in new waters, but he will not let you sink.

SET FREE

We can enter through a new and living way that Jesus opened for us. It leads through the curtain—Christ's body. And since we have a great priest over God's house, let us come near to God with a sincere heart and a sure faith, because we have been made free from a guilty conscience, and our bodies have been washed with pure water. Let us hold firmly to the hope that we have confessed, because we can trust God to do what he promised.

Let us think about each other and help each other to show love and do good deeds. You should not stay away from the church meetings, as some are doing, but you should meet together and encourage each other. Do this even more as you see the day coming.

Hebrews 10:20–25 NCV

Can you imagine being a pioneer woman, washing clothes with lye soap and a washboard? What about being a mother in the Victorian era, chasing your children while wearing a corset and stacked hair? Neither can we imagine being a woman in Old Testament times, serving as the "mom taxi" but on foot! We have many privileges and resources that mothers of old did not have.

Just as moms and women have been liberated in society by education, technology, and the right to vote, we also have been liberated from the guilt of sin through Christ. Before Jesus came, relationship with God depended on offering the necessary sacrifices and showing obedience. But after Jesus died for us, we have the opportunity for a relationship with God based solely on love's forgiveness and our faith.

Moms are free to vote, speak, and work, and we can be free to worship God. Take time this week to teach your daughter, niece, or granddaughter about the history of women's liberty and her freedom in Christ. By being a positive role model, you can help young girls become confident, Christian women like you.

JUST SAY IT

[Balaam] answered, "Shouldn't I say exactly what the LORD puts in my mouth?". . .

Balaam said to Balak, "Stay here by your burnt offering while I seek [the LORD] over there."

The LORD met with Balaam and put a message in his mouth. Then He said, "Return to Balak and say what I tell you."

So he returned to Balak, who was standing there by his burnt offering with the officials of Moab. Balak asked him, "What did the LORD say?"

Balaam proclaimed his poem: Balak, get up and listen; son of Zippor, pay attention to what I say! God is not a man who lies, or a son of man who changes His mind. Does He speak and not act, or promise and not fulfill? I have indeed received [a command] to bless; since He has blessed, I cannot change it.

Numbers 23:12, 15–20 HCSB

Life would be easier if we were never required to have a difficult talk with anyone. Sometimes, however, the right conversation is a challenging one.

Some of our most difficult experiences as mothers center around our children's involvement at school and in activities. We all want our children to succeed at learning, whether scholastics or skills. Part of a child's success depends on a parent's involvement in that learning. But conversations with teachers, principals, and coaches can be intimidating for even the most confident moms!

We don't have to be reluctant or overzealous in our children's learning. Follow Balaam's example; he was clear about what God wanted done. Notice what Balaam did before his conversation with Balak. He separated himself from the situation, and then he prayed about what God wanted him to do. Once he felt sure of an answer, he addressed the conversation.

You know your children better than anyone else with influence over them. If there is a matter you must confront, be sure to spend some time in prayer so that you can approach the situation confidently.

The Voice of Experience

"Be strong. Take courage. Don't be intimidated. Don't give them a second thought because God, your God, is striding ahead of you. He's right there with you. He won't let you down; he won't leave you."

Then Moses summoned Joshua. He said to him with all Israel watching, "Be strong. Take courage. You will enter the land with this people, this land that God promised their ancestors that he'd give them. You will make them the proud possessors of it. God is striding ahead of you. He's right there with you. He won't let you down; he won't leave you. Don't be intimidated. Don't worry."

Moses wrote out this Revelation and gave it to the priests, the sons of Levi, who carried the Chest of the Covenant of God, and to all the leaders of Israel.

Deuteronomy 31:6–9 MSG

We don't always get what we want in life. Moses wasn't granted his dream of entering the Promised Land with the Israelites. He could have complained; instead, he put Joshua in front of the people as the leader who would go into the land with them. His words instilled confidence; he didn't speaking theoretically but reminded everyone of God's help in the past.

Wherever you are in your experience as a mom, you can encourage other moms by telling them how God has been faithful to you. If you have entered your third trimester as a first-time mother, you can give hope to a newly pregnant mom that morning sickness does go away. If you are already a grandmother, you can share stories from your own life with younger mothers about how God helped you maneuver through the teen years and the empty nest.

You don't have to be an expert to be confident as a mother. When you see an opportunity to help another mother, ask, "Would you like to know what worked for me when I was experiencing that?" You will likely find an eager listener happy for a new perspective.

Confidants

With Lady Wisdom, God formed Earth; with Madame Insight, he raised Heaven. They knew when to signal rivers and springs to the surface, and dew to descend from the night skies.

Dear friend, guard Clear Thinking and Common Sense with your life; don't for a minute lose sight of them. They'll keep your soul alive and well, they'll keep you fit and attractive.

You'll travel safely, you'll neither tire nor trip. You'll take afternoon naps without a worry, you'll enjoy a good night's sleep. No need to panic over alarms or surprises, or predictions that doomsday's just around the corner, Because God will be right there with you; he'll keep you safe and sound.

Proverbs 3:19–26 MSG

A popular quote says, "Do what you can do, and let God do what he can do." Well, this portion of the book of Proverbs outlines what you can do and how you can do it. The answer to emotional and physical wellness and peace of mind lies in clear thinking and common sense.

These two attributes seem like pretty simple solutions that seemingly everyone would have. But notice that the passage cautions us to *guard* them so that they can benefit us.

With all our responsibilities inside and outside the home, we moms can easily become overworked without realizing it until we are depleted. To keep your body strong and your mind clear and confident, be proactive about taking care of yourself. You might want to combine some activities to help yourself in more than one area at the same time. For example, a brisk walk is a good workout and physically reduces stress. If talking to a friend helps you reduce emotional stress, combine the two and walk with a friend.

When you take care of yourself, you are partnering with God, who is with you, helping you accomplish your mothering with confidence.

PARTAKING OF PROMISES

Grace and peace be multiplied to you in the knowledge of God and of Jesus our Lord; seeing that His divine power has granted to us everything pertaining to life and godliness, through the true knowledge of Him who called us by His own glory and excellence. For by these He has granted to us His precious and magnificent promises, so that by them you may become partakers of the divine nature, having escaped the corruption that is in the world by lust. Now for this very reason also, applying all diligence, in your faith supply moral excellence, and in your moral excellence, knowledge, and in your knowledge, self-control, and in your self-control, perseverance, and in your perseverance, godliness, and in your godliness, brotherly kindness, and in your brotherly kindness, love.

2 Peter 1:2–7 NASB

Most moms spend significant hours doing math homework with their children. You are almost guaranteed to be asked this question at some point: "When will I ever use this, anyway?" Math is a good reminder that some things we learn are layers to prepare us for the next level of knowledge. We need to understand algebra before we tackle geometric equations, and this passage written by the apostle Peter tells us that some character traits help us master others.

You probably adopt this principle as a mother already. You don't expect your son to know how to clean his entire room by himself just because he turned seven. Instead, you begin teaching him how to pick up his toys after playtime when he is a toddler. Then when he's older, how to make his bed, and so on. Eventually he will be able to tackle the whole room.

Thankfully, God doesn't require us to learn everything we need to know for a godly life all at once. When you feel confident about mastering a consistent bedtime routine, you can tackle another area, like teaching your children to take turns leading family devotions.

WANT TO KNOW MY SECRET?

The time is coming when everything that is covered will be revealed, and all that is secret will be made known to all. What I tell you now in the darkness, shout abroad when daybreak comes. What I whisper in your ear, shout from the housetops for all to hear!

Don't be afraid of those who want to kill your body; they cannot touch your soul. Fear only God, who can destroy both soul and body in hell. What is the price of two sparrows—one copper coin? But not a single sparrow can fall to the ground without your Father knowing it. And the very hairs on your head are all numbered. So don't be afraid; you are more valuable to God than a whole flock of sparrows.

Matthew 10:26–31 NLT

Do you ever wonder what in the world God is up to in your life? You might think that if you just knew what his plan was for you, each day would be easier. Be assured that nothing happens that takes God by surprise. He knows exactly what we experience each moment of every day.

Some days bring challenges, even scares—a suspicious health report, a failed business, a spouse involved in an affair. We find some life situations difficult to understand with our limited human ability. But confidence in God balances reason. When we cannot rely on our own understanding, we *can* rely on God.

Jesus spoke the words in this passage to his disciples. He wanted them to be prepared for all that they would face as they began to tell others about the good news and to be assured of God's care and concern for them at all times, no matter the situation. Jesus' words are for you too. You can face any fear when you know that God is in control of your life. Trust that his plan is a good one and that he is always watching over you.

PUT IT IN PERSPECTIVE

"We went to the land where you sent us. It truly flows with milk and honey, and this is its fruit. Nevertheless the people who dwell in the land are strong." . . .

Caleb quieted the people before Moses, and said, "Let us go up at once and take possession, for we are well able to overcome it."

But the men who had gone up with him said, "We are not able to go up against the people, for they are stronger than we." And they gave the children of Israel a bad report of the land which they had spied out, saying, "The land through which we have gone as spies is a land that devours its inhabitants. . . . There we saw the giants . . . and we were like grasshoppers in our own sight, and so we were in their sight."

Numbers 13:27–28, 30–33
NKJV

The men who traveled with Joshua and Caleb to scout new territory lost their confidence when they saw who was awaiting them. They saw the wealth of opportunities in the land, but the challenge and obstacles seemed too great to attempt to attain them. But Caleb and Joshua had a different perspective. They were confident that God would empower his people to possess the land despite any hardships they might endure in the process.

Mothers encounter plenty of intimidating situations. You might see opportunities for a new career or promotion but wonder if the sacrifice of returning to school, with its extra financial and time commitments, will be worth it. You could have dismissed teaching your son's fifth-grade Sunday school class because it just seemed too much to tackle.

Give some thought to your hopes for the future. Is there something you want to accomplish? If you haven't seized certain opportunities because you've been intimidated by the process of achieving them, learn this lesson from Caleb. Have a positive perspective. You cannot let circumstances compromise your confidence if you want to have all that God offers you.

BOLD BELIEVER

The word of God is living and active, sharper than any two-edged sword, piercing to the division of soul and of spirit, of joints and of marrow, and discerning the thoughts and intentions of the heart. And no creature is hidden from his sight, but all are naked and exposed to the eyes of him to whom we must give account.

Since then we have a great high priest who has passed through the heavens, Jesus, the Son of God, let us hold fast our confession. For we do not have a high priest who is unable to sympathize with our weaknesses, but one who in every respect has been tempted as we are, yet without sin. Let us then with confidence draw near to the throne of grace, that we may receive mercy and find grace to help in time of need.

Hebrews 4:12, 14–16 ESV

Imagine what it would be like to meet an esteemed leader like the president of the nation or a modern-day king or queen. How much time would you spend planning what to wear, what to say, how to act? How many times would you rehearse the rules of etiquette with your children before the encounter?

What would it be like to meet Jesus face-to-face and make a request of him? Would you be nervous? This passage was written to encourage believers that Jesus is indeed the Messiah about whom the Old Testament teaches. The writer of the book of Hebrews invites us to enter into a relationship with God through Christ and tells us that we can do so confidently because of his grace!

Mothers cherish the blessings that come with their role in the family. But being a mom has its own stresses and challenges too that children and even spouses cannot fully understand. God does understand, and he invites us to share our lives with him. We don't have to be reluctant or anxious about asking him for help. We can be confident in approaching him because he is a gracious friend.

FINDING YOUR PLACE

To some who were confident of their own righteousness and looked down on everybody else, Jesus told this parable: "Two men went up to the temple to pray, one a Pharisee and the other a tax collector. The Pharisee stood up and prayed about himself: 'God, I thank you that I am not like other men. . . . I fast twice a week and give a tenth of all I get.'

"But the tax collector stood at a distance. He would not even look up to heaven, but beat his breast and said, 'God, have mercy on me, a sinner.'

"I tell you that this man, rather than the other, went home justified before God. For everyone who exalts himself will be humbled, and he who humbles himself will be exalted."

Luke 18:9–14 NIV

The Pharisees thought they were good people. They might even have had good intentions at one time. But the religious leaders of Jesus' day, like the Pharisee in this story, made two very big mistakes—they thought that what they did made them right with God, and they rejected Jesus, whom God had sent to truly make them good.

Many mothers find themselves in the same trap. There is no mistaking that we work hard. Laundry, helping with schoolwork, cleaning, cooking, nursing, employment, and volunteering—our tasks seem endless. But it isn't the amount of work we do or even how well we do it that makes us good moms. Our love for and nurturing of our children are what make us good moms.

Good deeds, no matter how many or how well accomplished, do not earn God's approval or forgiveness. Nothing we do makes God accept us more; we simply have to love him and submit to his will. Our relationships with our children work like this. Our love for them is unconditional; however, their lives and ours too run more smoothly when they are obedient and willing to follow our lead because they love and trust us.

CONFIDENT QUESTIONS

The one who does not believe God has made Him a liar, because he has not believed in the testimony that God has given concerning His Son. And the testimony is this, that God has given us eternal life, and this life is in His Son. He who has the Son has the life; he who does not have the Son of God does not have the life.

These things I have written to you who believe in the name of the Son of God, so that you may know that you have eternal life. This is the confidence which we have before Him, that, if we ask anything according to His will, He hears us. And . . . we know that we have the requests which we have asked from Him.

1 John 5:10–15 NASB

Mom! Mom!" How often have your children relentlessly called your name, impatiently awaiting your response? They want an immediate answer, not realizing that you are in a conversation or that they can't hear your answer because they keep yelling, "Mom!" When we call out to God, he does not ignore us, even if we don't hear his answer immediately.

For example, you might have the perfect teacher in mind for your child next year. You pray faithfully that your child will get into her class. But when you receive your child's assignment, you might be greatly disappointed. Just because you don't get the answer you were hoping for doesn't mean God didn't answer. You could learn a reason after a while (perhaps the preferred teacher gets transferred to another class midyear), or you might never know the purpose behind God's answer. You have to trust that just as you tell your child no or to wait, sometimes you will receive those same answers from God.

No matter the answer, we can trust that God always acts with our best interests in mind. He has already answered our request for salvation—could anything be more important?

WELL-ROOTED AND FRUIT-BEARING

Blessed is the person who trusts the LORD. The LORD will be his confidence. He will be like a tree that is planted by water. It will send its roots down to a stream. It will not be afraid in the heat of summer. Its leaves will turn green. It will not be anxious during droughts. It will not stop producing fruit.

"The human mind is the most deceitful of all things. It is incurable. No one can understand how deceitful it is. I, the LORD, search minds and test hearts. I will reward each person for what he has done. I will reward him for the results of his actions. A person who gets rich dishonestly is like a partridge that hatches eggs it did not lay." . . .

Our holy place is a glorious throne, highly honored from the beginning.

Jeremiah 17:7–12
GOD'S WORD

An old hymn says it this way: "I shall not be, I shall not be moved. . . . Just like a tree that's planted by the water . . ." *Immovable*—a proclamation of standing in a position of confident trust. We might prefer for this passage to compare our lives to a tree never exposed to heat or drought, but we are not promised we will never experience hardship or difficulties. Mothers can relate well to the figurative terms *heat*—intense pressure—and *drought*—shortage of needs.

Confidence would come easily if we were guaranteed that life would be full only of ease. But we are not guaranteed a perfect life, or even perfect children. A mom's day can go from relaxed to stressed with one phone call from a school principal. You might even awaken in the morning thinking of the financial strains that prevent you from funding your child's college. In any type of stressful situation, you can stay positioned with immovable confidence in God. He is not only someone to go to for help—like the stream feeds the tree, God is the actual source of your strength.

Self-Pride Causes Self-Destruction

In front of everyone Peter said, "That isn't so! I don't know what you are talking about!"

When Peter had gone out to the gate, another servant girl saw him and said to some people there, "This man was with Jesus from Nazareth."

Again Peter denied it, and this time he swore, "I don't even know that man!"

A little while later some people standing there walked over to Peter and said, "We know that you are one of them. We can tell it because you talk like someone from Galilee."

Peter began to curse and swear, "I don't know that man!"

Right then a rooster crowed, and Peter remembered that Jesus had said, "Before a rooster crows, you will say three times that you don't know me." Then Peter went out and cried hard.

Matthew 26:70–75 CEV

None of us like to disappoint others. We want to meet other people's expectations of us, especially our spouses' and children's. Sometimes that zeal to please others boosts our confidence to pride. When Jesus told Peter that he would deny him three times, Peter was adamant that he would remain a confident follower. But when grief, judgment, and fear set in, Peter was not as strong as he had convinced himself he would be.

Confidence is a good quality to have in motherhood. When you are confident in your relationship with Jesus and his strength in you, you realize that your capability to be successful relies on him. You want your children to know they can depend on you, but you also want them to realize your support and not take it for granted. You also must be aware that God's grace is so embracing that you can take it for granted.

Remember that you are mothering beyond your own ability because God helps you. One way to remind yourself is to thank him every day for his support in every aspect of your relationship with your children.

BOUND IN LOVE

Christ died and was raised to life, and now he is at God's right side, speaking to him for us. Can anything separate us from the love of Christ? Can trouble, suffering, and hard times, or hunger and nakedness, or danger and death? It is exactly as the Scriptures say, "For you we face death all day long. We are like sheep on their way to be butchered."

In everything we have won more than a victory because of Christ who loves us. I am sure that nothing can separate us from God's love—not life or death, not angels or spirits, not the present or the future, and not powers above or powers below. Nothing in all creation can separate us from God's love for us in Christ Jesus our Lord!

Romans 8:34–39 CEV

With career and educational opportunities available to us around the world, we have created somewhat of a transient society. A downside to such opportunity is that our familiy members become more detached from one another. Many grandparents are separated from their grandchildren, and sleepovers with cousins are reserved for only special occasions. The loss of family support that comes with the wedge of distance can cause difficulties and loneliness for mothers.

But neither place nor challenges can distance you from God's love. When your heart is troubled, you can count on God's love to comfort you. You do not have to fear handling financial hardships, family illnesses, or relationship struggles alone. Even if you are away from your own mom, you can be confident that God, your Father, is near to you. Just as you keep in touch with family through phone conversations and video chats, you can stay connected with God through prayer. When you spend time praying, be assured that he is interested in all your life, including your material needs and your emotional needs too. Be honest with him and ask him to provide what you need to be a confident, content mother.

SAFE PASSAGE

"When [the shepherd] gets them all out, he leads them and they follow because they are familiar with his voice. They won't follow a stranger's voice but will scatter because they aren't used to the sound of it."

Jesus told this simple story, but they had no idea what he was talking about. So he tried again. "I'll be explicit, then. I am the Gate for the sheep. All those others are up to no good—sheep stealers, everyone of them. But the sheep didn't listen to them. I am the Gate. Anyone who goes through me will be cared for—will freely go in and out, and find pasture. A thief is only there to steal and kill and destroy. I came so they can have real and eternal life, more and better life than they ever dreamed of."

John 10:4–10 MSG

The playground can be full of children near in age, giggling, yelling, sometimes crying. But when you hear your little one call out, "Mommy!" you discern it right away. A mother recognizes her own child's voice in a crowd and usually knows what the tone communicates: something scared her, he's mad, she is thrilled, he is hurt. How amazing to hear that one voice and one word and recognize the meaning, even above the noise of a crowd.

Did you know that you can learn to hear God in the same way? We can develop a keen ear to his voice very easily. First of all, spend time every week—or every day—reading the Bible. Like an author reveals himself in his autobiography, God reveals himself to us in the Bible. Also spend time praying. Just have a conversation with him. Tell him your feelings and ask him to guide you. Prayer is developing intimacy with God. It doesn't have to be eloquent.

The more time and attention you give to God, the more you know God's personality, thoughts, and intentions, and the more you will recognize his voice. He is always speaking.

Be Careful with Your Confidence

Do not trust a neighbor; put no confidence in a friend. Even with her who lies in your embrace be careful of your words. For a son dishonors his father, a daughter rises up against her mother, a daughter-in-law against her mother-in-law—a man's enemies are the members of his own household.

But as for me, I watch in hope for the LORD, I wait for God my Savior; my God will hear me.

Do not gloat over me, my enemy! Though I have fallen, I will rise. Though I sit in darkness, the LORD will be my light. . . . He will bring me out into the light; I will see his righteousness.

Micah 7:5–9 NIV

The people of Israel had to experience the correction of God because of poor decisions they had made. They had to experience some consequences, but difficulties did not stop them from looking to the future with a positive perspective. Even the most positive and peaceful people have disagreements and difficulties, sometimes even stemming from their own actions, like the people of Israel.

You have to learn to trust yourself and rely on your own ability to make good decisions, even when times are challenging. Many families are experiencing tough financial situations, some from their own poor decisions and some due to circumstances that they could not prevent. Who is to blame for your difficult situation is less important than resolving it. If you are struggling to provide all that your family needs financially, you can trust God to help you in your most difficult challenges—even your monthly bills. Be confident in your ability to sense his guidance in your life. You can ask him for the wisdom to tackle your situation, and expect that he will respond with creative ideas, practical strategies, or resources to help you.

STRONG FOUNDATION

"Everyone who hears these words of Mine and acts on them, may be compared to a wise man who built his house on the rock. And the rain fell, and the floods came, and the winds blew and slammed against that house; and yet it did not fall, for it had been founded on the rock. Everyone who hears these words of Mine and does not act on them, will be like a foolish man who built his house on the sand. The rain fell, and the floods came, and the winds blew and slammed against that house; and it fell— and great was its fall."

When Jesus had finished these words, the crowds were amazed at His teaching; for He was teaching them as one having authority, and not as their scribes.

Matthew 7:24–29 NASB

When you imagine your dream house, what do you envision? Maybe you see something as simple as clean bedrooms without toys strewn about, or a spacious kitchen with all the best appliances. Maybe you see a white picket fence.

Your home encompasses more than the structure, rooms, and decor of a house. Your dream home includes the people, activities, and ambience of family. You are the architect who must design the heart of the home. Bricks and mortar will provide only the exterior structure, but the Word of God will build the faith of a family.

Just as you would design a floor plan for your dream home, create a plan for your family. Write in a notebook your hopes and dreams for each family member as you discover his or her interests and abilities. You can also have a section for vacations you would like to take together and fun activities to do as a family. Most important, with the help of your spouse and children, create a section of family values that will be most important to each of you. These might include forgiveness, honesty, compassion. . . . These core values shape dreams.

Is That Really You?

The members of the council were amazed when they saw the boldness of Peter and John, for they could see that they were ordinary men with no special training in the Scriptures. They also recognized them as men who had been with Jesus. But since they could see the man who had been healed standing right there among them, there was nothing the council could say. So they ordered Peter and John out of the council chamber and conferred among themselves.

"What should we do with these men?" they asked each other. "We can't deny that they have performed a miraculous sign, and everybody in Jerusalem knows about it. But to keep them from spreading their propaganda any further, we must warn them not to speak to anyone in Jesus' name again."

Acts 4:13–17 NLT

Peter and John were not mothers, obviously, but they witnessed the power of Christ and were changed by what they observed. As their faith grew stronger, they became bolder, more confident men. There is no doubt that becoming a mother changes you. Your priorities seem to reshuffle the moment you hold your baby for the first time. Your maturity increases, your hope for the future is enhanced, your perspective is more global—the list of the effects of motherhood is endless. One thing that changes in mothers of faith is an increased awareness of the miraculous power of God. Once a mother hears the first cry of her child, she realizes that God has breathed life into a new person who is a part of her own body and soul.

As a mother, understand that you have a unique wisdom and revelation of God's creativity. Don't let the terrible twos or potty training or rebellious teens or driving lessons overshadow the day that you gave birth. Spend time reading your pregnancy journal, looking at first-year photos, and viewing the sonogram videos to remind yourself of the miracle of motherhood.

BE YOUR OWN ENCOURAGERS

David and his men burst out in loud wails—wept and wept until they were exhausted with weeping. David's two wives, Ahinoam of Jezreel and Abigail widow of Nabal of Carmel, had been taken prisoner along with the rest. And suddenly David was in even worse trouble. There was talk among the men, bitter over the loss of their families, of stoning him.

David strengthened himself with trust in his GOD. He ordered Abiathar the priest, son of Ahimelech, "Bring me the Ephod so I can consult God." Abiathar brought it to David.

Then David prayed to GOD, "Shall I go after these raiders? Can I catch them?"

The answer came, "Go after them! Yes, you'll catch them! Yes, you'll make the rescue!"

David went, he and the six hundred men with him.

1 Samuel 30:4–9 MSG

When we are tired and discouraged, people we count on to help us sometimes are dealing with their own life situations. David and his men had just discovered their home camp burned and their families taken into captivity. Every one of them was angry, sad, and exhausted. This passage shows us how David stirred up his own faith, exercised trust in God, and then led the others to do the same.

A mother sets much of the tone of the home for her family and children. If the adage "When momma's not happy, nobody's happy" is true, then maybe when momma *is* happy, everyone else will be too. You might have a good reason to be emotionally drained, just like David. Life can be especially difficult for single mothers who have experienced the loss of their partner in parenting. But after a time, you must gather your confidence and trust in God and encourage yourself. You might have to give yourself a time-out for reflection or rest. You might want to set the mood in your home by playing worship music while you prepare dinner. As you strengthen yourself, you will also strengthen your family.

YES! YES! YES!

Was I vacillating when I wanted to do this? Do I make my plans according to the flesh, ready to say "Yes, yes" and "No, no" at the same time? As surely as God is faithful, our word to you has not been Yes and No. For the Son of God, Jesus Christ, whom we proclaimed among you, Silvanus and Timothy and I, was not Yes and No, but in him it is always Yes. For all the promises of God find their Yes in him. That is why it is through him that we utter our Amen to God for his glory. And it is God who establishes us with you in Christ, and has anointed us, and who has also put his seal on us and given us his Spirit in our hearts as a guarantee.

2 Corinthians 1:17–22 ESV

When God presents you with a new opportunity, hopefully your response is yes. What punctuation is at the end of your yes to God? There are many ways to respond to God's call, and his request can come in many forms: lead a Bible study, cook a meal for a neighbor, send a card to a friend, pray about a difficult situation. Whenever you are given a chance to bring hope to someone or resolve a need other than your own, often that is God's voice inviting you. Busyness, shyness, or fear often tries to drown him out. But you can overcome time restraints and timidity.

When you are asked to help others in a way that might be new or uncomfortable for you, don't decline immediately. But don't say yes too easily either and then regret your response. Instead, prayerfully consider the request. If you determine that it is something God would want you to do, then do it confidently. Say "Yes!" with determination in your voice and spirit. Don't use a question mark or period in your answer to God. Always give him a hearty exclamation!

FRIENDSHIP & MENTORING

Regardless of the stage in life, everyone wants and needs friends. Caring people with common interests can boost our spirits with a simple conversation. The key is finding and cultivating friendships that are an asset to you emotionally, intellectually, or spiritually. Strong, loving friendships not only sharpen our minds but also nurture our souls.

A mentor is someone willing to help others grow into the people God created them to be by sharing her own experiences. Mentors vary in their personality traits, abilities, and passions. The Bible is full of examples of those who mentored and those who benefited from mentoring. As you look at the friendships in your life, you will most likely find mentors as well as someone waiting for you to mentor her.

As iron sharpens iron, friends sharpen the minds
of each other.

Proverbs 27:17 CEV

Absence Makes the Heart Grow Fonder

I appeal to you for my child, Onesimus, whose father I became in my imprisonment. (Formerly he was useless to you, but now he is indeed useful to you and to me.) I am sending him back to you, sending my very heart. I would have been glad to keep him with me, in order that he might serve me on your behalf during my imprisonment for the gospel, but I preferred to do nothing without your consent in order that your goodness might not be by compulsion but of your own accord. For this perhaps is why he was parted from you for a while, that you might have him back forever, no longer as a slave but more than a slave, as a beloved brother—especially to me, but how much more to you, both in the flesh and in the Lord.

Philemon 10–16 ESV

We all experience changes in relationships in our lives. We expect it when we move to a new city or change jobs. Our children have even more opportunities to experience such changes. Every school year with a new class of peers begins the process, as does a move to a new school or a different sports team or ballet class.

Your child has most likely never heard of Onesimus, but he can be a great example for you as you help your child navigate through seasons of friendships. Many transitions are evidenced in this passage and the events that led to it. Philemon lost a trusted relationship when Onesimus, his slave, ran away, but the relationship was restored in greater value later. Paul welcomed a stranger who became a dear friend, and then experienced the loss of that friendship when he sent Onesimus back to Philemon. Onesimus fled and then found a great friend in Paul, who helped him discover Jesus and a better way of living, and then was able to restore the former relationship in a positive way.

As your child experiences changes in friendships, help him to identify positive possibilities in new relationships.

CAN YOU GIVE ME A HAND?

I saw a man who had no family, no son or brother. He always worked hard but was never satisfied with what he had. He never asked himself, "For whom am I working so hard? Why don't I let myself enjoy life?" This also is very sad and useless.

Two people are better than one, because they get more done by working together. If one falls down, the other can help him up. But it is bad for the person who is alone and falls, because no one is there to help. If two lie down together, they will be warm, but a person alone will not be warm. An enemy might defeat one person, but two people together can defend themselves; a rope that is woven of three strings is hard to break.

Ecclesiastes 4:8–12 NCV

Your assumptions that your children will always get along with their brothers and sisters might be shattered when the adoring little brother becomes the aggravating pest. But mothers know that while friends will come and go throughout life, the sibling relationships among your children remain forever. Ecclesiastes reminds readers that relationships are more important in life than accomplishments. When siblings are connected in purpose, they have lifelong partners to help in difficulties as well as share in celebrations.

Sibling relationships, like any other friendship, must be nurtured. Rather than focusing on teaching your children to get along, focus on building the friendships between them. Find ways to increase their communication. Family dinners are a good place to start. Go around the table and ask everyone to tell the "pit," or low point, of his day. Then go around again and let each one share the "palace," or high, of the day. You'll be surprised how much you all learn about each other's daily lives.

Include some of the "pits" in family bedtime prayers. When you allow each child to take a turn praying for siblings, you build more empathy and camaraderie among them.

SANDPAPER

Be wise, my son, and make my heart glad so that I can answer anyone who criticizes me. Sensible people foresee trouble and hide. Gullible people go ahead and suffer. Hold on to the garment of one who guarantees a stranger's loan, and hold responsible the person who makes a loan in behalf of a foreigner. Whoever blesses his friend early in the morning with a loud voice—his blessing is considered a curse.

Constantly dripping water on a rainy day is like a quarreling woman. Whoever can control her can control the wind. He can even pick up olive oil with his right hand.

As iron sharpens iron, so one person sharpens the wits of another.

Proverbs 27:11–17
GOD'S WORD

Teens strongly desire to fit in with a group. But sometimes the attractive friends are not the right group. Even a teenager trying to choose good friends can be fooled by first impressions. This passage tells moms that it's wise for us to look ahead to foresee trouble and take action to avoid it.

Perhaps you can't quite identify your hesitation about one of your teen's friends. But take action anyway. Follow your intuition and impose your influence on the situation. Don't simply restrict your daughter from the friendship, at least not at first. Spend time in casual conversation with your teen about what value she thinks she is receiving from the friendship. A good time to have a nonthreatening talk with your child is while you are taxiing her around town. You can begin by asking what she thinks are the most important qualities in her friends, and then ask which of her friends demonstrate those qualities and how they do so.

Help your teen by leading her to identify the assets and hindrances in each of her relationships so that she grows to become a woman who chooses strong, positive friendships.

LIVE BIG

I can't tell you how much I long for you to enter this wide-open, spacious life. We didn't fence you in. The smallness you feel comes from within you. Your lives aren't small, but you're living them in a small way. I'm speaking as plainly as I can and with great affection. Open up your lives. Live openly and expansively!

Don't become partners with those who reject God. How can you make a partnership out of right and wrong? That's not partnership; that's war. Is light best friends with dark? Does Christ go strolling with the Devil? Do trust and mistrust hold hands? Who would think of setting up pagan idols in God's holy Temple? But that is exactly what we are, each of us a temple in whom God lives.

2 Corinthians 6:11–16 MSG

If you want your children to experience many opportunities in life, teach them how to meet new people and endeavors with enthusiasm. Consider these words that Paul wrote to the Corinthians and how they relate even to your family today. Sometimes children want to be part of a certain group, even to the point of exclusivity. But often those popular cliques that seem to offer liberty only box in their opportunities and shrink their worldview.

Children will benefit from distinguishing people first by their faith, then by their personality or popularity. You can encourage them to be comfortable with new people by giving them opportunities to reach out to others. Allow them to order their own meals at a restaurant, teach them to call people by name, encourage them to invite a lonely child on the playground to swing with them. Preteens sometimes begin to withdraw into themselves, but these are still great skills for them to practice. They may be more apt to speak up for themselves when they have had much practice as younger children. Later these skills will allow them to become welcoming young adults, confident about meeting people and making friends.

WALK, STAND, SIT

Blessed is the man who walks not in the counsel of the ungodly, nor stands in the path of sinners, nor sits in the seat of the scornful; but his delight is in the law of the LORD, and in His law he meditates day and night. He shall be like a tree planted by the rivers of water, that brings forth its fruit in its season, whose leaf also shall not wither; and whatever he does shall prosper. . . .

Therefore the ungodly shall not stand in the judgment, nor sinners in the congregation of the righteous.

For the LORD knows the way of the righteous, But the way of the ungodly shall perish.

Psalm 1:1–6 NKJV

Friendships exist on a spectrum, from acquaintances to casual friendships to best friends. Whatever the level of friendship, however, there is an effect on you and your reputation. Understanding this is important to us as mothers and also to our children.

Mothers can identify with this psalm because we long for our children to be immovable in their faith. This psalm cautions against the company of those who lack faith and encourages learning the truth of the Bible as a prescription for the kind of solid faith that your child needs to sustain beneficial friendships.

Walking, standing, and sitting represent the progression of developing a friendship. The influence of a friend strengthens, whether positively or negatively, as a friendship progresses. As they are getting to know others, help your children identify whether their friends have the same values they do. The more they spend time with friends, the more like their friends they will become. So it is important to let them know that every one of their acquaintances does not have to become a friend and that every friend may not become one of their best friends—and that this might be a good thing.

GOT TO BE REAL

Your love must be real. Hate what is evil, and hold on to what is good. Love each other like brothers and sisters. Give each other more honor than you want for yourselves. Do not be lazy but work hard, serving the Lord with all your heart. Be joyful because you have hope. Be patient when trouble comes, and pray at all times. Share with God's people who need help. Bring strangers in need into your homes. Wish good for those who harm you; wish them well and do not curse them. Be happy with those who are happy, and be sad with those who are sad. Live in peace with each other. Do not be proud, but make friends with those who seem unimportant. Do not think how smart you are.

Romans 12:9–16 NCV

Empathy is a powerful attribute that we can teach our children from a young age. Understanding another person's feelings and situation expands our capacity to love him. To genuinely love others without condition or pretention, we must develop respect for all humanity.

You can help your children develop consideration for others by allowing them to interact with many different types of people. Some ways to do this are having them donate and deliver some of their toys to a local homeless shelter, visiting ill children in the hospital on holidays, or participating in a fund-raiser for a need in the community. Seeing the needs of others, whether physical, material, or emotional, can create compassion in your child, which is a gateway to genuine love.

By meeting and communicating with people who are different from their usual circle of friends, your children can learn to appreciate and embrace differences in people as unique traits to be celebrated. You can also encourage friendships through your own modeling with friends. And if you have families from different walks of life over for dinner and games, your children will learn to embrace similarities rather than oppose differences.

DEPOSITS AND WITHDRAWALS

Owe no one anything except to love one another, for he who loves another has fulfilled the law. For the commandments, "You shall not commit adultery," "You shall not murder," "You shall not steal," "You shall not bear false witness," "You shall not covet," and if there is any other commandment, are all summed up in this saying, namely, "You shall love your neighbor as yourself." Love does no harm to a neighbor; therefore love is the fulfillment of the law.

And do this, knowing the time, that now it is high time to awake out of sleep; for now our salvation is nearer than when we first believed. The night is far spent, the day is at hand. Therefore let us cast off the works of darkness, and let us put on the armor of light.

Romans 13:8–12 NKJV

Often we think of the commandments as a list of don'ts, and we overlook the to-do list. But following the list of what not to do must be balanced with doing the right things too, like loving others. What if you could actually measure love in deposits and withdrawals just like your bank account? For every kind word, a deposit would be made, but for every selfish act a withdrawal would be registered.

For a family to be strong, love and friendship among the members of the family must be cultivated. One way you can be sure that each child receives the love he needs is to be certain you understand how he wants his deposits. One of your children might feel loved when others spend time with him, while another prefers hugs and cuddles. Once you know your child's "love economy," you can help each sibling to develop different ways of showing love by leading them in giving compliments, suggesting a hug, or teaching them to make gifts for one another. As your children learn to make these love deposits, your family will soon be rich in love.

Whatcha Talkin' 'Bout?

The same Lord is the Lord of all and gives many blessings to all who trust in him, as the Scripture says, "Anyone who calls on the Lord will be saved."

But before people can ask the Lord for help, they must believe in him; and before they can believe in him, they must hear about him; and for them to hear about the Lord, someone must tell them; and before someone can go and tell them, that person must be sent. It is written, "How beautiful is the person who comes to bring good news." But not all the Jews accepted the good news. Isaiah said, "Lord, who believed what we told them?" So faith comes from hearing the Good News, and people hear the Good News when someone tells them about Christ.

Romans 10:12–17 NCV

God uses several different people and plans to reach each person with the message of salvation. But somewhere in each plan, someone must tell the story of Jesus. Mothers have an unmatched influence on what our children hear beginning the very first day that we cradle them in our arms, singing softly about Jesus' love.

Throughout their lives, you can teach your children about the Bible and a life of faith without being a Bible scholar! Find teachable moments in everyday life to talk about godly things and your personal faith. When you are outdoors or even in the produce section of the grocery store, talk about Creation. When it's raining, remind your children of Noah's faith in building the ark. When you are enjoying a day at the beach, talk about Jonah, or the miracle of the loaves and fishes, or Jesus walking on the water. Endless topics surround you.

You can teach your children to share their faith too. Pray with your children for their friends and for situations at school. Your children will learn that faith is rightfully a part of every area of their lives.

SCRATCHING BACKS

I thank my God through Jesus Christ for all of you, because people everywhere in the world are talking about your faith. . . . I pray that I will be allowed to come to you, and this will happen if God wants it. I want very much to see you, to give you some spiritual gift to make you strong. I mean that I want us to help each other with the faith we have. Your faith will help me, and my faith will help you. Brothers and sisters, I want you to know that I planned many times to come to you, but this has not been possible. I wanted to come so that I could help you grow spiritually as I have helped the other non-Jewish people.

Romans 1:8, 10–13 NCV

One vital attribute of friendships for Christian mothers is reciprocity. It is important that the friendships you have include give-and-take among you. Even the great apostle Paul expressed in this passage that he needed others to help build his faith. You don't have to do it alone either. By encouraging others you will find your own faith strengthened too.

One edifying way to build your friends' faith is by beginning a prayer circle. If you have time to dedicate one morning a week or a month, have some moms over for an hour of prayer together. For most busy mothers, those extra few minutes are tough to squeeze in, but worth it.

If you just cannot afford the time, you don't even have to physically gather. You can start a circle with e-mail. On a specific day each week or month, send out an e-mail to your group of moms requesting their prayer needs. Compile them into one list and send them out to all in your circle to pray for during the month. In addition to building your faith, praying together will also build strong bonds of trust and friendship.

What Fruit Is in Your Salad?

Live your life as your spiritual nature directs you. Then you will never follow through on what your corrupt nature wants. What your corrupt nature wants is contrary to what your spiritual nature wants, and what your spiritual nature wants is contrary to what your corrupt nature wants. They are opposed to each other. As a result, you don't always do what you intend to do. . . .

The spiritual nature produces love, joy, peace, patience, kindness, goodness, faithfulness, gentleness, and self-control. There are no laws against things like that. Those who belong to Christ Jesus have crucified their corrupt nature along with its passions and desires. If we live by our spiritual nature, then our lives need to conform to our spiritual nature. We can't allow ourselves to act arrogantly and to provoke or envy each other.

Galatians 5:16–17, 22–26
GOD'S WORD

Just as natural fruit is a result of a seed that has been nurtured, spiritual fruit is the result of a growing relationship with God. The attributes listed in this passage, known as the fruit of the Spirit, are a reflection of the Holy Spirit who dwells within those with faith in Jesus. They serve as qualities to aspire to as our faith matures as well as proof of our spiritual growth. The friendships your children forge will help to mold their values and behavior, so it is vital that they surround themselves with positive influences. The fruit of the Spirit comprise nine key characteristics exhibited by a good friend. You can make it easy and fun for your children to understand friendship by teaching them the fruit of the Spirit.

Focus on one "fruit" for a week at a time. Play a game—think of and follow through on ways to be a good friend using that quality. For example, for patience, children might let their friends go first in every game they play. You can also use these nine areas as the focus for your family devotions and prayer times together.

Oh, How Sweet of You

Praise should come from another person and not from your own mouth, from a stranger and not from your own lips. . . .

Open criticism is better than unexpressed love. Wounds made by a friend are intended to help, but an enemy's kisses are too much to bear. . . .

Perfume and incense make the heart glad, but the sweetness of a friend is a fragrant forest. Do not abandon your friend or your father's friend. Do not go to a relative's home when you are in trouble. A neighbor living nearby is better than a relative far away.

Proverbs 27:2, 5–6, 9–10
GOD'S WORD

When you were growing up, did your mother ask you to run next door for a cup of sugar? Neighborhoods are not what they used to be; most of us don't even know the names of the people living on our block. But getting to know your neighbors offers many benefits.

One of the most important is knowing the families of the friends your children play with after school. You need to know the values and traditions of those who influence your children, and this will help you know how to guide your children in their friendships. You'll also gain peace of mind by knowing where your children are and that they are safe when they are out of your sight.

Befriend your neighbors by being, well, neighborly! Reach out to your neighbors on evening strolls. Stop and introduce yourself; get to know them a little. Being neighborly is about building relationships with others as an extension of your love for God and your family. As you open your home and your heart to those around you, you may find opportunities to make your own friendships as well as strengthen your children's.

Welcome Refreshment

Although I wrote to you, it was not for the sake of the offender nor for the sake of the one offended, but that your earnestness on our behalf might be made known to you in the sight of God. For this reason we have been comforted. And besides our comfort, we rejoiced even much more for the joy of Titus, because his spirit has been refreshed by you all. For if in anything I have boasted to him about you, I was not put to shame; but as we spoke all things to you in truth, so also our boasting before Titus proved to be the truth. His affection abounds all the more toward you, as he remembers the obedience of you all, how you received him with fear and trembling. I rejoice that in everything I have confidence in you.

2 Corinthians 7:12–16 NASB

When Paul told Titus about the Christians in Corinth, he must have said that they were full of hospitality. Evidently the Corinthians did not disappoint Titus when he spent time with them. Would you like to be known as someone whose presence refreshes others?

You might not be as domestic as Aunt Bee in Mayberry. She certainly had the gift of refreshing others. It seemed that she was always ready with iced tea and advice. The family always had room for one more at their table, even surprise guests. Hospitality might not be easy for you if you work outside your home. But being hospitable doesn't have to consume our days. We can incorporate small time- and budget-conscious gestures into our schedules and still serve others a good portion of encouragement.

How about uplifting a neighbor with a simple card of inspiration or a gift of spring flowers? If you don't have time for a meal, invite a friend to coffee and conversation after church. Keep some cookies on hand for when your kids have friends over and start teaching them to refresh others too.

SHOW ME SOME LOVE

We also ought to give up our lives for our brothers and sisters. If someone has enough money to live well and sees a brother or sister in need but shows no compassion—how can God's love be in that person?

Dear children, let's not merely say that we love each other; let us show the truth by our actions. Our actions will show that we belong to the truth, so we will be confident when we stand before God. Even if we feel guilty, God is greater than our feelings, and he knows everything.

Dear friends, if we don't feel guilty, we can come to God with bold confidence. And we will receive from him whatever we ask because we obey him and do the things that please him.

1 John 3:16–22 NLT

Share. Be kind. Wait your turn. Prefer others. Mothers recite these instructions from the time children are toddlers well into their teen years. Sometimes it's difficult to determine how to teach such intangible concepts to children who live in a culture that tells them to be concerned with their own desires and to look out for their own interests. Observe your children interacting with friends. Look for indications of patience, generosity, and kindness. You might identify some areas where your children need to grow.

Here's an activity that you might consider to help make the intangible concepts of compassion and giving more concrete. Schedule a play date for your child's friends. Ask each mom to provide a toy that her child no longer uses and have a swap. Pile them on a table and let the children take turns choosing a new toy. This works as your children become older too. Preteen boys love to exchange electronic games and music, and girls enjoy swapping clothing with their friends.

An added benefit to the joy of receiving "new" items is that your children learn to see the happiness that they can make for others through their giving.

REMEMBER THE LITTLE PEOPLE

[Joseph said,] "Only remember me, when it is well with you, and please do me the kindness to mention me to Pharaoh, and so get me out of this house. For I was indeed stolen out of the land of the Hebrews, and here also I have done nothing that they should put me into the pit.". . .

On the third day, which was Pharaoh's birthday, he made a feast for all his servants and lifted up the head of the chief cupbearer and the head of the chief baker among his servants. He restored the chief cupbearer to his position, and he placed the cup in Pharaoh's hand. But he hanged the chief baker, as Joseph had interpreted to them. Yet the chief cupbearer did not remember Joseph, but forgot him.

Genesis 40:14–15, 20–23 ESV

Because Joseph was forgotten, he remained in prison for a time longer. But eventually the cupbearer did remember him and mention him to the king. That remembrance started Joseph on his journey to the Egyptian palace. Ultimately it led to the growth of the nation of Israel from the family of Joseph and his brothers.

Who are the people who have impacted the course of your life? Who are the people who once were a big part of your life that you haven't connected with for some time?

With so many social networks available, it is easy to reconnect with past coworkers, high school friends, college buddies, or even a favorite cousin. You might want to track down a teacher or youth minister whose actions or words redirected your life at a critical time. Reach out and rekindle a friendship or two. You might have only one brief conversation to express your thanks, or you might establish a lifelong friend. Who knows, you might even find that your remembrance helps someone step out of a pit and make her way to the palace.

Timing Is Everything

Paul and Barnabas remained in Antioch, teaching and preaching the word of the Lord, with many others also.

And after some days Paul said to Barnabas, "Let us return and visit the brothers in every city where we proclaimed the word of the Lord, and see how they are." Now Barnabas wanted to take with them John called Mark. But Paul thought best not to take with them one who had withdrawn from them in Pamphylia and had not gone with them to the work. And there arose a sharp disagreement, so that they separated from each other. Barnabas took Mark with him and sailed away to Cyprus, but Paul chose Silas and departed, having been commended by the brothers to the grace of the Lord. And he went through Syria and Cilicia, strengthening the churches.

Acts 15:35–41 ESV

Barnabas introduced Paul—endorsing him, really—to the apostles after Paul committed himself to Jesus. Paul and Barnabas were pretty close pals for a while. But a time of disagreement came, and they parted ways. Have you experienced a turn in a friendship too? Often when life journeys us through various seasons, our relationships change with them.

If you have lost friendships during life transitions, don't despair. New seasons are opportunities for new friends. For example, if you have just become a mom, some of your friends without young children might not be excited about all the new experiences of motherhood. But you have great opportunities to become friends with other moms through your church, workplace, day care, or social groups for moms.

Changes in friendship can affect us deeply. The end of the story of Paul and Barnabas offers great encouragement, because later we learn that Paul reunited with Barnabas. He also traveled again with John Mark, the source of his disagreement with Barnabas.

So although some friendships change for a season, they can sometimes return and be even more fruitful. Life experiences provoke personal growth and shift relationships to significant matters of life.

I Choose You

You, Lord, are my choice, and I will obey you. With all my heart I beg you to be kind to me, just as you have promised. I pay careful attention as you lead me, and I follow closely. As soon as you command, I do what you say. Evil people may set a trap, but I obey your Law. Your laws are so fair that I wake up and praise you in the middle of the night. I choose as my friends everyone who worships you and follows your teachings. Our Lord, your love is seen all over the world. Teach me your laws.

I am your servant, Lord, and you have kept your promise to treat me with kindness.

Psalm 119:57–65 CEV

As we become adults, many of our friendships are formed through simple proximity. People we live near, work with, and attend church alongside are the people we befriend. We can't imagine how we would have become acquainted with some of our friends had we not been thrown together in the same environment. These friendships enhance our lives and expose us to personalities that we wouldn't have otherwise ever known.

But there are special friendships that we must choose to nurture. We must cultivate friendships with others who have the same beliefs that we have, especially those who share a love for God. The psalmist made a wise choice to befriend people who also worshipped God. This is the type of relationship that can become a committed friendship that lasts over time. When you discover this kind of friend, pay attention to her. Like marriage and parenting, we get out of friendship only as much as we put in.

Connect with one of your friends today for a moment of uplifting conversation. Make a commitment to nurture your friendships—even if you have to schedule a weekly phone call on your calendar.

CHERISHED CONVERSATIONS

Each time Moses went out to [the tent of meeting], everyone would stand at the entrance to their own tents and watch him enter. Then they would bow down because a thick cloud would come down in front of the tent, and the Lord would speak to Moses face to face, just like a friend. Afterwards, Moses would return to camp, but his young assistant Joshua would stay at the tent.

Moses said to the Lord, "I know that you have told me to lead these people to the land you promised them. But you have not told me who my assistant will be. You have said that you are my friend and that you are pleased with me. If this is true, let me know what your plans are, then I can obey and continue to please you."

Exodus 33:8–13 CEV

This account of Moses talking with God in the tent of meeting contains several threads that lead to great insight. One of the greatest nuggets found here is that God can be a friend to us!

When you talk with your children about their relationship with God, refer to him especially as a friend. Children understand the concept of friendship from a young age, because they experience it. They need to know that they can have some of the same experiences of friendship with God. Encourage your children to talk to God anywhere and anytime, but also to have a special place to meet with God, just as Moses did. Help them settle on where this place will be. Get them started in the habit of meeting with God there each day, talking to him just as they do with a friend with whom they like to spend time.

If your children learn from a young age that they can spend time with God as a friend and share their private thoughts and feelings, he will become a constant in their lives and they will learn to love him wholeheartedly, just as Moses did.

EASY LOVE

If someone slaps you on your right cheek, turn your other cheek to him as well. If someone wants to sue you in order to take your shirt, let him have your coat too. If someone forces you to go one mile, go two miles with him. Give to everyone who asks you for something. Don't turn anyone away who wants to borrow something from you.

You have heard that it was said, "Love your neighbor, and hate your enemy." But I tell you this: Love your enemies, and pray for those who persecute you. In this way you show that you are children of your Father in heaven. He makes his sun rise on people whether they are good or evil. . . . If you love those who love you, do you deserve a reward?

Matthew 5:39–46 GOD'S WORD

If a mother really wants to understand this passage, she could read it more like this: "If someone hits your child at school, tell your child not to fight back but to react humbly. If someone wants to blame your child for a bad situation or steal his lunch, offer his family a full meal too. . . ." When we ponder someone causing our child to suffer for any reason at all, it helps us to understand the fullness of what Matthew was conveying here in Jesus' teaching on how to deal with enemies. Regarding our children, we might not use the word *enemy* as much today. But this teaching still gives us insight on how to deal with bullies who try to intimidate or harm our children.

The instruction in this passage is not just to tolerate people you dislike but to love them and pray for their well-being. In essence, we are to change our attitudes and actions toward people we would call our enemies. Loving those who require effort to love is the real measure of how well we really love our neighbors.

LETTING GO

I said, "I wish I had wings like a dove. Then I would fly away and rest. I would wander far away and stay in the desert. I would hurry to my place of escape, far away from the wind and storm." . . .

It was not an enemy insulting me. I could stand that. It was not someone who hated me. I could hide from him. But it is you, a person like me, my companion and good friend. We had a good friendship and walked together to God's Temple. . . .

I will call to God for help, and the LORD will save me. Morning, noon, and night I am troubled and upset, but he will listen to me.

Psalm 55:6–8, 12–14, 16–17
NCV

Like adults, children experience changes and loss in their friendships. It seems that middle school years are some of the most difficult for children to encounter, and then come the teenage years and their frequent relationship ups and downs. Moms can forget just how painful these losses can be. Frankly, sometimes we know that our children are better off without certain friends, but even so we never desire for our children to experience the sting of rejection or separation.

Although you might not be able to prevent your children's pain, you can nurture them through it. When your children lose friends, you can help by understanding the loneliness and disappointment they are feeling and show them that David felt the same way. We often think of David fighting great battles, but he also had personal relationships that were difficult. Many of his friends and even his own son were disloyal to him. Encourage your children to express their feelings as David did, and really listen to them. Reassure them that God hears their cries too. Sometimes the warmest comfort a mother can bring is simply time and attention and maybe even a shared tear.

PRIMING THE PUMP

The Samaritan woman said to Him, "How is it that You, being a Jew, ask me for a drink since I am a Samaritan woman?" . . . Jesus answered and said to her, "If you knew the gift of God, and who it is who says to you, 'Give Me a drink,' you would have asked Him, and He would have given you living water." She said to Him, "Sir, You have nothing to draw with and the well is deep; where then do You get that living water?" . . . Jesus answered and said to her, "Everyone who drinks of this water will thirst again; but whoever drinks of the water that I will give him shall never thirst; but the water that I will give him will become in him a well of water springing up to eternal life."

John 4:9–11, 13–14 NASB

Jesus' interaction with this woman beside a well in Samaria was uncommon for several reasons. First, Jews looked down on Samaritans and did not associate with them, even adding miles to a journey to go around Samaria rather than through it. Second, Jewish tradition taught that sinners were to be avoided, and this woman's five divorces and current unmarried relationship labeled her a sinner in the eyes of any Jewish teacher. Finally, she was a woman, and Jewish men did not engage women in conversation.

But Jesus went through Samaria, not around it. And he saw this woman's need. He could offer her love, acceptance, and forgiveness. And he did. Sometimes God detours our paths during the day, not to frustrate us but so that we can cross paths with someone who needs a visit with us.

When you have an occasion to strike up a conversation with a stranger, be friendly as Jesus was to this woman at the well. Each person you meet has value. Don't let skin color, economic status, or the lifestyles others embrace stop you from showing interest in them or helping them find Jesus' "living water" for their needs.

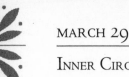

INNER CIRCLE

Jesus came with them to a place called Gethsemane, and He told the disciples, "Sit here while I go over there and pray." Taking along Peter and the two sons of Zebedee, He began to be sorrowful and deeply distressed. Then He said to them, "My soul is swallowed up in sorrow—to the point of death. Remain here and stay awake with Me." Going a little farther, He fell facedown and prayed, "My Father! If it is possible, let this cup pass from Me. Yet not as I will, but as You will."

Then He came to the disciples and found them sleeping. He asked Peter, "So, couldn't you stay awake with Me one hour? Stay awake and pray, so that you won't enter into temptation. The spirit is willing, but the flesh is weak."

Matthew 26:36–41 HCSB

Jesus had followers at different levels of intimacy. Of course you have heard of the Twelve. But as many as seventy people were counted as disciples in Luke 6. Even within the circle of twelve, Jesus had varying relationships with each one. On the evening before his death, they all (except Judas) went with him to the Mount of Olives, but he handpicked three to remain close to him while he prayed in the Garden of Gethsemane—Peter, James, and John. Of those three, John is known as "the disciple whom Jesus loved."

What can mothers learn from this? We too will experience different levels of intimacy with others. We might have many acquaintances, but not everyone should be invited into our prayer group to hear our deepest thoughts and feelings. Over time, friends will prove themselves to be trustworthy and loyal, as you will too; then you will naturally develop the deeper bond of close friends. And as much as we enjoy our inner circle, that one best friend whom we love dearly can be a gift from God with whom we can share our most precious dreams and concerns.

PRIORITY RELATIONSHIPS

Do not neglect to show hospitality to strangers, for by this some have entertained angels without knowing it. Remember the prisoners, as though in prison with them, and those who are ill-treated, since you yourselves also are in the body. Marriage is to be held in honor among all, and the marriage bed is to be undefiled; for fornicators and adulterers God will judge. Make sure that your character is free from the love of money, being content with what you have; for He Himself has said, "I will never desert you, nor will I ever forsake you," so that we confidently say, "The LORD is my helper, I will not be afraid. What will man do to me?"

Remember those who led you, who spoke the word of God to you; and considering the result of their conduct, imitate their faith.

Hebrews 13:2–7 NASB

Time is a commodity that we have to budget like any other valuable resource. This passage from the book of Hebrews reminds us that there are many relationships worthy of our attention. In friendships and family one way to do this is by prioritizing. Of course, we must first set aside time to spend with God. As the Bible tells us, he will be our constant helper. In particular, we must consider marriage first as a friendship to be developed. We also must prioritize time with family—not just our family as a group but with each family member as an individual. Family must remain our priority in every season of life.

You can prioritize friendships with others too. You might not be able to spend hours each week with every friend, but you can stay in touch with notes and calls throughout the month. One savvy mom keeps a stack of note cards handy. During commercials or while waiting in lines, she writes quick notes to friends to keep in touch. You might have to get creative with your time, but it will be worth it to build enduring and endearing friendships.

BEING NEIGHBORLY

Jesus answered and said: "A certain man went down from Jerusalem to Jericho, and fell among thieves, who stripped him of his clothing, wounded him, and departed, leaving him half dead. Now by chance a certain priest came down that road. And when he saw him, he passed by on the other side. Likewise a Levite, when he arrived at the place, came and looked, and passed by on the other side. But a certain Samaritan, as he journeyed, came where he was. And when he saw him, he had compassion. So he went to him and bandaged his wounds, pouring on oil and wine; and he set him on his own animal, brought him to an inn, and took care of him. . . . So which of these three do you think was neighbor to him who fell among the thieves?"

Luke 10:30–34, 36 NKJV

Imagining that this kind of scenario could really happen to us today makes us uncomfortable. But news reports tell stories of people driving past unnoticed victims of auto accidents or ignoring a woman's screams for help. Stories like these do happen. It is heartbreaking to think that humanity is so void of love. But when motivated by compassion, there is potential in each of us to do good.

This story says the injured man came down from Jerusalem. Samaritans were typically disliked by Jews because of their different religious practices. So the irony here is that someone who very likely would never be helped himself by a Jew was the hero. It is interesting to note who did not help the man as much as who did. As unlikely as it was for a Samaritan to be the person to stop and help, wouldn't you imagine that those who identified themselves as religious people would have been the first to help?

This parable certainly provokes us to think about our own reluctance or initiative to help others in need. Our neighbors include even strangers who are in need of our compassion.

GOOD COMPANY

Daniel said to the steward whom the chief of the eunuchs had assigned over Daniel, Hananiah, Mishael, and Azariah, "Test your servants for ten days." . . .

As for these four youths, God gave them learning and skill in all literature and wisdom, and Daniel had understanding in all visions and dreams. At the end of the time, when the king had commanded that they should be brought in, the chief of the eunuchs brought them in before Nebuchadnezzar. And the king spoke with them, and among all of them none was found like Daniel, Hananiah, Mishael, and Azariah. Therefore they stood before the king. And in every matter of wisdom and understanding about which the king inquired of them, he found them ten times better than all the magicians and enchanters that were in all his kingdom.

Daniel 1:11–12, 17–20 ESV

You might recognize the characters in this story by the new names that the chief official assigned three of them—Shadrach, Meshach, and Abednego. Together with Daniel, these young men were what mothers like to call good kids. In exile in Babylon, they were selected for the king's three-year training program because of their physical and intellectual potential.

The four young men in this story seemed to strengthen one another. They stuck together when challenges to their faith came. Imagine being offered a special regimen of exercise, education, and eating with proven results to make you healthier, wiser, and more attractive. The offer would be tempting. But the particular program prescribed for Daniel and his friends included foods that they would not eat because of their religious convictions. To them, it was denouncing their faith to participate. They aligned their behavior with their convictions.

You can teach your children to measure their actions by the Bible, even in matters that are seemingly unimportant to others. But with their choice of friends, they can be strengthened or weakened. It is important to help them build strong relationships with friends of the same character and courage.

Self-Protection

Do not let your good be spoken of as evil; for the kingdom of God is not eating and drinking, but righteousness and peace and joy in the Holy Spirit. For he who serves Christ in these things is acceptable to God and approved by men.

Therefore let us pursue the things which make for peace and the things by which one may edify another. Do not destroy the work of God for the sake of food. All things indeed are pure, but it is evil for the man who eats with offense. It is good neither to eat meat nor drink wine nor do anything by which your brother stumbles or is offended or is made weak. Do you have faith? Have it to yourself before God. Happy is he who does not condemn himself in what he approves.

Romans 14:16–22 NKJV

In the early years of the church, not all believers agreed that the food traditions in Old Testament law no longer were in effect. The real issue addressed in this passage, however, is not what we should eat or not eat; it is how we regard others and their beliefs. In our culture it might be less about food and more about lifestyle choices. Even within our churches, each family has its own convictions that might not be the same as another family's beliefs.

Times come when it is best to be able to agree to disagree on matters of personal conviction. When facilitating conflict resolution, one wise pastor poses this question: would you rather be happy or right? By demanding to be the one who is right about a matter, whether it is spiritual or relational, we build barriers to peaceful agreement.

It is not our responsibility to change other people's convictions. As mothers, we must be sure that our children develop their own convictions based on the Bible. We don't have to surround ourselves or our children only with people who share our opinions in order to live in harmony.

GOD'S SCRAPBOOK

GOD says, "You have spoken hard, rude words to me.

"You ask, 'When did we ever do that?'

"When you said, 'It doesn't pay to serve God. What do we ever get out of it?'" . . .

Then those whose lives honored GOD got together and talked it over. GOD saw what they were doing and listened in. A book was opened in God's presence and minutes were taken of the meeting, with the names of the GOD-fearers written down, all the names of those who honored GOD's name.

GOD-of-the-Angel-Armies said, "They're mine, all mine. They'll get special treatment when I go into action. I treat them with the same consideration and kindness that parents give the child who honors them. Once more you'll see the difference it makes between being a person who does the right thing and one who doesn't, between serving God and not serving him."

Malachi 3:13–14, 16–18 MSG

Some of the sweetest moments you can experience as a mother are when you listen unnoticed to your children's conversations. While watching your little girl pretend to be a mommy, you almost assuredly will hear familiar phrases that you have said. Can you imagine God doing the same thing with you? You might think of God hearing your conversations and judging your words. So remember instead that he delights when you talk about the wonderful things he does in your life. Malachi reminds us that God does indeed pay attention to our conversations—especially those about him. He notices when you honor his name, just as you do when your children talk about what a great mom you are!

Every day you have an awesome opportunity to give God something to add to his scrapbook about you. He notices the hope and grace you bring to others through your conversations. You can never run out of topics when you speak about God and his marvelous blessings in your life. When you speak of God positively, you not only bless your friends but you make him a proud parent too.

Faithful Friends

All these, having gained approval through their faith, did not receive what was promised, because God had provided something better for us, so that apart from us they would not be made perfect.

Therefore, since we have so great a cloud of witnesses surrounding us, let us also lay aside every encumbrance and the sin which so easily entangles us, and let us run with endurance the race that is set before us, fixing our eyes on Jesus, the author and perfecter of faith, who for the joy set before Him endured the cross, despising the shame, and has sat down at the right hand of the throne of God.

For consider Him who has endured such hostility by sinners against Himself, so that you will not grow weary and lose heart.

Hebrews 11:39–12:3 NASB

Childhood books intrigue little girls because of all the characters with whom they can identify as well as the relationships among the different characters in each story. A girl's longing to be intertwined with others' lives grows up with her, which could explain the popularity of best-selling books about friendships, movies about living in the city, or reality shows about housewives. But there are exciting epics and intriguing adventures about *real* lives within the Bible.

There is much to learn from the "great cloud of witnesses" this passage speaks of. These witnesses include heroes of the faith who encourage us with their own stories as we navigate through life. As we read their stories and learn how they overcame struggles and lived victoriously, our own faith is bolstered. They not only set the course before us but are at the sidelines cheering us on and at the finish line awaiting our victory leap into eternity.

Imagine yourself in conversations with some of your Bible heroes. Journal the advice that you think they would give to you as a mother, based on their lives of faith.

INTERLOCKED

Everyone I meet—it matters little whether they're mannered or rude, smart or simple—deepens my sense of interdependence and obligation. And that's why I can't wait to get to you in Rome, preaching this wonderful good news of God.

It's news I'm most proud to proclaim, this extraordinary Message of God's powerful plan to rescue everyone who trusts him, starting with Jews and then right on to everyone else! God's way of putting people right shows up in the acts of faith, confirming what Scripture has said all along: "The person in right standing before God by trusting him really lives." . . .

By taking a long and thoughtful look at what God has created, people have always been able to see what their eyes as such can't see: eternal power, for instance, and the mystery of his divine being.

Romans 1:14–17, 20 MSG

Paul realized that everyone has a place of importance, and that realization stirred his sense of purpose. Each person is linked to another, and together we strengthen one another as well as the whole group. Our friendships are the same.

Mothers understand missing pieces. We try everything to keep puzzle pieces together—plastic zip bags, containers with tight-fitting tops, boxes taped shut. No one ever knows where the missing pieces have gone; they just disappear, leaving an indelible void that affects the entire puzzle.

When you think of your relationships with other moms, what picture do you see? What part do you play? Most circles of friends have individuals in various roles—the caretaker, an adventurer, a scheduler, a jokester, an intellect. Each one fills a place in the group that all of the others need to depend on from time to time. The differences strengthen the whole group and its individuals. When your friends call for a get-together, don't hesitate to join in, regardless of your busy schedule or tasks yet to be done. You have value to add and a void to fill among friends. You just might be the missing piece of the puzzle.

Mind Your Own

Peter turned and saw the disciple whom Jesus loved following them, the one who had been reclining at table close to him and had said, "Lord, who is it that is going to betray you?" When Peter saw him, he said to Jesus, "Lord, what about this man?" Jesus said to him, "If it is my will that he remain until I come, what is that to you? You follow me!" So the saying spread abroad among the brothers that this disciple was not to die; yet Jesus did not say to him that he was not to die, but, "If it is my will that he remain until I come, what is that to you?"

This is the disciple who is bearing witness about these things, and who has written these things, and we know that his testimony is true.

John 21:20–24 ESV

Jesus had just alluded to how Peter would die for his faith. His response to Peter's question about John's fate was a kind but firm way of telling Peter to mind his own business. We cannot compare our lives of faith with someone else's, because God created each of us as individuals, with our own purposes.

It's tempting to watch how other mothers handle their faith and families and then to make comparisons. When you are going through a struggle with your child, you might look at other moms who seemingly have perfect relationships with their children and wonder what you are doing wrong. But every family has its own challenges and promises, so each of us must mother our children to the best of our ability in our own circumstances.

We must focus on our own relationship and journey with God. When we let other people or situations capture our attention, we can lose focus on our own family members. But if we concentrate on following Christ, he will keep us focused on the things that matter most. Whether we are experiencing success or challenges, we must stay on our own path.

NOT BLOOD, BUT FAMILY

The king said, "You inquire whose son the youth is."

When David returned from killing the Philistine, Abner took him and brought him before Saul with the Philistine's head in his hand.

Saul said to him, "Whose son are you, young man?" And David answered, "I am the son of your servant Jesse the Bethlehemite."

Now it came about when he had finished speaking to Saul, that the soul of Jonathan was knit to the soul of David, and Jonathan loved him as himself.

Saul took him that day and did not let him return to his father's house.

Then Jonathan made a covenant with David because he loved him as himself.

Jonathan stripped himself of the robe that was on him and gave it to David, with his armor, including his sword and his bow and his belt.

1 Samuel 17:56–18:4 NASB

Easing into motherhood can be a breeze when you have family to help you with babysitting, last-minute bailouts, moral support, and crisis control. But many moms do not have immediate family nearby to help them when needs arise or just to celebrate life's important occasions. David had a similar situation. He left his many brothers and parents behind when he was summoned to live at the king's palace. But God provided a new friend for him in Jonathan, who became like family to him.

What can you do when you do not have strong family support nearby? You can create family with your circle of friends as David did! Pray and ask God to connect you with the right relationships that can be mutually supportive. Weekends are the perfect time to reach out to others and invite friends over for family time.

If you are blessed to have your siblings or parents nearby, notice others around you who aren't as fortunate. Reach out to them with an offer of child care or just a nice family dinner. You might find that you expand your own family to embrace someone else for a lifetime.

He Looks Just Like His Dad

No one can see God, but Jesus Christ is exactly like him. He ranks higher than everything that has been made. Through his power all things were made—things in heaven and on earth, things seen and unseen, all powers, authorities, lords, and rulers. All things were made through Christ and for Christ. He was there before anything was made, and all things continue because of him. He is the head of the body, which is the church. Everything comes from him. He is the first one who was raised from the dead. So in all things Jesus has first place. God was pleased for all of himself to live in Christ. And through Christ, God has brought all things back to himself again—things on earth and things in heaven.

Colossians 1:15–20 NCV

When you look through the baby books and scrapbooks you've created for your children, you can't miss seeing how much your children look just like you and their father. Same eyes, same dimples, same smile . . . It is amazing to see the similarities develop throughout our children's growth. When we read the Bible, it is like reading a scrapbook about how much Jesus is like his Father. He shows us the attributes and character that we as God's children also can develop.

When your friends see you, how often do they recognize your Father, God, in you? Even more so, how are your children recognizing God through you? Your children follow your example just as you follow Christ. It is never too late for any of us to make changes in our lives. Spend a little time meditating about being like Christ and make a list of the areas in your life that need to be made more like him. As you allow God to help you develop those traits in your life, your children will likely notice the changes and follow your example to become more like Christ as well.

BLESSED HARVEST

Pay careful attention to your own work . . . and you won't need to compare yourself to anyone else. For we are each responsible for our own conduct.

Those who are taught the word of God should provide for their teachers, sharing all good things with them.

Don't be misled—you cannot mock the justice of God. You will always harvest what you plant. Those who live only to satisfy their own sinful nature will harvest decay and death from that sinful nature. But those who live to please the Spirit will harvest everlasting life from the Spirit. So let's not get tired of doing what is good. At just the right time we will reap a harvest of blessing if we don't give up. Therefore, whenever we have the opportunity, we should do good to everyone—especially to those in the family of faith.

Galatians 6:4–10 NLT

The old tradition of growing your own food provides many values, as does gardening for pleasure; one is the principle of the harvest: we are only going to grow what we plant. If you want beets, you don't plant tulip bulbs. If you want to eat salads, you plant lettuce, tomatoes, and maybe some cucumbers. The Bible tells us that like gardening, doing good yields its own crop. Also like gardening, doing good is a mind-set that requires constant attention; a garden fails if you don't tend it.

Most mothers wouldn't think of conducting their day-to-day affairs without anticipating the end result. We grocery shop according to our dinner menus, lunches to pack, afternoon snacks needed, and so forth. Though more important than our menus, spiritual matters function under the same principle. We must begin with the desired result. If you want forgiving children, you cannot plant judgment. If you want courageous children, you plant boldness. Think of the attributes you would like your children to possess. You might even ask them how they would like others to describe them. Then ask God to show you ways to help your children develop those characteristics.

ROAD CONSTRUCTION

Your God says, "Comfort, comfort my people. Speak kindly to the people of Jerusalem and tell them that their time of service is finished, that they have paid for their sins." . . .

This is the voice of one who calls out: "Prepare in the desert the way for the LORD. Make a straight road in the dry lands for our God. Every valley should be raised up, and every mountain and hill should be made flat. The rough ground should be made level, and the rugged ground should be made smooth. Then the glory of the LORD will be shown, and all people together will see it. The LORD himself said these things."

Isaiah 40:1–5 NCV

As your circle of friends increases through your children—other preschool moms, soccer moms, and PTA parents, for example—your realm of influence extends too. Some of these new friends might not know Christ in the same way you do. You might be eager to share Jesus' love with them, but others don't always welcome what they perceive as an aggressive approach to win them over to faith. Isaiah advised that encouragement was a good way to deliver the message of God's love to others. Words of kindness that demonstrate hope attune people to your words today too.

We cannot change other people. They have to make a personal decision to come to faith. Think of yourself as one who is clearing a path and building a roadway for them. They will have to travel that road themselves. Your part is simply to make the road appealing and easy to travel. You can do that by sharing your own story of hope with them. Simply tell them how God has met a need in your life. Your story might provide the hope that helps clear the path on their road to discovery.

SOUNDS LIKE FRIENDLY ADVICE . . . BUT IS IT?

Accept instruction from his mouth and lay up his words in your heart. If you return to the Almighty, you will be restored. . . .

Surely then you will find delight in the Almighty and will lift up your face to God. You will pray to him, and he will hear you, and you will fulfill your vows. What you decide on will be done, and light will shine on your ways. When men are brought low and you say, "Lift them up!" then he will save the downcast. He will deliver even one who is not innocent, who will be delivered through the cleanness of your hands.

Job 22:22–23, 26–30 NIV

Job had well-meaning friends. When he was grieving and suffering, they gave their opinions about the error of his ways and how to make things right. But as we read the entire story of Job, we realize there was much more going on behind the scenes than any of them understood, and God wasn't pleased with their advice.

Just because you face difficult situations does not mean God is displeased with you; he was not unhappy with Job. When you are experiencing challenges, rely on God as your source of wisdom, and he will give you the counsel and resources you need. Ask him to give you understanding of your situation and what you should do, and ask him to provide you with wise counsel from friends.

Our friends might have the best intentions, but their advice can be shaded by their own experiences or limited understanding. Be thankful for friends who care enough about you to give you counsel (even when you don't ask for it), but weigh their counsel against what the Bible teaches. Don't feel pressured to act upon every suggestion your friends have for you.

Deeper Than Skin-Deep

Who saw the LORD's power in this? He grew up like a small plant before the LORD, like a root growing in a dry land. He had no special beauty or form to make us notice him; there was nothing in his appearance to make us desire him. He was hated and rejected by people. He had much pain and suffering. People would not even look at him. He was hated, and we didn't even notice him.

But he took our suffering on him and felt our pain for us. We saw his suffering and thought God was punishing him. But he was wounded for the wrong we did; he was crushed for the evil we did. The punishment, which made us well, was given to him, and we are healed because of his wounds.

Isaiah 53:1–5 NCV

As children become tweens, teens, and young adults, their personal style seems to transition with them. Your daughter might go through many phases, leaving pink and lace as a forlorn memory. She is on a journey of self-discovery and self-expression that you may not always understand. Frankly, she might not either.

Keep this in mind about her taste in friends too. She might leave some of her childhood friends aside when she joins the cheerleading squad or enters high school. As her interests change, her friends can change. Guard against judging her friends on first impressions, their personal styles or differences. Many people misjudged Jesus. He didn't "look the part" that they expected of a hero. He didn't travel in popular, refined circles either. Yet he was the most compassionate and generous of any friend.

Try to be open-minded and openhearted toward your child's friends. You could find a genuine and loving young person hidden under a unique exterior, just waiting for an adult to accept her the way she is as well as to see who she can become, just as Jesus views each of us. Don't let individuality distract you from the individual.

Looking for a Missing Piece?

There are varieties of gifts, but the same Spirit; and there are varieties of service, but the same Lord; and there are varieties of activities, but it is the same God who empowers them all in everyone. To each is given the manifestation of the Spirit for the common good. To one is given through the Spirit the utterance of wisdom, and to another the utterance of knowledge according to the same Spirit, to another faith by the same Spirit, to another gifts of healing by the one Spirit, to another the working of miracles, to another prophecy, to another the ability to distinguish between spirits, to another various kinds of tongues, to another the interpretation of tongues. All these are empowered by one and the same Spirit, who apportions to each one individually as he wills.

1 Corinthians 12:4–11 ESV

No matter how much you know, how educated or experienced you are, there is always someone who can help you find your way through new experiences—and motherhood is full of new experiences. Many women are blessed with having a great example in their own mothers. But often even your own mother might not be able to help you in every area or might not be available to you every day in every way. Mentors can fill in the gap of what you know and what you have yet to learn.

God has dispersed many gifts to others around you. Learning from them can save you much time, effort, and heartache. The wonderful thing about the way God has connected you with others is that all of these powerful gifts complement one another. If gifts are given for the common good, it means that they are to be shared.

Maybe you aren't the most organized mom. That's OK. God has gifted someone around you with administrative gifts. Reach out to someone who has giftings that you can learn from. It's very likely that she might be able to learn from you too.

The Hard Way or the Easy Way . . . You Choose

Though you might have ten thousand instructors in Christ, yet you do not have many fathers; for in Christ Jesus I have begotten you through the gospel. Therefore I urge you, imitate me. For this reason I have sent Timothy to you, who is my beloved and faithful son in the Lord, who will remind you of my ways in Christ, as I teach everywhere in every church.

Now some are puffed up, as though I were not coming to you. But I will come to you shortly, if the Lord wills, and I will know, not the word of those who are puffed up, but the power. For the kingdom of God is not in word but in power. What do you want? Shall I come to you with a rod, or in love and a spirit of gentleness?

1 Corinthians 4:15–21 NKJV

Chastening does not feel good, but it is necessary at times. Even as moms we can lose sight of the big picture, loving God and serving him by loving others. Our humanness can make us resort to our own pride, relying on ourselves and gradually getting off course. This is why a good mentor is so important. A good mentor will not be afraid to "come with a rod" if need be, understanding that our time is short on earth and shouldn't be wasted with futile foolishness. Discipline is the accountability in our lives without which we struggle harder to become what God desires us to be.

In turn, if we do not also offer mentoring with accountability for those in our care, we withhold strength that can help them reach their potential with more ease. Remember that you must answer to God for all that he has given you, and if he has given you the opportunity to mentor others, including your children, consider with reverence that you are leading them as a representative of God. Being a mentor to your children is not only a responsibility but the privilege of destiny development.

LISTEN UP

Your teacher will no longer be hidden from you. You will see your teacher with your own eyes. You will hear a voice behind you saying, "This is the way. Follow it, whether it turns to the right or to the left." Then you will dishonor your silver-plated idols and your gold-covered statues. You will throw them away like clothing ruined by stains. You will say to them, "Get out!"

The Lord will give you rain for the seed that you plant in the ground, and the food that the ground provides will be rich and nourishing. When that day comes, your cattle will graze in large pastures. The oxen and the donkeys which work the soil will eat a mixture of food that has been winnowed with forks and shovels. There will be brooks and streams on every lofty mountain and every high hill.

Isaiah 30:20–25
GOD'S WORD

When the people of Israel were experiencing hard times, hearing the word of the Lord was scarce. It was quite a relief to know that after years of being submerged in a culture that worshipped other gods, the one true God would release teachers of his law and his ways to his people again. Mothers, just like the people of Israel, you are not alone. You do not have to figure things out for yourself, because God's Spirit teaches you. Just as God spoke to Israel, he speaks to you directly from the Bible and in your heart and indirectly through others like mentors.

Today if you do not have a mentor in your life, ask God for one. Pray specifically for what you and your family need and what is on your heart to accomplish in life. God is releasing teachers in these times, just as he did in Israel long ago, to give us direction for the future. If you already have a mentor in your life, thank God for her and take a moment today to bless her with a card, a cup of coffee, or another sentiment to show your appreciation!

Most Important Lesson

If I give everything I own to the poor . . . but I don't love, I've gotten nowhere. So, no matter what I say, what I believe, and what I do, I'm bankrupt without love.

Love never gives up. Love cares more for others than for self. Love doesn't want what it doesn't have. Love doesn't strut, doesn't have a swelled head, doesn't force itself on others, isn't always "me first," doesn't fly off the handle, doesn't keep score of the sins of others, doesn't revel when others grovel, takes pleasure in the flowering of truth, puts up with anything, trusts God always, always looks for the best, never looks back, but keeps going to the end.

1 Corinthians 13:3–7 MSG

When this passage was written, the Corinthian church was struggling, to say the least. The city of Corinth was a place where people came to seek immoral "love," and many in the church had only recently left that worldly culture. With this passage from what is known as the "Love Chapter," Paul set the record straight on what real love should look like. We must do the same in teaching our children about love; God's love conflicts with the images of love that our children are bombarded with daily.

If love is not the motivating factor for our actions, our work is in vain. The list in this passage is not primarily a task list of what we need to do to love but a word picture of what love inspired by God looks like. In a mentoring moment with your children, give them an assignment to find examples of what real love looks like versus what false love looks like. You can use magazines and television programs that they like as great discussion starters. Equip them to live God's real love each day by helping them to distinguish and deliver genuine love.

THE REAL HOUSEWIVES OF GOD'S KINGDOM

Titus, you must teach only what is correct. Tell the older men to have self–control and to be serious and sensible. Their faith, love, and patience must never fail.

Tell the older women to behave as those who love the Lord should. They must not gossip about others or be slaves of wine. They must teach what is proper, so the younger women will be loving wives and mothers. Each of the younger women must be sensible and kind, as well as a good homemaker, who puts her own husband first. Then no one can say insulting things about God's message.

Tell the young men to have self-control in everything.

Always set a good example for others. Be sincere and serious when you teach. Use clean language that no one can criticize.

Titus 2:1–8 CEV

We cannot help but think of some of the reality-television or situation-comedy wives who are currently on television when we read this passage. Some of them certainly do not fit the guidelines as outlined by Paul to be mentors, but they *have* opened their homes up for anyone to view their lives. Isn't that our job as Christian moms? What message would you show a generation of young women seeking a model of godly reality if cameras were following you around on a daily basis?

The world needs to see women who behave as those who love the Lord should behave. Young women are starving for the visual of practicality beyond the sermons they hear. Many women know what it is that they would like to accomplish but have no clue about how to arrive there or what their lives could and should look like in the process. As you are living the life of one who loves and serves the Lord, share it with the "viewers" around you, including your children, making sure that you conduct yourself in a way that will not make God want to take you off the show!

PRESCRIPTION FOR SUCCESS

Naomi, Ruth's mother-in-law, said to her, "My daughter, I must find a suitable home for you, one that will be good for you. Now Boaz, whose young women you worked with, is our close relative. Tonight he will be working at the threshing floor. Wash yourself, put on perfume, change your clothes, and go down to the threshing floor. But don't let him know you're there until he has finished his dinner. Watch him so you will know where he lies down to sleep. When he lies down, go and lift the cover off his feet and lie down. He will tell you what you should do."

Then Ruth answered, "I will do everything you say."

So Ruth went down to the threshing floor and did all her mother-in-law told her to do.

Ruth 3:1–6 NCV

Through wisdom and surrender to God's will, a good mentor will have the best interests of her students at heart. Ruth came to respect Naomi as her mother-in-law. So when Ruth became widowed, they remained close. Naomi had the knowledge of what to do, and she instructed Ruth with the desired outcome in mind. Mentoring is not simply telling someone what to do or attempting control over someone's life. Mentoring is assessing situations in someone's life and joining in a process for the desired results that they would like to achieve. A healthy mentor-protégé relationship allows the mentor to give suggestions and plans for success, but it is the protégé's responsibility to follow through and take the daily steps toward fulfillment of the goal.

Take a moment to give your mentoring relationships a checkup today. Determine if you are doing your part to the best of your ability in your mentor-mentee relationships. Begin every mentoring conversation with a prayer for wisdom and understanding. Then don't be afraid to share your ideas and advice with others who are seeking it. A great life and legacy is being built through your influence in the lives of others!

When You Build It, They Will Come

"Sing, barren woman, who has never had a baby. Fill the air with song, you who've never experienced childbirth! You're ending up with far more children than all those childbearing women." GOD says so! "Clear lots of ground for your tents! Make your tents large. Spread out! Think big! Use plenty of rope, drive the tent pegs deep. You're going to need lots of elbow room for your growing family. You're going to take over whole nations; you're going to resettle abandoned cities. Don't be afraid—you're not going to be embarrassed. Don't hold back—you're not going to come up short.

Isaiah 54:1–4 MSG

In the movie *Field of Dreams*, the main character is given a vision and encouraged to "build it; they will come." As he linked together with a mentor, the vision became more plain to him and indeed came to fruition. Many times when moms meet the challenging empty nest, they rediscover lost dreams. Do you feel barren, empty, as though you have lost aspirations you once longed to reach for? Get ready, because God has not overlooked you . . . but you must get ready.

You cannot do great things unless you prepare yourself to be able to care for and house great things. You may have to overhaul negative thinking, clear toxic relationships, or determine an attitude of tenacity. Build a home for your dreams by putting everything you aspire to on paper. Choose one dream to begin building today. Then pray and find a mentor to help you develop a plan of action. This takes hard work joined with great faith. Work it out; pray it through; rejoice that he who began a good work in you will be faithful to complete it (see Phil. 1:6) to the very end!

UNLIKELY CONNECTIONS

Mary responded, "I am the Lord's servant. May everything you have said about me come true." And then the angel left her.

A few days later Mary hurried to the hill country of Judea, to the town where Zechariah lived. She entered the house and greeted Elizabeth. At the sound of Mary's greeting, Elizabeth's child leaped within her, and Elizabeth was filled with the Holy Spirit.

Elizabeth gave a glad cry and exclaimed to Mary, "God has blessed you above all women, and your child is blessed. Why am I so honored, that the mother of my Lord should visit me? When I heard your greeting, the baby in my womb jumped for joy. You are blessed because you believed that the Lord would do what he said."

Mary responded, "Oh, how my soul praises the Lord."

Luke 1:38–46 NLT

It is wonderful when God makes a connection between people for the purpose of his kingdom, a prompting of the Holy Spirit that cannot be denied. Mary and Elizabeth were two women who at one time had only a family relationship in common. Elizabeth was well on in years; Mary was just embarking on adult life. The common thread that brought them together was the acceptance of carrying and bringing to fulfillment God's promise inside them. They both said yes to what God wanted to do in their lives, and when they next saw each other, a God connection took place. What he was doing inside them resonated with their spirits; baby John leaped inside his mother, Elizabeth was filled with the Holy Spirit, and Mary couldn't keep from expressing her praise to God.

The question today is this: Are we allowing these connections to happen in our lives today? Are we so in line with what God wants to do in our lives that we can recognize what he is doing in others that are surrendered to him? Make a list of possible God connections to nurture in your life today.

DO WHAT YOU HAVE TO DO

Elijah went and found Elisha son of Shaphat plowing a field. There were twelve teams of oxen in the field, and Elisha was plowing with the twelfth team. Elijah went over to him and threw his cloak across his shoulders and then walked away. Elisha left the oxen standing there, ran after Elijah, and said to him, "First let me go and kiss my father and mother good-bye, and then I will go with you!"

Elijah replied, "Go on back, but think about what I have done to you."

So Elisha returned to his oxen and slaughtered them. He used the wood from the plow to build a fire to roast their flesh. He passed around the meat to the townspeople, and they all ate. Then he went with Elijah as his assistant.

1 Kings 19:19–21 NLT

What do we do when God connects us with a potential mentor? Elisha recognized his mentor when Elijah threw his cloak on him. He knew that his life wasn't going to be the same (he recognized the God connection). Then he responded by finishing well what he was doing. There is something to be said for "ending well"; Elisha took time to say good-bye and give something to the people before he left.

Ending well in one season of life sets you up for continued success in the seasons that follow. It shows a maturity and responsibility that will show your mentor that you are capable and ready to take on the new opportunities that await you. Sometimes, like Elisha, we have to make quick assessments of the opportunities in front of us. Often we have just one chance to take advantage of the opportunity presented to us. Elisha recognized his moment of opportunity and seized it. Even though he was busy, he was ready to chase a new opportunity. As you are busy doing the mom thing, stay alert to new endeavors and relationships that herald new opportunities—you might even search out a few.

GENERATIONAL INFLUENCE

Paul arrived in the city of Derbe and then went to Lystra, where a disciple named Timothy lived. Timothy's mother was a Jewish believer, but his father was Greek. The believers in Lystra and Iconium spoke well of Timothy. Paul wanted Timothy to go with him. So he circumcised him because of the Jews who lived in those places and because he knew that Timothy's father was Greek.

As they went through the cities, they told people about the decisions that the apostles and spiritual leaders in Jerusalem had made for the people. So the churches were strengthened in the faith and grew in numbers every day.

Paul and Silas went through the regions of Phrygia and Galatia because the Holy Spirit kept them from speaking the word in the province of Asia.

Acts 16:1–6 GOD'S WORD

Timothy came from a believing mother and grandmother. He had been taught the Jewish scriptures since he was a child. He was set up his entire life for his moment and was ready when Paul came to Lystra and Iconium. He even had references!

We spend a lot of time and money preparing our children for college, sports, careers, and marriage. How much do we spend preparing our children for their future with God? How much have you invested in making your child a strong disciple of Jesus? Do not limit your child's experience with God to the four walls of the church; home is the prime area for children to build their faith and knowledge of God in great one-on-one sessions with you.

You are the greatest influencer throughout your child's life. If you need help in how to cultivate a Christ-centered home, the children's pastor of your church can be a great resource with ideas for you. Then the Internet, mommy-and-me groups, and experienced moms can all offer practical tips on how to best nurture your child's relationship with God. Most moms love to share their ideas! Don't be afraid to ask.

The Risk Taker

When Saul arrived in Jerusalem, he tried to meet with the believers, but they were all afraid of him. They did not believe he had truly become a believer! Then Barnabas brought him to the apostles and told them how Saul had seen the Lord on the way to Damascus and how the Lord had spoken to Saul. He also told them that Saul had preached boldly in the name of Jesus in Damascus.

So Saul stayed with the apostles and went all around Jerusalem with them, preaching boldly in the name of the Lord. . . .

The church then had peace . . . and it became stronger as the believers lived in the fear of the Lord. And with the encouragement of the Holy Spirit, it also grew in numbers.

Acts 9:26–28, 31 NLT

Whenever we take a chance on working with someone, whether being a mentor or choosing a mentor, we take a risk. We never really know the full scope of what we are getting ourselves into. Barnabas didn't have the luxury of a private investigator or the Internet to check out Saul before he brought him to the apostles. All Barnabas had to help him spring into action was his relationship with God, obedience to the Spirit, and faith that it would all come together. It was a risk the other believers did not want to take, but thank God that Barnabas did!

Do you have your reservations about starting or continuing a mentor relationship? Ask God to confirm in your spirit what to do, and act on that. Trust the Holy Spirit in you to point you in the right direction. Paul wasn't welcomed by many, but God sent Barnabas to befriend him. Don't allow the fears or expectations of others to dissuade you from reaching out to someone else. You may find a Barnabas of your own, or you might find that you are the support someone else has been waiting for.

EXPANSION

The Lord now chose seventy-two other disciples and sent them ahead in pairs to all the towns and places he planned to visit. These were his instructions to them: "The harvest is great, but the workers are few. So pray to the Lord who is in charge of the harvest; ask him to send more workers into his fields. Now go, and remember that I am sending you out as lambs among wolves. Don't take any money with you, nor a traveler's bag, nor an extra pair of sandals. And don't stop to greet anyone on the road.

"Whenever you enter someone's home, first say, 'May God's peace be on this house.' If those who live there are peaceful, the blessing will stand; if they are not, the blessing will return to you."

Luke 10:1–6 NLT

Every mother should understand and remember the practical lesson in this passage. At the very core of what you do daily, you must be continuously working on duplicating yourself—not creating carbon copies but multiplying yourself in the sense of passing on your wisdom and instruction. Jesus had a side job along with his great purpose. He was equipping his followers to be able to continue his mission beyond his personal time with them. He understood that his time on earth was short; in order to get the gospel out to the world, he was going to have to duplicate himself and send out others to carry on the mission.

Have you ever worked with a babysitter, assistant, or volunteer who was so awesome that you wished you had five like her with the same spirit or commitment? If you can teach one person a day each week, you will touch seven. If you can teach one each day to teach one more, then you can touch fourteen with the same effort. The world needs an expansion of godly mothers to develop positive and effective influencers to follow.

KEY INGREDIENTS

The disciples had forgotten to bring any bread when they crossed the lake. Jesus then warned them, "Watch out! Guard against the yeast of the Pharisees and Sadducees."

The disciples talked this over and said to each other, "He must be saying this because we didn't bring along any bread."

Jesus knew what they were thinking and said: You surely don't have much faith! Why are you talking about not having any bread? Don't you understand? Have you forgotten about the 5,000 people and all those baskets of leftovers from just five loaves of bread? And what about the 4,000 people and all those baskets of leftovers from only seven loaves of bread? Don't you know by now that I am not talking to you about bread? Watch out for the yeast of the Pharisees and Sadducees!

Matthew 16:5–11 CEV

Shortly before the conversation in this passage, the disciples had just witnessed Jesus' miracle of the feeding of four thousand, which was the second time Jesus had multiplied food to feed many. Despite seeing those miracles, however, the disciples were back to focusing on the daily tasks of maintaining life. They had to be reminded that God takes care of those things.

Mothers, God is not just a resource but *the source* of all you need. Do not allow your earthly responsibilities to distract you or your little ones from what God wants to teach you in the moments of mothering. Do as Jesus did; use everyday situations to minister. Cook dinner with the help of your children with the sole purpose of having time with them to talk about God; don't worry if the preparation takes longer or the meal isn't as good as if you did it yourself. The key ingredients to effective mothering are not bread and fish (or food and fashion) but faith and obedience in teaching your children how to listen to God. Trust God as the source who provides all the other essential ingredients in life.

It's Time

Jesus' mother was there, and Jesus and His disciples were invited to the wedding as well. When the wine ran out, Jesus' mother told Him, "They don't have any wine."

"What has this concern of yours to do with Me, woman?" Jesus asked. "My hour has not yet come."

"Do whatever He tells you," His mother told the servants.

Now six stone water jars had been set there for Jewish purification. Each contained 20 or 30 gallons.

"Fill the jars with water," Jesus told them. So they filled them to the brim. Then He said to them, "Now draw some out and take it to the chief servant." And they did.

When the chief servant tasted the water (after it had become wine), he did not know where it came from—though the servants who had drawn the water knew.

John 2:1–9 HCSB

How hard it must have been to be the mother of Jesus! Would you have been intimidated when Jesus said that it wasn't his time yet? Or would you have given him a continued nudge as Mary did? God had chosen Mary for her role and gave her grace and wisdom. She didn't sit there and argue with Jesus, she just prepared those around her for a miracle by telling the servants to do whatever Jesus told them to do. She also allowed Jesus to solve the wedding host's problem his way, without imposing her own way of completing the task.

Seek God for the same wisdom and grace to discern the time for your children to step into their destinies. When that time comes, be sure to exhibit self-control and operate as God leads you, allowing your children the freedom to find their own way. Begin today to pray for the right people to surround them and that your children will be rooted in Christ and be ready to minister in their time. Get ready, mom! Your children will do great things for God in their time!

RECIPROCAL REWARDS

"May he also be to you a restorer of life and a sustainer of your old age; for your daughter-in-law, who loves you and is better to you than seven sons, has given birth to him." Then Naomi took the child and laid him in her lap, and became his nurse. The neighbor women gave him a name, saying, "A son has been born to Naomi!" So they named him Obed. He is the father of Jesse, the father of David.

Now these are the generations of Perez: to Perez was born Hezron, and to Hezron was born Ram, and to Ram, Amminadab, and to Amminadab was born Nahshon, and to Nahshon, Salmon, and to Salmon was born Boaz, and to Boaz, Obed, and to Obed was born Jesse, and to Jesse, David.

Ruth 4:15–22 NASB

Are you going through something in your life that you feel disqualifies you as a mentor? Have you recently had a death in the family, experienced foreclosure, or maybe lost your job? Be encouraged by the story of Naomi today. Life isn't going to be perfect because you are a mentor. Things within and outside your control may fail, and your students have a front-row seat to it—let them learn through your experiences. The pain you are experiencing in your time of trouble will be long forgotten when you get to see the fruit of your labor with your mentees. Their successes, marriages, new babies, and graduations will be reasons to celebrate, and you will feel a swell of motherly pride over it all.

Enjoy those rewards; God has allowed you to experience the pleasures of goals accomplished. They are one of the perks he designed for a mentoring relationship. So if today you are feeling ready to quit, refocus. Look at the line of blessing that came through Naomi's decision to guide Ruth. Your life experiences build a treasure box of wisdom to be shared with others.

Help Is on the Way

The job is too much for one person; you can't do it alone. God will help you if you follow my advice. You should be the one to speak to God for the people, and you should teach them God's laws and show them what they must do to live right.

You will need to appoint some competent leaders who respect God and are trustworthy and honest. Then put them over groups of 10, 50, 100, and 1,000. These judges can handle the ordinary cases and bring the more difficult ones to you. Having them to share the load will make your work easier. This is the way God wants it done. You won't be under nearly as much stress, and everyone else will return home feeling satisfied.

Moses followed Jethro's advice.

Exodus 18:18–24 CEV

Was Jethro intimidated because God had Moses leading a nation of people? Did Jethro keep silent thinking that Moses could figure it out himself or that Moses was not going to listen to his advice? Not at all. He was interested enough in Moses' life that he noticed when Moses was becoming weary. Jethro offered unsolicited advice to his son-in-law, who eagerly accepted it. Jethro's interaction with Moses shows how wisdom can be passed on from one generation to the next.

Believe it or not, we face a deficit of mentors in the church today. Many moms are so tired, busy, or intimidated that they will not share their God-given wisdom with the younger generation. Whether or not those we influence choose to follow our advice is not in our control as mentors, but we have a responsibility to share our wisdom. Don't stand by silently watching young people struggle when you can rescue them with godly counsel. Your wisdom can help your children but can also reach beyond them to their friends, their spouses, and their children too. Reach out to them today; your words could be the answer to their prayers.

NEXT . . .

I pleaded with the LORD and said, "O Sovereign LORD, you have only begun to show your greatness and the strength of your hand to me, your servant. Is there any god in heaven or on earth who can perform such great and mighty deeds as you do? Please let me cross the Jordan to see the wonderful land on the other side, the beautiful hill country and the Lebanon mountains."

But the LORD was angry with me because of you, and he would not listen to me. "That's enough!" he declared. "Speak of it no more. But go up to Pisgah Peak, and look over the land in every direction. Take a good look, but you may not cross the Jordan River. Instead, commission Joshua and encourage and strengthen him, for he will lead the people across the Jordan."

Deuteronomy 3:23–28 NLT

The Israelites would soon enter the Promised Land. Moses knew that he would soon die and that God was not going to allow him to cross over with them for his rebellious act back in the wilderness. God did allow him to see the land from a distance, but he could not enter in. He had to prepare Joshua and the people to go and then release them to continue on to their destiny without him. Ouch, that stings! Moses would experience his protégé's victory and blessing only from a distance due to his own rebellion.

Not everything that happens for the kingdom is going to include you. Can you be OK with that while you are preparing the next generation? At some point you will stand at the door of your home and watch your children drive off into the distance, into their future. Be faithful now so when that time comes, you can know that you obeyed to the very best of your ability, providing the best foundation possible for your children's future. Even though their independence may sting a little, you are a partaker in their successes too.

PEER PERSUASION

When Peter came to Antioch, I had to oppose him to his face, for what he did was very wrong. When he first arrived, he ate with the Gentile Christians, who were not circumcised. But afterward, when some friends of James came, Peter wouldn't eat with the Gentiles anymore. He was afraid of criticism from these people who insisted on the necessity of circumcision. As a result, other Jewish Christians followed Peter's hypocrisy, and even Barnabas was led astray by their hypocrisy.

When I saw that they were not following the truth of the gospel message, I said to Peter in front of all the others, "Since you, a Jew by birth, have discarded the Jewish laws and are living like a Gentile, why are you now trying to make these Gentiles follow the Jewish traditions?"

Galatians 2:11–14 NLT

Peter's actions, reported by Paul in this passage, show us that old habits indeed die hard. Peter was again having issues with peer pressure, and Paul confronted him. Peter's fear of criticism was leading believers, including leaders, astray. Like Paul, mothers confront challenges daily.

Confrontation is rarely if ever enjoyable, but it is extremely necessary, especially among Christians. When character flaws go unchecked in relationships, people are affected. The unchecked behavior is seen by less-mature Christians as acceptable behavior that they in turn can and should engage in. Mothers sometimes even refrain from disciplining their children because of the reaction that the confrontation will ignite.

Approach bringing correction carefully. A hasty rebuke might make matters worse. A mentor, parent, or other respected person who has a relationship with the person being confronted should initiate the conversation. If you have been avoiding a challenging conversation that you know needs to take place, spend some time in prayer asking God to guide you, and then invite the conversation. Always remember that any confrontation is to help the individual and the church as a whole, because there is always a ripple effect to confrontation.

SPREAD THE WORD

My child, find your source of strength in the kindness of Christ Jesus. You've heard my message, and it's been confirmed by many witnesses. Entrust this message to faithful individuals who will be competent to teach others.

Join me in suffering like a good soldier of Christ Jesus. Whoever serves in the military doesn't get mixed up in nonmilitary activities. This pleases his commanding officer. Whoever enters an athletic competition wins the prize only when playing by the rules. A hardworking farmer should have the first share of the crops. Understand what I'm saying. The Lord will help you understand all these things.

Always think about Jesus Christ. He was brought back to life and is a descendant of David. This is the Good News that I tell others.

2 Timothy 2:1–8 GOD'S WORD

Paul wrote these words to Timothy, whom he mentored, from prison. Waiting for his execution, he encouraged Timothy to continue sharing the gospel. Paul knew that there wasn't much time to waste, and he wanted to be certain to leave Timothy with as much mentoring and direction as possible.

Can you still encourage and build even when you are facing your own life crisis? Can you still point others to where their source of strength lies when you are in one of your darkest moments? Paul's true focus is explained with his illustration of the good soldier. He reminded Timothy that no matter what our circumstances, there is a larger battle raging and we all have an assignment to follow through on. A good soldier stays focused and pleases his commander.

Can you do this? No matter what you are facing today, can you still encourage, build up, and point others to Jesus? If you need help, remember that the source of your strength is in the kindness of Jesus, who is working things out on your behalf. Let Christ be your encourager as you strengthen others.

What's Your Story?

[Jesus] presented another parable to them, saying, "The kingdom of heaven is like a mustard seed, which a man took and sowed in his field; and this is smaller than all other seeds, but when it is full grown, it is larger than the garden plants and becomes a tree, so that the birds of the air come and nest in its branches."

He spoke another parable to them, "The kingdom of heaven is like leaven, which a woman took and hid in three pecks of flour until it was all leavened."

All these things Jesus spoke to the crowds in parables, and He did not speak to them without a parable. This was to fulfill what was spoken through the prophet: "I will open my mouth in parables; I will utter things hidden since the foundation of the world."

Matthew 13:31–35 NASB

Stories can be great "visuals" for the message you are trying to convey to your children. Everything Jesus did on earth was to teach about the kingdom of God, how to enter it and how to live in it. His stories presented his purpose. What is your story? What is the message that you are continually conveying to the children in your home? Take some time to write it down today, not what you want to say but what you have currently been "saying" both in words and in your actions. Does this match what you want your message to be? Be honest, because in order to change your story, you first need to know exactly what message you are currently telling.

Once you are aware of your story, find verses in the Bible that identify with your story and meditate on them. If your story is unconditional love, for example, you can find countless ways to express it. Brainstorm some of the different ways that you could tell your story. What flows naturally will be in line with the message you want to convey, just as Jesus' parables flowed from his message.

PROFITABLE PARTNERSHIPS

Summoning the Twelve, He gave them power and authority over all the demons, and [power] to heal diseases. Then He sent them to proclaim the kingdom of God and to heal the sick.

"Take nothing for the road," He told them, "no walking stick, no traveling bag, no bread, no money; and don't take an extra shirt. Whatever house you enter, stay there and leave from there. If they do not welcome you, when you leave that town, shake off the dust from your feet as a testimony against them." So they went out and traveled from village to village, proclaiming the good news and healing everywhere.

Herod the tetrarch heard about everything that was going on. He was perplexed, because some said that John had been raised from the dead, . . . and others that one of the ancient prophets had risen.

Luke 9:1–8 HCSB

Jesus did not simply tell the disciples to go out and preach; he first gave them power and authority over all the demons and to heal diseases. He equipped them to not just speak, but to act. Jesus' protégés were expected to minister just as he did and were given all they needed to do so. In fact, he told them that he expected them to do even greater things than he had done.

As a mentoring mom, your objective should be to equip those under your influence with power to live the life of authority they are called to live for God. This type of investment is reserved for those who are ready and willing to use all that is given to them. Remember, you are the example for your mentees, and you must be willing to make the same effort in obediently seeking God that you expect from them.

More personally, are you operating in power? Are you operating with everything that has been given to you by God? Take two new actions today, perhaps taking a long walk and writing an entry in your journal, that you have not taken lately to empower yourself.

147

CHECK YOURSELF BEFORE YOU WRECK YOURSELF

Do not judge so that you will not be judged. For in the way you judge, you will be judged; and by your standard of measure, it will be measured to you. Why do you look at the speck that is in your brother's eye, but do not notice the log that is in your own eye? Or how can you say to your brother, "Let me take the speck out of your eye," and behold, the log is in your own eye? You hypocrite, first take the log out of your own eye, and then you will see clearly to take the speck out of your brother's eye.

Do not give what is holy to dogs, and do not throw your pearls before swine, or they will trample them under their feet, and turn and tear you to pieces.

Matthew 7:1–6 NASB

Most of us would say that we are not judgmental people. But Jesus knew our tendency to determine how we think others should handle their lives. That's judging, and it's especially insidious when we have no understanding of their situations. The most potent form of judgment is when we compare ourselves to others. Comparisons can compel us to see others or ourselves more harshly than needed. Judging and comparing can even inhibit compassion toward others.

Every mother's experience is not the same. Each of us has our own set of experiences and circumstances that prevents a one-size-fits-all method of parenting. One way to change our perspective of others is to become more self-aware through time with God, asking the Holy Spirit to check our hearts and motives. We must be aware of not just what we do but what we are capable of doing—both good and bad. This keeps our hearts pliable before God and tender for others. Keep your sight clear of any "planks," and you will find your clear perspective will have you looking at your brothers and sisters in Christ through a lens of compassion rather than judgment.

REFOCUS FORWARD

The following week almost the entire city turned out to hear [Paul and Barnabas] preach the word of the Lord. But when some of the Jews saw the crowds, they were jealous; so they slandered Paul and argued against whatever he said.

Then Paul and Barnabas spoke out boldly and declared, "It was necessary that we first preach the word of God to you Jews. But since you have rejected it and judged yourselves unworthy of eternal life, we will offer it to the Gentiles. For the Lord gave us this command when he said, 'I have made you a light to the Gentiles, to bring salvation to the farthest corners of the earth.'"

When the Gentiles heard this, they were very glad and thanked the Lord for his message; and all who were chosen for eternal life became believers.

Acts 13:44–48 NLT

Paul and Barnabas had a great many people coming to hear the gospel from them, so much so that others felt jealous. There might be times where the one (or a group) that you have invested in completely rejects you. This can be painful, but you cannot let it stop you from ministering. Being hurt in ministry is unavoidable; we are working with humans, and none of us are perfect. Mistakes will be made, feelings will be hurt, and jealousy will sprout. It takes time for people to learn how to respond to these feelings in a godly way, and until they get it right, offenses will come.

You must not allow this to stop you from being healed or stop you from being used to heal others. There are other people who need your wisdom and time. Seek God's direction on what the next step is and move on. For every person who rejects you, there are multitudes waiting to hear the word of the Lord. The salvation of many rests in your ability to move forward with the gospel. Will you move forward?

A TEAM OF GIFTS

These are the gifts Christ gave to the church: the apostles, the prophets, the evangelists, and the pastors and teachers. Their responsibility is to equip God's people to do his work and build up the church, the body of Christ. This will continue until we all come to such unity in our faith and knowledge of God's Son that we will be mature in the Lord, measuring up to the full and complete standard of Christ.

Then we will no longer be immature like children. We won't be tossed and blown about by every wind of new teaching. We will not be influenced when people try to trick us with lies so clever they sound like the truth. Instead, we will speak the truth in love, growing in every way more and more like Christ, who is the head of his body, the church.

Ephesians 4:11–15 NLT

Look again at this passage from a letter the apostle Paul wrote to the church at Ephesus. Notice what it does *not* say. It does not say that one type of leader has sole responsibility for equipping God's people. Rather, this passage gives us a list of people who are described as gifts to the church. Other similar Bible passages list abilities given to believers as gifts for the purpose of building church unity and growth.

You are a gift! Your gift matters; it has purpose. Working together in unity matures us as a group and keeps us from adopting wrong teaching. Acknowledging that we need one another to reach our goals helps keep love at the forefront of our intentions.

The principle applies in your home also. Who are your teammates in your home? Have you identified what gifts God has given your children and your spouse? What about in your church? Are you doing all that you can to help foster a team environment with the purpose of building people up? Pray for your teammates today; pray that you all will be given wisdom to grow together, speaking the truth in love.

Uh-Oh!

The first day of the week we met to break bread together. Paul spoke to the people until midnight because he was leaving the next morning. In the upstairs room where we were meeting, there were a lot of lamps. A young man by the name of Eutychus was sitting on a window sill. While Paul was speaking, the young man got very sleepy. Finally, he went to sleep and fell three floors all the way down to the ground. When they picked him up, he was dead.

Paul went down and bent over Eutychus. He took him in his arms and said, "Don't worry! He's alive." After Paul had gone back upstairs, he broke bread, and ate with us. He then spoke until dawn and left. Then the followers took the young man home alive and were very happy.

Acts 20:7-12 CEV

At first glance, a mother might look at this account and think, Who let that boy sit in the window? But this scenario teaches us something about mentoring. Around us every day are Christians who are falling asleep spiritually. They have diminished their service to others and lagged in attendance at church; the enthusiasm for the Lord that once glowed in their eyes has clouded over through years of dealing with problems. Unfortunately, often nothing is done for these people until they have fallen completely away, intentionally becoming invisible. To the church they seem gone, lost forever, but there is still life in them.

Eutychus died when he fell from that window. Paul picked him up and brought him back to life. Ask God to show you someone in your church who has fallen asleep; ask him for eyes to see the life remaining in those who have been left for dead. Pray for the words to speak to encourage them. Invite them to attend church with you once again and treat them to lunch and conversation afterward. Someone is out there lifeless but waiting for your prayers, positive affirmation, and words of faith.

BE ON YOUR BEST BEHAVIOR

The rod of correction imparts wisdom, but a child left to himself disgraces his mother.

When the wicked thrive, so does sin, but the righteous will see their downfall.

Discipline your son, and he will give you peace; he will bring delight to your soul.

Where there is no revelation, the people cast off restraint; but blessed is he who keeps the law.

A servant cannot be corrected by mere words; though he understands, he will not respond.

Do you see a man who speaks in haste? There is more hope for a fool than for him.

If a man pampers his servant from youth, he will bring grief in the end.

Proverbs 29:15–21 NIV

You have probably heard the old saying "If you give a man a fish, you have fed him for a day; if you teach a man to fish, you have fed him for lifetime." This saying also applies to correcting and disciplining, as we can also see in these *proverbs*—"wise sayings"—of King Solomon. Correction for correction's sake doesn't offer the tools that equip us not to fall into the same sin again. God's way of correction doesn't simply punish for the moment but trains so that the person being corrected does not make that particular bad choice again. The purpose of correction is to broaden the perspective of the guilty party to understand the implications of his disobedience. That is how discipline and correction can bring peace into a household and delight to the very soul of a parent or mentor.

Is your style of discipline balanced? Spend some time reviewing how you correct your children. Whether they are toddlers or have toddlers of their own, you have opportunities to bring correction to their ways. Revamp your plan to transition from discipline for the moment to correction for the future.

WALK THIS WAY

I, too, am an elder and a witness to the sufferings of Christ. And I, too, will share in his glory when he is revealed to the whole world. As a fellow elder, I appeal to you: Care for the flock that God has entrusted to you. Watch over it willingly, not grudgingly—not for what you will get out of it, but because you are eager to serve God. Don't lord it over the people assigned to your care, but lead them by your own good example. And when the Great Shepherd appears, you will receive a crown of never-ending glory and honor.

In the same way, you younger men must accept the authority of the elders. And all of you, serve each other in humility, for "God opposes the proud but favors the humble."

1 Peter 5:1–5 NLT

Any mentor serious about leading people into their God-given destiny should know that we cannot expect from people what we would not do ourselves. In this passage, Peter applies that leadership principle, reminding the church leaders three times that he speaks from experience. Peter learned from his own mentor, Jesus, and his own experiences of struggle and triumph. He makes sure that those he is mentoring know he's in the trenches with them and working for the same purpose they are, caring for the flock.

It has been said that familiarity breeds contempt, but a lack of familiarity breeds doubt and a loss of respect. Making the connection between your purpose and another person's shows the integrity of your wisdom, providing hope to the one you wish to help.

When was the last time you made sure that your children or the women you're mentoring know that you are right there with them? This might take a little bit of vulnerability on your part, but that is what provides a safe place for them to reciprocate. A little vulnerability on your part may be just what they need to take their next step of growth today.

153

UNDER THE DUST

Jesus asked his disciples if they understood all these things. They said, "Yes, we do."

So he told them, "Every student of the Scriptures who becomes a disciple in the kingdom of heaven is like someone who brings out new and old treasures from the storeroom."

When Jesus had finished telling these stories, he left and went to his hometown. He taught in their meeting place, and the people were so amazed that they asked, "Where does he get all this wisdom and the power to work these miracles? Isn't he the son of the carpenter? Isn't Mary his mother, and aren't James, Joseph, Simon, and Judas his brothers? Don't his sisters still live here in our town? How can he do all this?" So the people were unhappy because of what he was doing.

Matthew 13:51–57 CEV

Surely the people in Jesus' hometown, his own people, would cheer him on! But not only did Jesus not receive support, he met resistance. How do you handle rejection, and how are you teaching your children to handle it? Disappointment will come, many times from the most unlikely sources. Jesus handled rejection with good boundaries and with reliance on God and his closest friends. Teach this plan to your children and model it for them when you face rejection or disappointment.

Jesus taught in his hometown, sharing the good news, but the Bible says that because of the lack of faith among the people in his hometown, Jesus could not perform any miracles there. Teach your little ones to give their best, but if rejection comes, to set boundaries and move on. Setting a boundary differs from building a wall because with a boundary we are still able to communicate and be open to reconciliation. A wall completely cuts off any interaction, which is not what Jesus came to do. But healthy boundaries are like fences, with gates that allow access in both directions. Show your children the difference in your own healthy boundaries.

Good Answer!

Each of the twelve regional officers brought food to Solomon and his household for one month of the year. They provided everything he needed, as well as barley and straw for the horses.

Solomon was brilliant. God had blessed him with insight and understanding. He was wiser than anyone else in the world, including the wisest people of the east and of Egypt. He was even wiser than Ethan the Ezrahite, and Mahol's three sons, Heman, Calcol, and Darda. Solomon became famous in every country around Judah and Israel. Solomon wrote 3,000 wise sayings and composed more than 1,000 songs. He could talk about all kinds of plants, from large trees to small bushes, and he taught about animals, birds, reptiles, and fish. Kings all over the world heard about Solomon's wisdom and sent people to listen to him teach.

1 Kings 4:27–34 CEV

Wisdom given by God is true and like no other wisdom on earth. Most people are desperate for true wisdom; are you? We were never meant to operate solely on what we gain through our own achievements. Solomon is a great example of this. He was a king, which made him important but not necessarily brilliant. Without the wisdom given by God, Solomon could not have accomplished all that he did. When we look at Solomon's life, we have to wonder, Are we living out our full potential in God? Yes, we are raising children; yes, we mentor others. But are we giving them the fullness of what we could through God? When asked by God what he wanted, Solomon recognized what he needed to do well was the job he had been given.

Motherhood is not about maintaining a busy life for our families; it is about building and equipping our children to go further than we ever did. Recognize the task that God has set before you and ask him today for unending wisdom for your "little kingdom." You may soon find other people looking to learn from you, opening new opportunities to mentor others!

HANGING ON FOR DEAR LIFE

The time had come for the LORD to take Elijah up to heaven in a whirlwind. Elijah and Elisha were traveling from Gilgal, and Elijah said to Elisha, "Stay here; the LORD is sending me on to Bethel."

But Elisha replied, "As the LORD lives and as you yourself live, I will not leave you." So they went down to Bethel.

Then the sons of the prophets who were at Bethel came out to Elisha and said, "Do you know that today the LORD will take your master away from you?"

He said, "Yes, I know. Be quiet."

Elijah said to him, "Elisha, stay here; the LORD is sending me to Jericho."

But Elisha said, "As the LORD lives and as you yourself live, I will not leave you." So they went to Jericho.

2 Kings 2:1–4 HCSB

Elisha recognized that his time with Elijah would soon end. He decided that he was not going to miss one second of his mentor's presence. Do you recognize the time at hand around you? For years people have been saying that we are living in the last days, so much that many have become jaded and tired. The word for today is to hang on to God for dear life. Do not get tired of chasing after God; do not miss one second in his presence. You need him. Your children need him. Your community needs him.

Picture yourself hanging from a window in a high-rise building. Your arms gradually feel fatigue from the weight they are supporting; your knuckles turn white as they grasp the window ledge for dear life. No matter what you feel at that time, it can't be worse than letting go—quitting. Do not give up on yourself or those around you. Even if circumstances are strained or relationships are struggling, strengthen yourself. Let hope invigorate you with renewed energy and hang on. You might just find that you have a double portion of blessing awaiting you as Elisha did.

FAITH

Roller coasters, haunted houses, and scary fireside stories give us a rush of adrenaline that can be fun in the moment. But when the real-life unknown frightens us, that's not quite the same, is it? We're told to face our fears, but how do we do that, really?

Find your courage in God through faith. Get to know God's character and his wonderful promises. Believe that he is who he says and that he does what he promises to do. Find strength in the grace—the favor—God provides because of his love poured out on us through Jesus. Knowing God's goodness and love is all you need to stand in faith with confidence against any circumstance or fear.

Faith is being sure of what we hope for and certain of what we do not see.

Hebrews 11:1 NIV

God Needs You

I also remember the genuine faith of your mother Eunice. Your grandmother Lois had the same sort of faith, and I am sure that you have it as well. So I ask you to make full use of the gift that God gave you when I placed my hands on you. Use it well. God's Spirit doesn't make cowards out of us. The Spirit gives us power, love, and self-control.

Don't be ashamed to speak for our Lord. And don't be ashamed of me, just because I am in jail for serving him. Use the power that comes from God and join with me in suffering for telling the good news.

God saved us and chose us to be his holy people. We did nothing to deserve this, but God planned it because he is so kind.

2 Timothy 1:5–9 CEV

This passage is taken from a letter the apostle Paul wrote to a young minister named Timothy. Paul wasn't trying to paint a pretty picture. He didn't say that Timothy should go out, preach, and expect everyone to be accepting and loving or even tolerant of him or his message. Instead, Paul told Timothy not to be intimidated but to recognize and use with full confidence the gifts God had given him for the sake of those who would hear the gospel message he was preaching.

God has given you gifts to be used in the raising of your children in a godly home. Especially if you are young, you might find the task intimidating, but God wants you to use your gifts with confidence and rely on your strong faith to keep you on track.

God has promised to provide you with the clear mind, power, and love you need to teach your children. Whether they accept everything you tell them isn't your primary concern. Your responsibility is to recognize your gifts and use them with confidence, full of faith that it is God working through you for their good.

I Love Your Outfit!

Put on the full armor of God so that you can fight against the devil's evil tricks. Our fight is not against people on earth but against the rulers and authorities and the powers of this world's darkness, against the spiritual powers of evil in the heavenly world. That is why you need to put on God's full armor. Then on the day of evil you will be able to stand strong. And when you have finished the whole fight, you will still be standing. So stand strong, with the belt of truth tied around your waist and the protection of right living on your chest. On your feet wear the Good News of peace to help you stand strong. And also use the shield of faith with which you can stop all the burning arrows of the Evil One.

Ephesians 6:11–16 NCV

When foul weather is predicted, you make certain your children are dressed appropriately before heading outside. You supply the appropriate gear—mittens, boots, an umbrella—whatever offers them the protection they'll need.

The Bible says God's children head into battle every day—a spiritual battle that you might not even be aware is going on all around you. But there's no need to be afraid. God, our loving Father, provides the protective gear we need. All we need to do is put it on!

In this passage from a letter to the Ephesians, Paul lists that spiritual armor. By searching out the truth found in the Bible, doing what's right, and freely sharing with others how God has changed your life, you're equipped to fight off anything that might hinder your relationship with God. But one piece of equipment isn't designed for solo use—the shield of faith. The shields of Roman soldiers interlocked with one another, forming a barrier that couldn't be easily broken. Joining with other mothers to pray and study the Bible is one way to strengthen your own shield of faith. Side by side, you'll find victory is close at hand.

FULL HOUSE

If the LORD doesn't build the house, the builders are working for nothing. If the LORD doesn't guard the city, the guards are watching for nothing. It is no use for you to get up early and stay up late, working for a living. The LORD gives sleep to those he loves. Children are a gift from the LORD; babies are a reward. Children who are born to a young man are like arrows in the hand of a warrior. Happy is the man who has his bag full of arrows. They will not be defeated when they fight their enemies at the city gate.

Psalm 127:1–5 NCV

There's a time-honored Jewish proverb that says, "God couldn't be everywhere; that's why he created mothers." There is a major flaw in the truth of this fine old adage. The Bible tells us God *is* everywhere and that he's certainly powerful enough to handle anything and everything on his own. But as mothers, sometimes we act as though the saying were true. We act as though the health and happiness of our family rest on our own shoulders.

Each child God entrusts to our care is a uniquely precious blessing. Working hard to provide and care for our children is a wonderful thing. But without faith the foundation of the family is built on shaky ground. We cannot offer our children what matters most—unwavering and unconditional love, absolute forgiveness, and eternal life. Only God can do that.

Relying on God, instead of trying to "play God," allows us to trade overwork and overconfidence for peace of mind. Faith gives us and our families a security we could never muster on our own. Allow God to do his job, and you do yours. That's the best gift you could ever give the children you love.

CLOSE DOESN'T COUNT

This is true for all who believe in Christ, because all people are the same: Everyone has sinned and fallen short of God's glorious standard, and all need to be made right with God by his grace, which is a free gift. They need to be made free from sin through Jesus Christ. God sent him to die in our place to take away our sins. We receive forgiveness through faith in the blood of Jesus' death. This showed that God always does what is right and fair, as in the past when he was patient and did not punish people for their sins. And God gave Jesus to show today that he does what is right. God did this so he could judge rightly and so he could make right any person who has faith in Jesus.

Romans 3:22–26 NCV

Even good kids are disobedient now and then. Sometimes they pretend they don't hear a word you say. You offer one cookie and they grab two. You turn your back and one sibling hits the other, just because.

Moms are just like their kids, disobedient now and then. But when we choose to ignore what God says, there are always consequences. Eternal ones. The word for *sin* in the New Testament means "to miss the mark." It's like when your kids are asked to put their dirty clothes in the hamper, but they toss them somewhere near the hamper. No matter how close the clothes land, the action falls short of what was asked.

Whether you consider your sins big or small is irrelevant. As Paul explains in this passage, anything that misses God's mark for what's pure and good falls short of what's needed for a right relationship with him. But Jesus took upon himself the consequences for everywhere you've fallen short. When you put your faith in Jesus, you acknowledge what he's done. You accept God's free gift of forgiveness. Everything's been set right. Nothing stands between you and God—or this life and eternity.

Soul Food

Jesus answered, "I have food to eat that you know nothing about."

So the followers asked themselves, "Did somebody already bring him food?"

Jesus said, "My food is to do what the One who sent me wants me to do and to finish his work. You have a saying, 'Four more months till harvest.' But I tell you, open your eyes and look at the fields ready for harvest now. Already, the one who harvests is being paid and is gathering crops for eternal life. So the one who plants and the one who harvests celebrate at the same time. Here the saying is true, 'One person plants, and another harvests.' I sent you to harvest a crop that you did not work on. Others did the work, and you get to finish up their work."

John 4:32–38 NCV

Faith starts out as a tiny seed. The desire to know God and the choice to accept his forgiveness break that seed open so a bud can sprout. But plants, like people, need nourishment to continue to grow. Your faith grows tall and strong when you work with God to do the things he asks you to do.

One thing God asks you to do is help other seeds of faith sprout. These seeds may be planted in your children, your spouse, your friends and neighbors, or even a stranger you happen to meet along the road of life. Every time you pray for others or encourage them in ways that help them grow closer to God, you're contributing to a future harvest of faith.

When it comes to spiritual growth, every child of God has a part to play in God's family, even your own children. No matter how young they are, God gave them a soul that hungers for him. Talk to them about God. Encourage them to pray for their friends. Help them make choices that please their heavenly Father. Eat, reap, and sow spiritual soul food as a family.

What's Your Story?

By faith we understand that the universe was formed at God's command, so that what is seen was not made out of what was visible.

By faith Abel offered God a better sacrifice than Cain did. By faith he was commended as a righteous man, when God spoke well of his offerings. And by faith he still speaks, even though he is dead.

By faith Enoch was taken from this life, so that he did not experience death; he could not be found, because God had taken him away. For before he was taken, he was commended as one who pleased God. And without faith it is impossible to please God, because anyone who comes to him must believe that he exists and that he rewards those who earnestly seek him.

Hebrews 11:3–6 NIV

Everyone has faith in something. Some put their faith in science. Others in karma. Some rest their faith solely in themselves. Yet only those who trust in God have faith in the truest sense of the word. That's because the core meaning of the word *faith* is "a belief in the truth." You can have faith you're Superwoman, but no matter how strongly you believe it, that faith will never let you fly.

Faith in God enables you to do things you might never choose to do on your own. Look at the lives of Abel and Enoch. Abel was murdered by his brother, jealous because Abel chose to offer God a better sacrifice. Enoch "walked" with God, meaning his life was in line with what God wanted him to do. Then, we're told, "he was no more." Two people of faith with two very different endings to their stories.

How one mom lives out her faith will look different from another. One might homeschool while another will not. One might work outside the home; another will not. Your journey of faith is unique. Put your faith in what's true; then live what you believe.

SURE AND STEADY

"Those who do not stumble in their faith because of me are blessed!"

When John's followers left, Jesus began talking to the people about John: "What did you go out into the desert to see? A reed blown by the wind? What did you go out to see? A man dressed in fine clothes? No, people who have fine clothes and much wealth live in kings' palaces. But what did you go out to see? A prophet? Yes, and I tell you, John is more than a prophet. This was written about him: 'I will send my messenger ahead of you, who will prepare the way for you.'

"I tell you, John is greater than any other person ever born, but even the least important person in the kingdom of God is greater than John."

Luke 7:23–28 NCV

Motherhood isn't a popularity contest. Sometimes other mothers or your own children question your choices, but a good parent cares more about doing the right thing than winning the approval of others.

God's prophets cared about the same thing. The only approval John the Baptist wanted to win was God's. John had done what God asked—encouraged people to turn away from sin and toward God in preparation for the arrival of the Messiah. Throughout the Old Testament, other prophets had spoken of a Messiah who would come to save God's people. John had the privilege of delivering the message that Jesus had finally arrived. But now John was in prison, and the Messiah wasn't quite what John had expected. Jesus hadn't led a revolution or freed John from jail. So just before Jesus spoke the words in this passage, John sent his followers to ask Jesus if he was indeed the expected one. Jesus told them to look at what he'd done and decide.

Both prophets and moms can struggle without stumbling. When you have questions and doubts, do what John did—look at Jesus, and forget about living for anyone's approval other than God's.

WHICH KIND OF CHILD ARE YOU?

From the days of John the Baptist until now the kingdom of heaven has suffered violence, and the violent take it by force. For all the Prophets and the Law prophesied until John, and if you are willing to accept it, he is Elijah who is to come. He who has ears to hear, let him hear.

But to what shall I compare this generation? It is like children sitting in the marketplaces and calling to their playmates,

"We played the flute for you, and you did not dance; we sang a dirge, and you did not mourn."

For John came neither eating nor drinking, and they say, "He has a demon." The Son of Man came eating and drinking, and they say, "Look at him! A glutton and a drunkard, a friend of tax collectors and sinners!" Yet wisdom is justified by her deeds.

Matthew 11:12–19 ESV

Being a mom gives you the opportunity to closely observe what it means to be a child. It's easy to forget what it's like to be young, to overlook how trusting, worry-free, and spontaneous a child can be. But childhood is a mixed bag of qualities. Some characteristics are worth emulating, while others are worth eradicating.

In Matthew 18 we see Jesus talking about the importance of having a child*like* faith, and in this passage we see him illustrate the problem of being child*ish* in our faith. Here God's people apparently couldn't make up their minds as to what they expected of God or his prophets. John the Baptist lived an austere life in the desert. Jesus reached out to those who needed God most by talking and dining with them. God's people, particularly their leaders, ridiculed both Jesus and John. Like stubborn, self-centered children, they wanted God to do things their way. They wanted to pick and choose who could enter God's kingdom—and they didn't want to change anything about themselves.

Are you more childlike or childish in your faith? Ask God to help you know how best to grow.

The Promise Keeper

Without becoming weak in faith he contemplated his own body, now as good as dead since he was about a hundred years old, and the deadness of Sarah's womb; yet, with respect to the promise of God, he did not waver in unbelief but grew strong in faith, giving glory to God, and being fully assured that what God had promised, He was able also to perform. Therefore it was also credited to him as righteousness. Now not for his sake only was it written that it was credited to him, but for our sake also, to whom it will be credited, as those who believe in Him who raised Jesus our Lord from the dead, He who was delivered over because of our transgressions, and was raised because of our justification.

Romans 4:19–25 NASB

How old were you when you first became a mom? Sarah was eighty-nine. Her husband, Abraham, was ninety-nine at the time of their son's birth. Obviously, Sarah's and Abraham's biological clocks started ticking once more long after they'd biologically come to a stop. How could that happen? Faith.

In this passage from the book of Romans, the apostle Paul compares the resurrection of Abraham's body to the resurrection of Christ. Abraham needed to be dead reproductively, so that everyone would know that only through faith in God could he have fathered a child. For those of us born after Christ's resurrection, we need to recognize we are truly dead without Christ, because of how we've turned our backs on God through sin. Only then, through faith in Jesus, can we be born again spiritually and step into eternal life.

Though Abraham was obedient in doing what God asked, it wasn't his actions that made him right before God—it was the fact that Abraham believed God would do what he'd promised. You can trust that God will be as true to his promises to you as he was to Abraham.

Introducing . . . YOU!

God chose me to be an apostle, and he appointed me to preach the good news that he promised long ago by what his prophets said in the holy Scriptures. This good news is about his Son, our Lord Jesus Christ! As a human, he was from the family of David. But the Holy Spirit proved that Jesus is the powerful Son of God, because he was raised from death.

Jesus was kind to me and chose me to be an apostle, so that people of all nations would obey and have faith. You are some of those people chosen by Jesus Christ. . . . God loves you and has chosen you to be his very own people.

I pray that God our Father and our Lord Jesus Christ will be kind to you and will bless you with peace!

Romans 1:1–7 CEV

Introductions are important. They're like a verbal snapshot that helps others get a clearer picture of who you really are. You're more than just a name and a face. You're a mother, with a unique background and a variety of interests and abilities. You're also a child of God who through faith has been chosen to fill a very special role in history.

In Paul's letter to the Roman church, Paul introduces himself by name. Then he takes time to put a few of his credentials, as well as Christ's, on display. Next he does the unexpected—he recites a few of the audience's own credentials to them, credentials they might not even be aware of.

The Greek word for *nations* Paul uses here means "Gentiles." Gentiles were anyone who was not a Jew. Paul was the first apostle to be sent to tell the Gentiles the "good news" of Jesus. Previously, God's chosen people had exclusively been the Jews. But thanks to Jesus, now the Gentiles were God's chosen people as well.

Like the people of Rome, you are chosen and cherished by God. That's a credential worth celebrating.

MOUNTAIN MOVERS

"Lord, have mercy on my son. He has seizures and suffers terribly. He often falls into the fire or into the water. So I brought him to your disciples, but they couldn't heal him."

Jesus said, "You faithless and corrupt people! How long must I be with you? How long must I put up with you? Bring the boy to me." Then Jesus rebuked the demon in the boy, and it left him. From that moment the boy was well.

Afterward the disciples asked Jesus privately, "Why couldn't we cast out that demon?"

"You don't have enough faith," Jesus told them. "I tell you the truth, if you had faith even as small as a mustard seed, you could say to this mountain, 'Move from here to there,' and it would move. Nothing would be impossible."

Matthew 17:15–20 NLT

As a parent, it's easy to put yourself in this father's shoes. You'd do anything to help your child. This father's first attempt at finding healing, by bringing his son to Jesus' disciples, had failed, but this dad didn't give up. He risked taking his son straight to Jesus.

The disciples who had been unable to help the boy were Jesus' "second string." They were the nine who stayed behind while Jesus took James, John, and Peter up to a mountaintop where they witnessed Moses and Elijah speaking with Jesus. Perhaps the nine were jealous of Jesus' extra attention for his favorite few. Or perhaps they'd failed to pray. Whatever the reason, their faith needed to grow.

Faith doesn't provide us with superpowers. Faith gives us the power to accomplish what God asks. Period. If God asks you to move mountains, you can. Like a seed, your faith may be small, but it's alive. As you step out in faith to do what God asks, that seed expands and grows. Whatever God asks of you today—from moving a mountain of laundry to disciplining a rebellious child—faith says, "With God, I can."

Home Sweet Home

While we live in these earthly bodies, we groan and sigh, but it's not that we want to die and get rid of these bodies that clothe us. Rather, we want to put on our new bodies so that these dying bodies will be swallowed up by life. God himself has prepared us for this, and as a guarantee he has given us his Holy Spirit.

So we are always confident, even though we know that as long as we live in these bodies we are not at home with the Lord. For we live by believing and not by seeing. Yes, we are fully confident, and we would rather be away from these earthly bodies, for then we will be at home with the Lord. So whether we are here in this body or away from this body, our goal is to please him.

2 Corinthians 5:4–9 NLT

To a baby accustomed to her mother's womb, birth must seem a drastic change. The only home she's ever known vanishes. Her once-dark world now floods with light. The way she breathes and receives nourishment has all changed. She's entered a new world.

One day, you'll experience a new birth. The body you've grown accustomed to will give way to a new kind of life—one that will never end. The thought of that transition may be unsettling. Change often is. But faith tells us this transition is something to celebrate, not fear. The groans Paul talks about are not because we're currently in an aging body or nervous about what's ahead. We groan because we long for home.

We can have faith there's a home waiting beyond this one because we've been given a guarantee. In Greek, the word *guarantee* can be translated "engagement ring." God's Spirit is like an engagement ring, a promise we'll be joined with the One we love to make a permanent home together. Through faith we can anticipate that day with confidence. Since God's Spirit lives in us, our hearts know the way home.

REACH FOR JESUS

While Jesus was still speaking, an official came and knelt in front of him. The man said, "My daughter has just now died! Please come and place your hand on her. Then she will live again."

Jesus and his disciples got up and went with the man.

A woman who had been bleeding for twelve years came up behind Jesus and barely touched his clothes. She had said to herself, "If I can just touch his clothes, I will get well."

Jesus turned. He saw the woman and said, "Don't worry! You are now well because of your faith." At that moment she was healed.

When Jesus went into the home of the official and saw the musicians and the crowd of mourners, he said, "Get out of here! The little girl isn't dead. She is just asleep."

Matthew 9:18–24 CEV

A mature woman and a young girl—two different stages of life, two miracles, both the result of faith. By reading the Gospels of Luke and Mark along with Matthew, we get a better picture of what transpired between Jesus and these two. One suffered from hemorrhagic bleeding. This meant she was considered unclean and ostracized from her Jewish community. The other was the young daughter of a Jewish leader named Jairus. When Jairus first met Jesus, his daughter was ill. Before Jesus arrived at Jairus's home, she had died.

Jairus believed Jesus could not only cure the sick but raise the dead. The bleeding woman believed even Jesus' clothing held more power than the doctors who'd treated her. Both received what they believed: physical healing.

Not every prayer for healing is answered with an instantaneous yes as in this passage. But God still works miracles. You can trust he hears, cares, and answers every prayer you pray. Whether you're praying for the health of your children or for a friend to know Jesus, follow these examples of faith. Reach out to Jesus. His power will provide all you need to face whatever lies ahead.

VICTORY'S NOT ALWAYS VISIBLE

What more should I say? I don't have enough time to tell you about Gideon, Barak, Samson, Jephthah, David, Samuel, and the prophets. Through faith they conquered kingdoms, did what God approved, and received what God had promised. They shut the mouths of lions, put out raging fires, and escaped death.

They found strength when they were weak. They were powerful in battle and defeated other armies. Women received their loved ones back from the dead. Other believers were brutally tortured but refused to be released so that they might gain eternal life. Some were made fun of and whipped, and some were chained and put in prison. Some were stoned to death, sawed in half, and killed with swords. Some wore the skins of sheep and goats. Some were poor, abused, and mistreated. The world didn't deserve these good people.

Hebrews 11:32–38
GOD'S WORD

Chapter 11 of Hebrews is nicknamed the "Hall of Faith." It reads like a who's who of Bible heroes. Some names are familiar, others obscure. Some people's names aren't mentioned at all. But everyone listed here shares something in common. They were all victorious in the face of great difficulties because they put their faith in God.

Not every circumstance listed reads like a victory celebration. Some of God's children didn't see the victory they hoped for. Some were tortured, imprisoned, and killed. But faith trusts there is more to their stories than what the world sees as a happy ending.

As a mother you long for your children to win over all difficulties. But sometimes they rebel. They make poor choices. They head in the opposite direction you prayed they would go. From where you're standing today, victory may not be in sight. That doesn't mean all is lost! Staying consistent in discipline, guidance, love, forgiveness, and prayer is living a Hebrews 11 kind of life. Only God knows your children's whole story. But as you faithfully follow God's lead, you can help weave a theme of faith into their lives.

WATCH AND PRAY

Elijah said to Ahab, "Go up, eat and drink; for there is the sound of abundance of rain." So Ahab went up to eat and drink. And Elijah went up to the top of Carmel; then he bowed down on the ground, and put his face between his knees, and said to his servant, "Go up now, look toward the sea."

So he went up and looked, and said, "There is nothing." And seven times he said, "Go again."

Then it came to pass the seventh time, that he said, "There is a cloud, as small as a man's hand, rising out of the sea!" So he said, "Go up, say to Ahab, 'Prepare your chariot, and go down before the rain stops you.'"

Now it happened in the meantime that the sky became black with clouds and wind, and there was a heavy rain.

1 Kings 18:41–45 NKJV

Elijah was an Old Testament prophet who challenged people to turn from worshipping false idols to worship the one true God. But spiritually wishy-washy King Ahab allowed his wife, Jezebel, to finance 850 false prophets to worship the idols Baal and Asherah. Elijah responded by pronouncing a drought on the land, significant because Baal was supposedly the god of rain.

After three years, Elijah announced the drought would end—not because the people had returned to God but because it would demonstrate God's power and the false idols' powerlessness. Then Elijah waited for God to fulfill his promise. Though there wasn't a cloud in the sky, Elijah continued to pray and wait, wait and pray. When Elijah saw the smallest sign that God's answer was on its way, he started celebrating. That's praying in faith.

Prayer takes patience and persistence. Sometimes you may feel as though God isn't listening, because you haven't yet seen an answer. Don't give up. Keep praying, watching, and waiting. In the same way that you wouldn't give your children gifts they aren't yet old enough for, God sends his gifts of answered prayer to arrive at just the right time.

FAITHFULLY FRUITFUL

Early in the morning, as He was returning to the city, He was hungry. Seeing a lone fig tree by the road, He went up to it and found nothing on it except leaves. And He said to it, "May no fruit ever come from you again!" At once the fig tree withered.

When the disciples saw it, they were amazed and said, "How did the fig tree wither so quickly?"

Jesus answered them, " I assure you: If you have faith and do not doubt, you will not only do what was done to the fig tree, but even if you tell this mountain, 'Be lifted up and thrown into the sea,' it will be done. And if you believe, you will receive whatever you ask for in prayer."

Matthew 21:18–22 HCSB

Do your kids ever think you're angry with them when negative feelings about a totally different situation rise to the surface? That's similar to what happened in this passage. Jesus seems angry with a fig tree, but what he's actually frustrated about is the condition of the people of Israel.

The day before, Jesus had visited the temple and seen people more concerned with making a profit from worship than worshipping God. On this morning, Jesus was headed back into Jerusalem. The fig tree's fruitlessness reminded Jesus of God's fruitless children. On the outside, the "green leaves" of their religious behavior looked like they were growing. But they were not producing any spiritual fruit. Inside, they were already withered and dead.

Faith grows fruit. One kind of fruit is prayer that has power. If you feel God isn't answering your prayers, take time to ask why. He might be answering in a different way than you expect, or perhaps it's not the right time. Or maybe your faith is flagging. If you're only praying out of habit or you don't believe God can or will answer, your prayers—like the fig tree—will be fruitless.

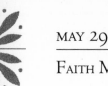

Faith Makes It Happen

The officer said, "Lord, I'm not good enough for you to come into my house. Just give the order, and my servant will get well." . . .

When Jesus heard this, he was so surprised that he turned and said to the crowd following him, "I tell you that in all of Israel I've never found anyone with this much faith! Many people will come from everywhere to enjoy the feast in the kingdom of heaven with Abraham, Isaac, and Jacob. But the ones who should have been in the kingdom will be thrown out into the dark." . . .

Then Jesus said to the officer, "You may go home now. Your faith has made it happen."

Matthew 8:8, 10–13 CEV

A centurion—a Roman officer in charge of one hundred soldiers—came to Jesus with a request. That wasn't surprising; people came to Jesus all the time, asking for things. But this man's faith so surprised Jesus that he used it as an object lesson for his followers.

This prestigious leader asked Jesus to heal his sick servant. When Jesus offered to follow the centurion home, the man refused. He felt he wasn't deserving of such an honor. The officer said he believed Jesus had the authority to merely speak and his servant would be healed. So Jesus did what the centurion believed he could do.

Not only was the centurion compassionate and humble, he was also a Gentile. He didn't have a religious upbringing. But he did have faith, and that was enough. You might feel spiritually inadequate because you don't know a lot about the Bible, or maybe you believe your children's faith is weak or ineffective because they're young. It's faith, not knowledge, that pleases God. While it's important to continue to learn more about God, it's even more important to believe and act on what he says. That's the kind of faith that made a centurion worth emulating.

SAFE IN ANY STORM

It happened, on a certain day, that He got into a boat with His disciples. And He said to them, "Let us cross over to the other side of the lake." And they launched out. But as they sailed He fell asleep. And a windstorm came down on the lake, and they were filling with water, and were in jeopardy. And they came to Him and awoke Him, saying, "Master, Master, we are perishing!"

Then He arose and rebuked the wind and the raging of the water. And they ceased, and there was a calm. But He said to them, "Where is your faith?"

And they were afraid, and marveled, saying to one another, "Who can this be? For He commands even the winds and water, and they obey Him!"

Luke 8:22–25 NKJV

Sudden storms are common on the Sea of Galilee. The surrounding mountains channel winds down to the lake's surface, six hundred feet below sea level. When cold and warm air meet, a storm is born. But even the Sea of Galilee's most violent winds grew still at Jesus' command.

Though the elements obeyed him, Jesus' own disciples were less compliant. They'd witnessed miracles and heard profound spiritual teaching, but their faith continued to waver. Their master had told them they would "cross over to the side of the lake," but they believed a storm had the power to hinder Jesus' plans.

Are there any tempests in your life threatening to blow you off the path God has placed you on? Every stage of motherhood has its own set of challenges and joys. Squalls like toddler-sized temper tantrums or adolescent angst can put your faith to the test. But faith that is tested teaches you God can be trusted. When a storm is raging, focus on God instead of the size of the waves. Cling closely to him, trusting that through his power you and your children will make it safely to the other shore.

THE FAITH TO FORGIVE

Peter, remembering, said to Him, "Rabbi, look! The fig tree which You cursed has withered away."

So Jesus answered and said to them, "Have faith in God. For assuredly, I say to you, whoever says to this mountain, 'Be removed and be cast into the sea,' and does not doubt in his heart, but believes that those things he says will be done, he will have whatever he says. Therefore I say to you, whatever things you ask when you pray, believe that you receive them, and you will have them.

"And whenever you stand praying, if you have anything against anyone, forgive him, that your Father in heaven may also forgive you your trespasses. But if you do not forgive, neither will your Father in heaven forgive your trespasses."

Mark 11:21–26 NKJV

Jesus' action in this passage could be called a living parable. He had seen a fig tree leafed out and went to pick something from it to assuage his hunger. Finding the tree barren, he pronounced a judgment on it that immediately came to pass—it died. The tree wasn't fulfilling the purpose for which it was created.

The followers of Jesus were astonished at his authority to do such mighty works. Taking note of them, he spoke a profound truth: spiritual insight combined with a genuine trust in God's willingness to work through people will result in the power to bring God's will to pass on the earth. However, there is one caveat, according to Jesus: your attitude in prayer is the key to it all. The kingdom of God is all about grace, so if there isn't faith enough to extend grace, neither will there be much power in prayer.

The key to a life of power for your child lies in the faith to forgive. Teach your child the grace of forgiveness, and you've handed him the keys to the kingdom.

FAITH, THE FREEDOM FIGHTER

Does this mean that the law is against God's promises? Never! That would be true only if the law could make us right with God. But God did not give a law that can bring life. Instead, the Scriptures showed that the whole world is bound by sin. This was so the promise would be given through faith to people who believe in Jesus Christ.

Before this faith came, we were all held prisoners by the law. We had no freedom until God showed us the way of faith that was coming. In other words, the law was our guardian leading us to Christ so that we could be made right with God through faith. Now the way of faith has come, and we no longer live under a guardian.

Galatians 3:21–25 NCV

In the world in which Paul's readers lived, parents with means customarily appointed slaves as guardians of their children. The guardian's job involved general oversight of the child, including instruction in ethics and the responsibility of finding a respectable teacher for the child's education. The child wasn't free to make independent decisions until coming of age. It isn't difficult to see why Paul used this metaphor in reference to God's law. It kept Israel under instruction and under restraints until Jesus came to fulfill the law and open the way to a life of promise. Jesus is "the way of faith" who sets us free from the tension that exists between the law and our violation of it.

As a mom, you have a role very similar to that of Israel's law. You keep your children under instruction and restraint until they come into faith of their own . . . faith that is mature enough to take hold of the way of Jesus responsibly and joyfully.

It is critical that as an adult you demonstrate the freedom of faith that results in a life of abundance, peace, and fulfillment.

ENERGIZER BUNNY

Think back on those early days when you first learned about Christ. Remember how you remained faithful even though it meant terrible suffering. Sometimes you were exposed to public ridicule and were beaten, and sometimes you helped others who were suffering the same things. You suffered along with those who were thrown into jail, and when all you owned was taken from you, you accepted it with joy. You knew there were better things waiting for you that will last forever.

So do not throw away this confident trust in the Lord. Remember the great reward it brings you! Patient endurance is what you need now, so that you will continue to do God's will. Then you will receive all that he has promised.

"For in just a little while, the Coming One will come and not delay."

Hebrews 10:32–37 NLT

Many first-century Christians suffered for claiming Jesus as Lord. It might come as a surprise that they were fully aware of this danger prior to confessing their faith, for the persecution of those who followed Jesus was widely publicized. At first, the new believers endured it admirably. However, since the suffering did not end in a timely fashion, they began to get weary and threatened to abandon the faith. They were counseled to hang on with words like these: "Look how far you've come and look at where you're headed; this is no time to give up!"

In training your children to have the faith to persevere through hard times and difficult circumstances, you'll find this counsel very effective. Help each child remember the journey that has led him or her to the present. Accentuate the victories you've experienced together in terms of authentic joy despite real heartache. Try to cast a hopeful vision for the good things that lie ahead, helping your child see the value of pressing through current circumstances, however difficult they may be, in order to cross the finish line as a winner.

THE GREATEST SHOW ON EARTH

I will pour out my Spirit upon all people. Your sons and daughters will prophesy. Your old men will dream dreams, and your young men will see visions. In those days I will pour out my Spirit even on servants—men and women alike. And I will cause wonders in the heavens and on the earth—blood and fire and columns of smoke. The sun will become dark, and the moon will turn blood red before that great and terrible day of the LORD arrives. But everyone who calls on the name of the LORD will be saved . . . just as the LORD has said.

Joel 2:28–32 NLT

The words of the prophet Joel held important implications for Israel just after Jesus' crucifixion, and still do for us today. Spoken approximately four hundred years prior to the death of Jesus, these words were fulfilled when, after the Resurrection, the Holy Spirit was released from heaven in a lavish outburst like an abundant rain, just as Joel had predicted. The followers of Jesus experienced amazing things: the ability to speak in languages they had not learned, to prophesy, to heal the sick, and to cast out evil spirits. Their faith in Jesus was what marked them as those who were to receive this gift of power for ministry.

The amazing thing about prophecy is that it can telescope out into the future with more than one point of fulfillment. The words in this passage indicate that there are more wonders to occur before the end of this age.

As a mom, it is critical to teach your children that God is capable of doing uncommonly powerful things in the interest of advancing his kingdom on the earth. Faith in God's desire to work through humans may determine how effectively your child participates in God's mission.

CHUGGING ALONG

You, who once were alienated and hostile in mind, doing evil deeds, he has now reconciled in his body of flesh by his death, in order to present you holy and blameless and above reproach before him, if indeed you continue in the faith, stable and steadfast, not shifting from the hope of the gospel that you heard, which has been proclaimed in all creation under heaven, and of which I, Paul, became a minister.

Now I rejoice in my sufferings for your sake, and in my flesh I am filling up what is lacking in Christ's afflictions for the sake of his body, that is, the church, of which I became a minister according to the stewardship from God that was given to me for you, to make the word of God fully known, the mystery hidden for ages and generations but now revealed to his saints.

Colossians 1:21–26 ESV

The mystery that was "hidden for ages" came packaged as a first-century Jewish peasant residing in the rural town of Nazareth in Israel. No one expected God to show up that way. Furthermore, no one expected him to unhinge the gates of his abundant kingdom for a bunch of alienated scoundrels by laying his life down for their sake. But that is precisely what happened, and the door of hope remains wide open to those who are true to him in spite of the scandalous development of his plot—in other words, to those who are faithful to his person and his cause.

Moms have the sobering responsibility to demonstrate this "steadfast" faith to their children while living in the midst of a culture that is moving further away from biblical truth. One proof of your steady faith is the way you handle hardship, conflict, and suffering. It is easy to be "faithful" when things are going your way, but the true test of commitment is staying with Jesus when the going gets tough. As Paul said, by living this way we have the opportunity to fill up what is lacking in someone else's faith.

Emancipation

Jesus said to the Jews who had believed in him, "If you abide in my word, you are truly my disciples, and you will know the truth, and the truth will set you free." They answered him, "We are offspring of Abraham and have never been enslaved to anyone. How is it that you say, 'You will become free'?"

Jesus answered them, "Truly, truly, I say to you, everyone who commits sin is a slave to sin. The slave does not remain in the house forever; the son remains forever. So if the Son sets you free, you will be free indeed. I know that you are offspring of Abraham; yet you seek to kill me because my word finds no place in you. I speak of what I have seen with my Father, and you do what you have heard from your father."

John 8:31–38 ESV

Faith is not merely what you know, it's the receptivity and response that allow what you know to take root, develop, and eventually define who you are and how you live in the world. Jesus referred to this process as allowing his words to take up residence in your life. The leaders to whom Jesus spoke in this passage accepted his words at first, but they rejected the way his words played out in life. The pious elite held the power to oppress others with their rigid legalism. Freedom threatened to dismantle the control they had over the common folks. Those oppressed by the religious strongholds that kept people in shame, however, were liberated by Jesus' way.

As a mother, you can teach your children the liberating truth to which your faith lays claim. Empowered to resist the temptation to do wrong, you can wave the banner of freedom before your children by following through on your convictions. Your children will see that no one—nothing—can leverage the power to make them a slave to wrongdoing. Living responsibly is truly emancipating! Living responsibly as a witness to others will help set others free as well.

181

TIME TO RETREAT

When the man saw Jesus, he bowed with his face to the ground, begging to be healed. "Lord," he said, "if you are willing, you can heal me and make me clean."

Jesus reached out and touched him. "I am willing," he said. "Be healed!" And instantly the leprosy disappeared. Then Jesus instructed him not to tell anyone what had happened. He said, "Go to the priest and let him examine you. Take along the offering required in the law of Moses for those who have been healed of leprosy. This will be a public testimony that you have been cleansed."

But despite Jesus' instructions, the report of his power spread even faster, and vast crowds came to hear him preach and to be healed of their diseases. But Jesus often withdrew to the wilderness for prayer.

Luke 5:12–16 NLT

By the common folks, Jesus was perceived as a prophet. Yet by the religious and scholarly leaders of Jerusalem, he was held in suspicion as a heretic and a troublemaker, and they launched a campaign to discredit him.

In the history of Israel, there had been only one case of the healing of a leper on record. No one dreamed that the rural prophet from Nazareth could do what the great Elisha had done centuries before. When the healing in this passage occurred, it affirmed to the people that Jesus was deeply empowered by God.

Because Jesus was aware that this healing would pose such a threat to the religious leaders, he warned the man to use discretion and restraint in reporting the incident—"Just go seek sanction from the local priest and be reunited with your family." But the news spread like wildfire, and people flocked to Jesus from every region.

Your children will benefit from seeing Jesus' response to public acclaim. Never exploiting his popularity as a celebrity, Jesus distanced himself from the crowds regularly in the interest of solitude, seeking the wisdom of God in prayer and contemplating his mission without distraction.

SAY WHAT YOU MEAN, MEAN WHAT YOU SAY

My friends, be patient until the Lord returns. Think of farmers who wait patiently for the spring and summer rains to make their valuable crops grow. Be patient like those farmers and don't give up. The Lord will soon be here! Don't grumble about each other or you will be judged, and the judge is right outside the door.

My friends, follow the example of the prophets who spoke for the Lord. They were patient, even when they had to suffer. In fact, we praise the ones who endured the most. You remember how patient Job was and how the Lord finally helped him. The Lord did this because he is so merciful and kind. . . .

"Yes" or "No" is all you need to say. If you say anything more, you will be condemned.

James 5:7–12 CEV

Using a familiar metaphor, James impresses the need for a no-nonsense faith like that of a man having just sown seed. Evidence of an abundant crop won't come instantaneously. The farmer must respect the natural order of things and trust that the seed and soil will do what they are supposed to do. Though there is some anxiety in waiting, it must be kept in perspective.

Sustained periods of anxiety and stress can take a toll on the best of us, causing our patience to wear thin. It is in these times that moms and children tend to lapse into careless habits. Children are particularly vulnerable to one of those reckless tendencies—careless words.

As a mom, you are aware of your child's inclination to say more than should be said. We all have a responsibility to tame our tongues. Those who learn to exercise discipline in speech become influential in communication, rising above the status quo, just like the prophets of old. Teach your children that it isn't necessary or wise to sling words about in a careless manner. Words are an arsenal of power; they should be chosen and deployed with great care.

PROTOTYPE FOR PRAYER

Pray to your Father in private. He knows what is done in private, and he will reward you.

When you pray, don't talk on and on as people do who don't know God. They think God likes to hear long prayers. Don't be like them. Your Father knows what you need before you ask.

You should pray like this: Our Father in heaven, help us to honor your name. Come and set up your kingdom, so that everyone on earth will obey you, as you are obeyed in heaven. Give us our food for today. Forgive us for doing wrong, as we forgive others. Keep us from being tempted and protect us from evil. If you forgive others for the wrongs they do to you, your Father in heaven will forgive you.

Matthew 6:6–14 CEV

Many mothers feel inadequate to teach their children to pray. Do your prayers seem ineffective? Perhaps the reason prayer is often ineffective is because it is often self-centered. Jesus presented his followers with a powerful conversation starter for prayer.

Begin in the context of relationship: "Father . . . Papa." Praying this way will give your child a feeling of intimacy and security. Move immediately into the motive of prayer: "We want to bring honor to your name." Place yourself in submission to God's mission: "We want to participate in your plan for today." Elaborate on how that might happen.

Align yourself with God's strategies: "We want to put your priorities first today." Help your children learn the importance of praying about obedience.

Teach your children to be conscientious citizens of the earth: "We ask you to provide all of us—the world over—with sustenance for survival." Teach your children that we are agents of God's provision when we have "bread" to share with others.

End where you began, in relationship again, only this time with the human race: "May we live to forgive!" Grace is the ground of true prayer.

STOP AND ASK FOR DIRECTIONS

By faith Abraham obeyed God's call to go to another place God promised to give him. He left his own country, not knowing where he was to go. It was by faith that he lived like a foreigner in the country God promised to give him. He lived in tents with Isaac and Jacob, who had received that same promise from God. Abraham was waiting for the city that has real foundations—the city planned and built by God.

He was too old to have children, and Sarah could not have children. It was by faith that Abraham was made able to become a father, because he trusted God to do what he had promised. This man was so old he was almost dead, but from him came as many descendants as there are stars in the sky.

Hebrews 11:8–12 NCV

Any mom can relate to Abraham's journey into the unknown: you set out by faith not knowing who your children will become or how you'll reach your goal together. However, as in Abraham's situation, you do have something at which to aim.

God counseled Abraham to go to a specific geographical region in which God was going to build an amazing city. Little did Abraham know that city lay in the far-distant future—at the end of this age—and had meaning far beyond what Abraham could imagine in his day.

As a mother, you have the counsel of God recorded in the Bible, which indicates not a specific geographical goal but a desired spiritual destination for each of your children. The development of each child—like Abraham's city—is dependent upon certain architectural blueprints and materials. The construction of a child's character is your main responsibility, and you'll find adequate tooling in Scripture to get the job done. For instance, in the Bible you'll find instruction regarding integrity, diligence, work ethic, honest government, justice, compassion, economics, peacemaking, purity of heart, and more.

Seeking guidance from the Lord daily, you'll reach the goal!

BETTER THAN IT SEEMS

Moses answered, "Don't be afraid! Stand still and you will see the LORD save you today. You will never see these Egyptians again after today. You only need to remain calm; the LORD will fight for you."

Then the LORD said to Moses, "Why are you crying out to me? Command the Israelites to start moving. Raise your walking stick and hold it over the sea so that the sea will split and the people can cross it on dry land. I will make the Egyptians stubborn so they will chase the Israelites, but I will be honored when I defeat the king and all of his chariot drivers and chariots. When I defeat the king, his chariot drivers, and chariots, the Egyptians will know that I am the LORD."

Exodus 14:13–18 NCV

This passage was of great import throughout ancient Israel's colorful history. God's deliverance of Israel from the oppression of Egypt became the event that fueled hope for every adverse situation in which the people found themselves from there forward.

Through a visible column of fire and smoke, God had intentionally led the nation to the brink of the Red Sea with the Egyptian army following close on their heels. Despite the miracles that they had already witnessed, the people despaired when they saw that they were hemmed in on both horizons. They panicked and blamed Moses, saying, "Didn't we tell you to leave us alone while we were in Egypt? We were better off slaves there than dead in this wilderness."

This story is a perfect vehicle through which you can teach your children a profound element of faith concerning times of trial: if you find yourself in difficult circumstances because you were following God, then trust that he can and will deliver you safely through it.

Blaming others for adversity shows our lack of faith. When you're in difficulty, train your eyes instead to focus on the power and mercies of God.

Hang in There

If what you have heard from the beginning remains in you, then you will remain in the Son and in the Father. And this is the promise that He Himself made to us: eternal life. I have written these things to you about those who are trying to deceive you.

The anointing you received from Him remains in you, and you don't need anyone to teach you. Instead, His anointing teaches you about all things, and is true and is not a lie; just as it has taught you, remain in Him.

So now, little children, remain in Him, so that when He appears we may have boldness and not be ashamed before Him at His coming. If you know that He is righteous, you know this as well: everyone who does what is right has been born of Him.

1 John 2:24–29 HCSB

John was part of Jesus' intimate entourage throughout his ministry and witnessed Jesus alive after his crucifixion. The words in this passage were written as many as sixty years later. Although he'd been exposed to many other philosophies during those years, John insisted on sticking with the simple gospel as the substance of true faith: the story of Jesus as told in the books written by Matthew, Mark, Luke, and John.

Particularly in today's world, it is critical to build a foundation of faith that your children can hang on to no matter what comes. The macro story that reveals God's plan to rescue his creation comes to its culmination in the micro story of Jesus. He came, he died, he was resurrected, he ascended to a position of authority, and he will return in order to reestablish the reign of God on earth. This story is a defining story for those who follow Jesus, for when he returns, he'll come to claim his faithful friends. Meanwhile, we are left to advance his mission here on earth. We moms must help our children find their place in the story . . . in the mission.

Decisions & Balance

Sometimes does it seem that you are the one making all the decisions—dinner, chores, outfits, even minute-by-minute activities? Being a lone voice making decisions for everyone all day can be overwhelming, even intimidating. Be confident knowing that you are a strong voice of persuasion. Be guided by God's words to you in the Bible—helping you discern good from bad, wise from unwise.

With good decisions, you can find balance. How did she do it, that Proverbs 31 lady? She seemed to have her hands busy at everything with her priorities perfectly aligned and her heart engaged. Many women look at her with envy, maybe even with a little disbelief. Can anyone really have it all together like that? The way to blend both for a little balance is to make God the focus of everything we do—from cooking and cleaning to excelling as an employee and a friend.

> With all this going for us, my dear, dear friends, stand your ground. And don't hold back. Throw yourselves into the work of the Master, confident that nothing you do for him is a waste of time or effort.

1 Corinthians 15:58 MSG

SHINE THE LIGHT

Light brings every kind of goodness, right living, and truth. Try to learn what pleases the Lord. Have nothing to do with the things done in darkness, which are not worth anything. But show that they are wrong. It is shameful even to talk about what those people do in secret. But the light makes all things easy to see, and everything that is made easy to see can become light. This is why it is said: "Wake up, sleeper! Rise from death, and Christ will shine on you."

So be very careful how you live. Do not live like those who are not wise, but live wisely. Use every chance you have for doing good, because these are evil times. So do not be foolish but learn what the Lord wants you to do.

Ephesians 5:9–17 NCV

It sometimes seems the Bible was written only for those who need to know right from wrong. But in this passage the apostle Paul addresses those who already know the truth. He is encouraging those who know Christ, or who have begun to understand God's forgiveness, to be wise in their behavior. He warns us that participating in ungodly things, even talking about them, can lead to destruction.

The best way to be sure you're doing the right thing is to have your mind set on doing good—not only for yourself, but for others. Our thinking controls our beliefs, and our beliefs lead our behavior. So when we are concentrating on what pleases God, actions that please him will follow.

In challenging situations when you wonder if you should take part, ask yourself, *Am I bringing truth here, or will I have to hide this choice?* Even the best of moms can find themselves in precarious circumstances—at the soccer field, at a dance recital, or at your children's school. When you find yourself in a sticky situation, you don't have to flee. Your purpose might be to bring light into that moment of darkness.

SUPERNATURAL SYNERGY

In view of all we have just shared about God's compassion, I encourage you to offer your bodies as living sacrifices, dedicated to God and pleasing to him. This kind of worship is appropriate for you. Don't become like the people of this world. Instead, change the way you think. Then you will always be able to determine what God really wants—what is good, pleasing, and perfect. . . .

Your thoughts should lead you to use good judgment based on what God has given each of you as believers. Our bodies have many parts, but these parts don't all do the same thing. In the same way, even though we are many individuals, Christ makes us one body and individuals who are connected to each other.

Romans 12:1–5 GOD'S WORD

Most moms can think of a few things we would like to change about ourselves. Most likely you have a list too. Maybe you would like to be thinner or stronger or taller or shorter. Few people are satisfied with how God made them. This passage tells you how to handle your list: allow your mind to transform into new ways of thinking. If you are willing to change your thought patterns, then God will bring about the transformation you want in your life.

Specifically, you should be honest in your estimate of yourself. When you look at your abilities (and inabilities) realistically, you appreciate your strengths as well as the gifts in others. Don't be afraid to ask others what they think are your greatest attributes. Change the way you think about your abilities, so that your part can contribute to the whole.

Don't let an underestimate of your gifts and talents hold you back. Decide to put your strengths to good use for the kingdom of God. Several members of the body working together ignite a supernatural synergy. Connect with others who are using their gifts, and the results can be exponential.

READY AND ABLE

The ways of God are without fault. The LORD's words are pure. He is a shield to those who trust him. Who is God? Only the LORD. Who is the Rock? Only our God. God is my protection. He makes my way free from fault. He makes me like a deer that does not stumble; he helps me stand on the steep mountains. He trains my hands for battle so my arms can bend a bronze bow. You protect me with your saving shield. You support me with your right hand. You have stooped to make me great. You give me a better way to live, so I live as you want me to.

Psalm 18:30–36 NCV

Ideally, a mother has all the help she needs raising her children. But in many families moms are filling the gap for spouses who travel, or work more than one job to make ends meet, or serve in the military, or maybe the gap is the absence of a spouse altogether. Whether you are single or married, you sometimes can find yourself feeling as if you are parenting all alone.

One of the biggest challenges in this situation is making all the decisions yourself. The unanswered questions can be overwhelming at times. Take comfort in this psalm that reassures you that God is someone you can rely on. He will guide you in the daily decisions that you must make.

He is a great protector. So you don't have to worry about making mistakes or doubting yourself. When you are feeling overwhelmed with decisions, connect with God. Ask him to guide you and reveal the right answers to you. Keep a journal of your requests to him and what you feel he is leading you to do. Trust that you can rely on him to partner with you in all of your parenting decisions.

Enticement Entangles

God will bless you, if you don't give up when your faith is being tested. He will reward you with a glorious life, just as he rewards everyone who loves him. Don't blame God when you are tempted! God cannot be tempted by evil, and he doesn't use evil to tempt others. We are tempted by our own desires that drag us off and trap us. Our desires make us sin, and when sin is finished with us, it leaves us dead.

Don't be fooled, my dear friends. Every good and perfect gift comes down from the Father who created all the lights in the heavens. He is always the same and never makes dark shadows by changing. He wanted us to be his own special people, and so he sent the true message to give us new birth.

James 1:12–18 CEV

As mothers we want to do everything we can to give our children a wonderful life, with the most opportunities we can provide. When children want to participate in sports, lessons, or other good activities, we want to accommodate all of their interests. Sometimes that drive may compel you to overschedule your commitments both in time and finances. It's easier to identify what the big commitments will require of you, but the daily requests for attendance or assistance with events have an impact too.

The consequences of overcommitting can strain your family budget, causing you to work extra hours or cut back on other family expenses. The commitment can also impose on your time not only as individuals but as a family.

When you or your children are invited to participate in new activities or events, be careful to determine the value in the opportunity. Ask yourself what is enticing you to say yes to the decision to add more to your family schedule. You or your child should gain a positive impact for the commitment. Agree to the obligation only if you determine that you will receive a positive return for your investment.

THE BEST ADVISER

Protect me, God, because I trust in you. I said to the LORD, "You are my LORD. Every good thing I have comes from you." As for the godly people in the world, they are the wonderful ones I enjoy. . . .

The LORD is all I need. He takes care of me. My share in life has been pleasant; my part has been beautiful.

I praise the LORD because he advises me. Even at night, I feel his leading. I keep the LORD before me always. Because he is close by my side, I will not be hurt. So I rejoice and am glad.

Psalm 16:1–3, 5–9 NCV

When you awaken each day, you know that the day will be full of decisions, but you just don't always know all of the specific decisions you will have to make. So it is best to be prepared at all times, ready to make the right choice at the right moment. This psalm offers a great meditation for each time of the day: morning, afternoon, and evening.

When you rise in the morning, remind yourself of all the blessings in your life that have been given to you by God. Pray for God's protection over you and your family for the day. The afternoon is a wonderful time to take a moment of reflection on the decisions in front of you for the remainder of the day and how you can be a blessing to others through your choices. Then in the evening, be mindful of and thankful for how the Lord has directed you throughout the day.

Remember that your children are bombarded by choices everyday too. Share this psalm with them and help them learn how to look to God for his advice throughout the day too.

I Shall and I Will

Shout with joy to the Lord, all the earth! Worship the Lord with gladness. Come before him, singing with joy. Acknowledge that the Lord is God! He made us, and we are his. We are his people, the sheep of his pasture. Enter his gates with thanksgiving; go into his courts with praise. Give thanks to him and praise his name. For the Lord is good. His unfailing love continues forever, and his faithfulness continues to each generation.

I will sing of your love and justice, Lord. I will praise you with songs. I will be careful to live a blameless life—when will you come to help me? I will lead a life of integrity in my own home.

Psalm 100:1–101:2 NLT

One of the most important decisions we must make each day concerns our attitude. Mothers cannot control or even predict all the challenges that will be encountered each day. But you can pre-determine your reaction to every situation you will face—expected or unexpected.

Whether you are making decisions from a corporate boardroom that affect hundreds of people or you are deciding which lesson to teach your homeschooler, don't let daily pressure or others' expectations of you impede your attitude. A joyful attitude of praise is a choice. We have to decide every morning to keep our outlook positive.

Some days are so challenging that you will have to remind yourself several times of your determination to keep a pleasant and peaceful attitude. One thing you can do is take a few minutes during the transitions of your day. Just before you pick the children up from school, on your drive home from work, or maybe while you are preparing dinner, listen to a few minutes of worship music and thank God for his blessings in your life. A few minutes to refocus can renew your joyful spirit.

INVESTING IN FUTURES

How joyful are those who fear the LORD and delight in obeying his commands. Their children will be successful everywhere; an entire generation of godly people will be blessed. They themselves will be wealthy, and their good deeds will last forever. Light shines in the darkness for the godly. They are generous, compassionate, and righteous. Good comes to those who lend money generously and conduct their business fairly.

Such people will not be overcome by evil. Those who are righteous will be long remembered. They do not fear bad news; they confidently trust the LORD to care for them. . . . Their good deeds will be remembered forever. They will have influence and honor.

Psalm 112:1–7, 9 NLT

Have you ever caught yourself thinking, *I sound just like my mother?* Sometimes that moment brings back a fond memory that evokes a chuckle; sometimes it might be a moment of regret that you said something you vowed to never say. In either case you are powerfully reminded that your mother's influence in your childhood still impacts you today.

There is no doubt that today's actions have an eternal impact on your children, just as your mother's had on you. This sobering thought will make even small parts of your daily routine seem significant. Small decisions can have a powerful impact. You would never think to let your children go without food, because their bodies need it. With that same conviction, you can feed their spirits daily with encouragement, compassion, and love. What effect do you want to have on your children today? Do you want them to feel important, courageous, or nurtured? Then plan your words and actions to achieve that result. Your daily decisions and interactions with your children carry forward into the future generation; so assign eternal intention to even the most mundane moments of motherhood.

A Mom's Hope

It is only natural for me to feel the way I do. All of you have helped in the work that God has given me, as I defend the good news and tell about it here in jail. God himself knows how much I want to see you. He knows that I care for you in the same way that Christ Jesus does.

I pray that your love will keep on growing and that you will fully know and understand how to make the right choices.

Then you will still be pure and innocent when Christ returns. And until that day, Jesus Christ will keep you busy doing good deeds that bring glory and praise to God.

My dear friends, I want you to know that what has happened to me has helped to spread the good news.

Philippians 1:7–12 CEV

A strong-willed young boy was standing in his mother's grocery cart, so she asked him to be seated. Wanting to be independent, he continued to stand. She repeated her request, and then insisted, but he responded with folded arms and tightened knees. Finally, after his mother threatened no grocery store prize for good behavior, he reluctantly took his seat and proclaimed, "I may be sitting on the outside, but I am standing on the inside!"

So often we pray for our children to make the right choices. We want to protect them from the consequences of bad decisions and see them reap the rewards of good ones. Even though we might be able to coax, impose, or control their compliance, the real goal is for them to want to embrace the right choice. Whether our children are two, twelve, or twenty, we can expand our prayers for them to fully understand how to make decisions that honor God.

A wonderful prayer to pray over your children is nestled in this passage. Pray not only that they make right decisions but that God continues to increase their insight and ability in the process.

CROWNED A WINNER

Whoever loves instruction loves knowledge, but one who hates correction is stupid.

The good obtain favor from the LORD, but He condemns a man who schemes.

Man cannot be made secure by wickedness, but the root of the righteous is immovable.

A capable wife is her husband's crown, but a wife who causes shame is like rottenness in his bones.

The thoughts of the righteous [are] just, but guidance from the wicked [leads to] deceit.

The words of the wicked are a deadly ambush, but the speech of the upright rescues them.

The wicked are overthrown and perish, but the house of the righteous will stand.

A man is praised for his insight, but a twisted mind is despised.

Proverbs 12:1–8 HCSB

But is a powerful word that this passage uses to illustrate the opposing elements within choices and actions. Every day we have the opportunity and privilege of making choices about where we go, whom we befriend, how we conduct business, and whom we will love. Each of the couplets in this passage addresses a different area of thought, but they all weave together a common insight.

Parents sometimes try to protect their children from the challenges of life by keeping big decisions and challenges hidden. But you can contribute to your children's confidence in decision making by teaching them to weigh the options of choices carefully. You might not want to share your entire family budget planning session with them, but you can ask how they think you should spend the entertainment fund for the month. It is good for children to understand reasons for and consequences of decisions.

Whether you are making decisions yourself or with the help of your family, remember that every action has the potential to cause a reaction. When you are making decisions, think through not only the options but also the results of each action.

THANK-YOU GIFT

In the course of time Hannah conceived and gave birth to a son. She named him Samuel, saying, "Because I asked the LORD for him." . . .

After he was weaned, she took the boy with her, young as he was, along with a three-year-old bull, an ephah of flour and a skin of wine, and brought him to the house of the LORD at Shiloh. When they had slaughtered the bull, they brought the boy to Eli, and she said to him,

"As surely as you live, my lord, I am the woman who stood here beside you praying to the LORD. I prayed for this child, and the LORD has granted me what I asked of him. So now I give him to the LORD. For his whole life he will be given over to the LORD." And he worshiped the LORD there.

1 Samuel 1:20, 24–28 NIV

Hannah's response to God's blessing in her life seems illogical, doesn't it? How could a woman who so desperately wanted a child send him away? However, Hannah knew exactly what she was doing when she made the decision to take what was most precious to her and put it back in the hands of God. She was so grateful to God, and she put action to her gratitude and was blessed richly because of it. Her soul was blessed by her giving without the knowledge that God would later bless her with more children.

This was not just a nice gesture on Hannah's part; this was a solid decision to bless God for blessing her. She sacrificed the very thing she wanted. Little did she know that in turn her thank-you gift ended up blessing a nation! Little Samuel grew up to become one of Israel's most influential leaders.

We can never outgive God. When was the last time you made a conscious decision to bless him with a most precious sacrifice on your part? Allow your mind to follow through on what your heart longs to express to the Lord today.

HAVE YOU CONSIDERED THE TIME?

[Jesus] was also saying to the crowds, "When you see a cloud rising in the west, immediately you say, 'A shower is coming,' and so it turns out.

"And when you see a south wind blowing, you say, 'It will be a hot day,' and it turns out that way.

"You hypocrites! You know how to analyze the appearance of the earth and the sky, but why do you not analyze this present time?

"And why do you not even on your own initiative judge what is right?

"For while you are going with your opponent to appear before the magistrate, on your way there make an effort to settle with him, so that he may not drag you before the judge, and the judge turn you over to the officer, and the officer throw you into prison."

Luke 12:54–58 NASB

There are just some days when we have to say to ourselves, "It's time to seriously get it together." This passage is one of those cold cups of water we need to wake us up from our routines of life.

It is easy to forget that this world is not eternal as we juggle laundry, sibling conflicts ("She hit me! . . . He's looking at me!"), doctor appointments, parent-teacher conferences, meetings at work . . . you get the idea. Just as we look out the window to judge what kind of outerwear to suit our children up in during the morning rush, we must stop to think about what spiritual climate our children are walking into as they leave the warm nest of our homes. Have you considered the time? Are you experiencing God on a daily basis and training your child to do the same? Are you teaching them to do their part to live peacefully with each other? Are you showing them through your own actions how to treat others with love? Consider the times! This world needs a real generation of Christ followers now more than ever before.

BATTLE OF WILL

What I don't understand about myself is that I decide one way, but then I act another, doing things I absolutely despise. So if I can't be trusted to figure out what is best for myself and then do it, it becomes obvious that God's command is necessary.

But I need something *more*! For if I know the law but still can't keep it, and if the power of sin within me keeps sabotaging my best intentions, I obviously need help! I realize that I don't have what it takes. I can will it, but I can't *do* it. I decide to do good, but I don't *really* do it; I decide not to do bad, but then I do it anyway. My decisions, such as they are, don't result in actions.

Romans 7:15–20 MSG

We often know what is best for us, but we don't always go that direction. Some moms have silently cried while putting the dishes away about the seemingly endless tasks of caring for their family, let alone the tasks and sacrifice it will take to bring their children into all God has for them. It would be easy to just go with routines and not strive for more in everyday life, but that is not what life is about.

Jesus gave us life so that we may live abundantly, friends! That means richly and with freedom. An inner battle rages between settling for monotony and forging ahead for more. We cannot move forward on our own, which is why God gave us the Holy Spirit. Mothers have a tremendous capacity for strength, but we can never be all that God has created us to be without the work of the Holy Spirit in our lives. Make the decision today to invite the Holy Spirit into all that you do. Make each day better and stronger knowing that you are living at full capacity because of the Spirit's influence and leading in your life!

SETTLE DOWN

This world as we know it will soon pass away.

I want you to be free from the concerns of this life. An unmarried man can spend his time doing the Lord's work and thinking how to please him. But a married man has to think about his earthly responsibilities and how to please his wife. His interests are divided. In the same way, a woman who is no longer married or has never been married can be devoted to the Lord and holy in body and in spirit. But a married woman has to think about her earthly responsibilities and how to please her husband. I am saying this for your benefit, not to place restrictions on you. I want you to do whatever will help you serve the Lord best, with as few distractions as possible.

1 Corinthians 7:31–35 NLT

God does not desire that marriage and family take a backseat to any career, including ministry. Having a career is not a bad thing at all; it is a wrong priority placed on our work that this passage is speaking to. We all know that our first ministry is in our homes to our husbands and children, but do we practice it? This is one of the most difficult things to balance when you are a mom with a full-time job outside the home, and particularly full-time ministry.

Work will always be there, but your time with your family will not. Children grow old and gain lives of their own, and if your marriage has indeed taken a backseat to your ministry . . . well, it will not continue to thrive. Choosing how to prioritize comes with tough decisions, because you cannot please everyone. However, you can do your best to make certain that your family members are not the ones constantly being disappointed. Give God your best by giving your family your best! And if you are in full-time ministry, lead others in this by your example.

Take Charge

My child, never forget the things I have taught you. Store my commands in your heart. If you do this, you will live many years, and your life will be satisfying. Never let loyalty and kindness leave you! Tie them around your neck as a reminder. Write them deep within your heart. Then you will find favor with both God and people, and you will earn a good reputation.

Trust in the Lord with all your heart; do not depend on your own understanding. Seek his will in all you do, and he will show you which path to take.

Don't be impressed with your own wisdom. Instead, fear the Lord and turn away from evil. Then you will have healing for your body and strength for your bones.

Proverbs 3:1–8 NLT

Do you want to take charge of your life? Then give it away . . . give it to God. Many moms give their lives away to something else—a career, unhealthy relationships, or hobbies. These mothers ultimately find only an aching heart from disappointments and a high level of dissatisfaction in life due to overexhaustion. Take charge of your life by putting your trust in God for everything and following him where he leads.

This passage is one of the most vital Bible passages for mothers because this confident decision to trust God must be done daily, like taking a prenatal vitamin. Without the vitamin, your baby will most likely survive but will not be as healthy as she could have been, with a big chance for deformity. It is the same with your life—don't be reckless about trusting God and moving forward in your faith according to what he says in the Bible, knowing that his leading is the best for you and your family. Unlike anything else that women give their lives to, you will not be found in want; instead, you will build a legacy of wholeness.

Just Do It

Don't just listen to God's word. You must do what it says. Otherwise, you are only fooling yourselves. For if you listen to the word and don't obey, it is like glancing at your face in a mirror. You see yourself, walk away, and forget what you look like. But if you look carefully into the perfect law that sets you free, and if you do what it says and don't forget what you heard, then God will bless you for doing it.

If you claim to be religious but don't control your tongue, you are fooling yourself, and your religion is worthless. Pure and genuine religion in the sight of God the Father means caring for orphans and widows in their distress and refusing to let the world corrupt you.

James 1:22–27 NLT

The world is filled with useless religion as it is described in this passage. Unfortunately, so many people have been affected in a negative way by false faith that it has given Christianity a stained reputation. Fortunately, this can be reversed through those who choose to live what the Bible says before quoting it.

James uses the analogy of someone seeing herself in the mirror and walking away, forgetting who she is or what she looks like. The Bible confronts us in many ways just as a mirror does, but if we choose to ignore it and act like those who don't know what it says, we confuse those around us about what it means to be a Christ follower . . . including our impressionable children. A very wise mother once said to model the Christianity that you want your children to live. Our children will mimic our actions before they can even speak, as seen with any toddler. So do yourself and your children a favor—after you sit in church, live the rest of the week in line with what you just spent an hour or more professing to believe.

Do You See What I See?

The king sent horses and chariots and a large fighting unit there. They came at night and surrounded the city.

When the servant of the man of God got up in the morning and went outside, he saw troops, horses, and chariots surrounding the city. Elisha's servant asked, "Master, what should we do?" Elisha answered, "Don't be afraid. We have more forces on our side than they have on theirs." Then Elisha prayed, "LORD, please open his eyes so that he may see." The LORD opened the servant's eyes and let him see. The mountain around Elisha was full of fiery horses and chariots. As the Arameans came down to get him, Elisha prayed to the LORD, "Please strike these people with blindness." The LORD struck them with blindness, as Elisha had asked.

2 Kings 6:14–18 GOD'S WORD

Life comes with its share of battles, and no matter how much we want to shelter our children, they will see and pick up a lot more than we would like them to. In these intense situations the stance as a mother should be one of mentoring, just as this passage shows in the relationship between the prophet Elisha and his servant. Elisha did not panic. Before he prayed for God to take care of the situation, he stopped and prayed that his servant would be able to see where God was in all of what was happening.

We are raising a generation that desperately needs to see God as he is; our children need to see that the One who is in them is greater than the one who is in the world (see 1 John 4:4). Take time out in every storm or battle to ask God to open the eyes of your children to see him in that situation, and you will build a legacy of faith for your family. This will train your children to look for God in all situations, even when mom is not there to point him out.

SPEAK FOR YOURSELF

Joshua told the people: Worship the LORD, obey him, and always be faithful. Get rid of the idols your ancestors worshiped when they lived on the other side of the Euphrates River and in Egypt. But if you don't want to worship the LORD, then choose right now! Will you worship the same idols your ancestors did? Or since you're living on land that once belonged to the Amorites, maybe you'll worship their gods. I won't. My family and I are going to worship and obey the LORD!

The people answered: We could never worship other gods or stop worshiping the LORD. The LORD is our God. We were slaves in Egypt as our ancestors had been, but we saw the LORD work miracles to set our people free and to bring us out of Egypt.

Joshua 24:14–17 CEV

After reviewing all that God had done for the Israelites, Joshua called the people to make the decision that needed to be made in order to thrive in the new land God was giving them. Joshua's own often-quoted declaration, "As for me and my house, we will serve the Lord," set the precedent.

Making the decision to serve the Lord is not a one-time decision; it is a daily decision to do things according to God's will as outlined in the Bible. Our children know that we serve God, but it is important to stop and declare to them *why* we live for God. Make it a practice in your home to stop every once in a while and reflect with your family why you all have chosen to serve God. As your children mature, they will need deeply rooted reasons to continue living by faith, especially as they enter high school and college. You can record family members' prayer requests and testimonies in their Bibles as landmarks. You can even read them as bedtime stories to your children to serve as memoirs of times that God has "come through" for your family.

WILL THE REAL MOMMY PLEASE STAND UP?

They argued back and forth in front of Solomon, until finally he said, "Both of you say this live baby is yours. Someone bring me a sword."

A sword was brought, and Solomon ordered, "Cut the baby in half! That way each of you can have part of him."

"Please don't kill my son," the baby's mother screamed. "Your Majesty, I love him very much, but give him to her. Just don't kill him."

The other woman shouted, "Go ahead and cut him in half. Then neither of us will have the baby."

Solomon said, "Don't kill the baby." Then he pointed to the first woman, "She is his real mother. Give the baby to her."

Everyone in Israel was amazed when they heard how Solomon had made his decision. They realized that God had given him wisdom to judge fairly.

1 Kings 3:22–28 CEV

The real mother in this story had the most to lose in this case—her child. The other woman had stolen the child and was willing to let him die. Let's be honest. Not everyone is going to have the best interest of your family at heart. There might be times when you feel as if someone is trying to take away everything you have worked so hard to nurture. A very real enemy is after the souls and the future of you and your household, and there will be times when you feel as though that enemy is gaining ground. It is at these times you must respond in faith and love, even if it means releasing what you hold most dear.

Remember that the One who sits on the throne and judges loves you and has good plans for you and your family. During times of testing, stand firm in your knowledge of God and who you are. Show your godly character by laying aside your desires and making decisions for the advancement of his kingdom. Standing firm as a woman of God seeking his desires will reveal that this promise of God belongs to you.

That Must Have Cost a Fortune

While [Jesus] was eating dinner, a woman came up carrying a bottle of very expensive perfume. Opening the bottle, she poured it on his head. Some of the guests became furious among themselves. "That's criminal! A sheer waste! This perfume could have been sold for well over a year's wages and handed out to the poor." They swelled up in anger, nearly bursting with indignation over her.

But Jesus said, "Let her alone. Why are you giving her a hard time? She has just done something wonderfully significant for me. You will have the poor with you every day for the rest of your lives. Whenever you feel like it, you can do something for them. Not so with me. She did what she could when she could—she pre-anointed my body for burial."

Mark 14:3–8 MSG

She did what she could when she could." That is what made this act of worship so precious, intimate, and sincere. Many times we see our present situations as limitations to worshipping God. There are times mothers of very young children are disappointed because they cannot spend as much time on a daily or weekly basis in praying, reading the Bible, or worshipping God as they did before having children. A mother's worship is even more precious because of the sacrifice she must make to engage in it, whether that means going without sleep, pressing past all the caregiver tasks floating in her mind, or playing a little less with her children, her most precious gems.

Moms, do not miss moments of worship, thinking that you have limits. The woman in this passage did not belong at this dinner at that moment in the cultural sense, but she did not miss her moment to worship and gave what she had when she could. God is not waiting for you to give him what you wish you had; he is waiting for you to come with all that you do have! Do not miss your moment!

Fall in Line, Soldier

I [Moses] took the heads of your tribes, wise and experienced men, and set them as heads over you, commanders of thousands, commanders of hundreds, commanders of fifties, commanders of tens, and officers, throughout your tribes. And I charged your judges at that time, "Hear the cases between your brothers, and judge righteously between a man and his brother or the alien who is with him. You shall not be partial in judgment. You shall hear the small and the great alike. You shall not be intimidated by anyone, for the judgment is God's. And the case that is too hard for you, you shall bring to me, and I will hear it."

Deuteronomy 1:13–17 ESV

If there is one person who can understand the need for organization within a large group of people, it is a mother. Moms can also understand the gravity of judging a case righteously in order to avoid bloodshed! It is so comforting to know that God is ultimately in control as you keep your mind focused on what he desires in each situation. Mothers must make impromptu judgment calls on a daily basis. The choices we make should be just responses in all matters, and when something is beyond our jurisdiction, we can bring it to God.

Although believers have been given authority, we are not left alone on this earth to figure it all out. Any authority that is not surrendered to the ultimate authority of God is counterfeit and will eventually fall apart. Women understanding true authority will exercise sound wisdom and are mature enough to acknowledge that they don't have it all figured out all of the time. Women of wisdom know to whom they report to get their answers. Don't feel pressured to make a judgment decision prematurely. Enjoy your time of conversation with God and let him direct your decision.

ONE MORE QUESTION

Gideon said to God, "If you will save Israel by my hand as you have promised—look, I will place a wool fleece on the threshing floor. If there is dew only on the fleece and all the ground is dry, then I will know that you will save Israel by my hand, as you said." And that is what happened. Gideon rose early the next day; he squeezed the fleece and wrung out the dew—a bowlful of water.

Then Gideon said to God, "Do not be angry with me. Let me make just one more request. Allow me one more test with the fleece. This time make the fleece dry and the ground covered with dew." That night God did so. Only the fleece was dry; all the ground was covered with dew.

Judges 6:36–40 NIV

Let's make one thing clear—Gideon was not stalling for time! There is a big difference between asking God for guidance and stalling. Stalling is when we know what God wants us to do, but we pray about it until we can justify why we will not obey. That is not what was happening in this passage. God had told Gideon that he would use Gideon to deliver the whole nation out of bondage! Gideon had to make sure that he heard correctly, because of the gravity of the situation. Things would not go well if God wasn't with him.

In your decision making, you must include God if you are planning to live your life for him. God wasn't angry with Gideon, because he knew that this questioning was coming from an obedient heart that needed assurance. It is the same with you; if you need assurance, if you need wisdom, ask God for it. If you are unsure, you can ask God to accomplish his will for you. While you are at it, also ask for the courage and stamina to be obedient to his direction when you receive it!

There Is a Method to It

When a farmer plows for planting, does he plow continually? Does he keep on breaking up and harrowing the soil? When he has leveled the surface, does he not sow caraway and scatter cumin? Does he not plant wheat in its place, barley in its plot, and spelt in its field? His God instructs him and teaches him the right way.

Caraway is not threshed with a sledge, nor is a cartwheel rolled over cumin; caraway is beaten out with a rod, and cumin with a stick. Grain must be ground to make bread; so one does not go on threshing it forever. . . . All this also comes from the Lord Almighty, wonderful in counsel and magnificent in wisdom.

Isaiah 28:24–29 NIV

Be encouraged by processes and order today. God has blessed us and given us much responsibility during our time on earth. It is so comforting to know that he also gives us direction on how to get the job done. Consider the toast that you may have had this morning . . . a loaf of bread did not just pop out of the ground, waiting to be packaged. Ground was plowed, seeds were planted, plants were cared for until the time of harvest; then came the threshing, the baking, the packing—you get it; there was a process to get that seemingly insignificant item to your table.

How much more is God involved in the process of your life and the lives of your loved ones? He has an unending supply of wisdom and knowledge and waits to speak with you today concerning all that you need to get done and all that you desire to accomplish as a mom and in life. Do not be intimidated by it all; your life has been designed to go through processes to get to your desired destination. Seek God's counsel and embrace your unique process today.

CONSIDER IT CAREFULLY

[The serpent] asked the woman, "Did God really say you must not eat the fruit from any of the trees in the garden?"

"Of course we may eat fruit from the trees in the garden," the woman replied. "It's only the fruit from the tree in the middle of the garden that we are not allowed to eat. God said, 'You must not eat it or even touch it; if you do, you will die.'"

"You won't die!" the serpent replied to the woman. "God knows that your eyes will be opened as soon as you eat it, and you will be like God, knowing both good and evil."

The woman was convinced. She saw that the tree was beautiful and its fruit looked delicious, and she wanted the wisdom it would give her. So she took some of the fruit and ate it.

Genesis 3:1–6 NLT

It is so hard to read this passage of Scripture and not wince at the moment that Eve took the fruit. Her decision to disobey changed the entire world for eternity. Daily we face choices that might not have life-or-death impact every time, but each decision has many unseen effects that we must stop to consider. Choosing what we desire but God opposes never brings a positive result for anyone, not even for ourselves.

Look at how the serpent convinced Eve to compromise. The truth was contorted in a way that made the wrong choice seem right. There were considerations that Eve missed: Yes, your eyes will be opened, Eve, but is that what you want out of life? You will know both good and evil, but don't you already know goodness walking with the Lord each day? Why would you want to know evil? Why be like God when you already have God?

It might seem the only person being affected by our decisions is us, but that is rarely the case. Somewhere someone is affected by the choices we make—and often it is our children. So consider your decisions carefully.

You Mean I Can Pick Anything?

[Solomon said,] "O LORD my God, you have made me king instead of my father, David, but I am like a little child who doesn't know his way around. And here I am in the midst of your own chosen people, a nation so great and numerous they cannot be counted! Give me an understanding heart so that I can govern your people well and know the difference between right and wrong. For who by himself is able to govern this great people of yours?" . . .

So God replied, "Because you have asked for wisdom in governing my people with justice and have not asked for a long life or wealth or the death of your enemies—I will give you what you asked for! . . . And I will also give you what you did not ask for—riches and fame!"

1 Kings 3:7–13 NLT

It is very interesting that God asked Solomon the questions in this passage through a dream. Our best decisions are made when our hearts and minds are quieted and we can hear God clearly.

The God of the universe asked Solomon his heart's desire! How would you answer that question? Solomon answered well; his answer was well thought out. He wasn't greedy, thinking, *How can I get the most out of this?* Instead, he answered out of maturity.

Solomon wanted from God the ability to best care for what God had given him. Many times we think the answer to a situation is to have more of something—more money, more beauty, more time—when really what we need is an understanding of the best way to care for all that we've been given—including our children! We all have limitations: the latest balance in our checkbook, our physical abilities, the number of hours in a day, and more. But concentrate on what you already have to best care for and use your resources, rather than their limits. The next time you want to pray for more of something, consider praying for more wisdom first.

SIESTA

The Lord GOD, the Holy One of Israel, has said: "You will be delivered by returning and resting; your strength will lie in quiet confidence. But you are not willing." You say, "No! We will escape on horses"—therefore you will escape! . . . One thousand [will flee] at the threat of one, at the threat of five you will flee, until you alone remain like a [solitary] pole on a mountaintop or a banner on a hill.

Therefore the LORD is waiting to show you mercy, and is rising up to show you compassion, for the LORD is a just God. Happy are all who wait patiently for Him.

Isaiah 30:15–18 HCSB

This passage gives moms such a reason to rejoice today! Think about these two words for a moment . . . "quiet confidence." Not loud boasting, not doing your best to take care of everything yourself, but in return and rest you will be delivered; in quiet confidence your strength lies. When you are facing one of the many storms in life that mothers face, this can be hard to do. In fact, just being able to lay your head down at night and not think or worry about your situation takes faith to accomplish!

Although you feel that you are doing nothing by resting in God, you are actually allowing a spiritual power to move. Leaving a situation in God's hands, praying about it, refusing to retaliate on your own or relying on your own strength is like moving yourself into the safest place possible. Possibly the best thing that you can do about a difficult situation today is to say a prayer and then deliberately take a nap or do something completely restful. Do not allow yourself to doubt that God can and will move on your behalf today.

KNOW THE AGENDA

[Samuel said,] "Why didn't you obey the LORD? Why did you take the best things? Why did you do what the LORD said was wrong?"

Saul said, "But I did obey the LORD. I did what the LORD told me to do. I destroyed all the Amalekites, and I brought back Agag their king. The soldiers took the best sheep and cattle to sacrifice to the LORD your God at Gilgal."

But Samuel answered, "What pleases the LORD more: burnt offerings and sacrifices or obedience to his voice? It is better to obey than to sacrifice. It is better to listen to God than to offer the fat of sheep. Disobedience is as bad as the sin of sorcery. Pride is as bad as the sin of worshiping idols. You have rejected the LORD's command. Now he rejects you as king."

1 Samuel 15:19–23 NCV

Saul, Israel's first king, thought he was doing something good for God. All throughout Saul's reign he confused his religion and culture with a relationship with God, and it got him in trouble repeatedly. He did not have a faithful relationship with God, so he did not rely on him or heed his voice. Saul ended up being tormented by spirits and acting out of his own suspicion and paranoia.

There are many like Saul today, week to week going to church out of tradition without any expectation of hearing from God. They are not engaging in a relationship with God and daily are relying on their own strength. It's easy for moms to fall into this, and thank God there is a way out! Engage in a relationship with God, speak to him and read the Bible, wait for him to speak to you and obey when he does. Attend church with an expectation that he will be there to meet with you. Serve others so that they may be led into a relationship with him as well. Live life obediently, knowing God will save you from yourself and influence your children as well!

CHOOSE

See, I have set before you today life and good, death and evil, in that I command you today to love the LORD your God, to walk in His ways, and to keep His commandments, His statutes, and His judgments, that you may live and multiply; and the LORD your God will bless you in the land which you go to possess. . . . I call heaven and earth as witnesses today against you, that I have set before you life and death, blessing and cursing; therefore choose life, that both you and your descendants may live; that you may love the LORD your God, that you may obey His voice . . . that you may dwell in the land which the LORD swore to your fathers, to Abraham, Isaac, and Jacob, to give them.

Deuteronomy 30:15–16, 19–20 NKJV

God poses the question to each person: will you choose life or death? Thankfully, he does not limit us to only one response. Choosing to live for God is not a one-time decision but a decision made repeatedly with every choice taken in our lives. Decisions that we mothers make in front of our families impact those around us, and our children in turn learn from us how to live.

When you choose to follow God, you are shaping the lives of those around you and building a legacy of people who serve the Lord. God takes care of everything that you and your family need and desire. Your job is to keep his commandments out of love for him. Do it. The alternative is not worth the lessened effort of following God. Some compromise and try to justify their wavering obedience. But there are only two ways to go—toward God or away from him. Moving consistently toward him produces growth in many ways—spiritually, emotionally, and physically. God gives you the choice of promise or compromise. By choosing the promise of life, you strengthen your legacy. The results of your faithfulness will impact generations.

RETURN REQUIRES INVESTMENT

The servant with the one bag of silver came and said, "Master, I knew you were a harsh man, harvesting crops you didn't plant and gathering crops you didn't cultivate. I was afraid I would lose your money, so I hid it in the earth. Look, here is your money back."

But the master replied, "You wicked and lazy servant! If you knew I harvested crops I didn't plant and gathered crops I didn't cultivate, why didn't you deposit my money in the bank? At least I could have gotten some interest on it."

Then he ordered, "Take the money from this servant, and give it to the one with the ten bags of silver. To those who use well what they are given, even more will be given, and they will have an abundance."

Matthew 25:24–29 NLT

At the beginning of this parable, Jesus stated that the master gave to each servant according to his own ability. So that knocks out the theory that the servant in this passage was given more than he could handle. Of all the master's servants, he was given the least to care for, but he refused to do the little required to invest what was given to him.

The parable applies to moms who are part of God's kingdom. God has given you all that you need to bring forth blessing in your family. Some are given the opportunity to give more, some less. Our job is never to judge who is not doing enough or too much; all we are to do is make certain that what we are doing falls in line for a proper return of what was given to us.

Everything you have been given, the good and the not so good, is useful for some sort of return. You must decide how you will make use of everything to benefit your life. What can you do with what you have today to bless the kingdom of God, beginning with your children?

A Work of Faith

My brothers and sisters, what good does it do if someone claims to have faith but doesn't do any good things? Can this kind of faith save him? Suppose a believer, whether a man or a woman, needs clothes or food and one of you tells that person, "God be with you! Stay warm, and make sure you eat enough." If you don't provide for that person's physical needs, what good does it do? In the same way, faith by itself is dead if it doesn't cause you to do any good things.

Another person might say, "You have faith, but I do good things." Show me your faith apart from the good things you do. I will show you my faith by the good things I do. You believe that there is one God. That's fine! The demons also believe that, and they tremble with fear.

You fool! Do you have to be shown that faith which does nothing is useless?

James 2:14–20 GOD'S WORD

Mothers have a wonderful ability to multitask to blend several areas of life together. We can cook dinner, talk on the phone, help children finish their homework, and complete folding laundry all at the same time. When it comes to meeting others' needs, most moms move into quick action. However, you can't please your family just by working extra hard for them.

God says something similar. You can't please him just by doing good things. But you can't please him just by acknowledging that he exists, either. In this passage from James's very practical how-to letter, we learn that what we do shows what we believe and what we believe must balance what we do. James explains that faith without action has no life, but action without faith degenerates into busyness.

Whether you are a working mom, a stay-at-home mom, or a mom taking care of your own parents, you are a woman with many responsibilities. Be careful that everything you do doesn't bury your faith. Check the motives of your heart regularly. Make sure that what you are doing grows your faith, and find out how God's ways create balance.

MORE THAN RULES

Through Christ Jesus the law of the Spirit that brings life made you free from the law that brings sin and death. The law was without power, because the law was made weak by our sinful selves. But God did what the law could not do. He sent his own Son to earth with the same human life that others use for sin. By sending his Son to be an offering for sin, God used a human life to destroy sin. He did this so that we could be the kind of people the law correctly wants us to be. Now we do not live following our sinful selves, but we live following the Spirit.

Those who live following their sinful selves think only about things that their sinful selves want. But those who live following the Spirit are thinking about the things the Spirit wants them to do.

Romans 8:2–5 NCV

Rule keepers don't reproduce God's heart. That was Jesus' message to anyone who tried to legislate God's approval. Because Paul had been a fanatical rule follower before accepting Jesus' message, he could speak to the Roman Christians about God's desire to free them from believing that following rules could save them.

Mothers use rules to bring balance and safety to the way family members live together. We make rules about bedtime, crossing the street, approved snacks, and taking turns. Without rules, chaos wins. But push rules too hard and we create another imbalance—conformity without heart change. As you use rules, teach how they provide more freedom than confinement. Connect rules to principles of appropriate and kind behavior.

God wants us to live life with more substance than a list of rules can give. He showed us his heart by sending Jesus. We can't accept Jesus' model without keeping some rules; however, the emphasis becomes how the life of Jesus shapes our hearts. Let God's life bring you freedom from everything that would make you ineffective and fill you with everything you need to be complete. Live God's life, and following his rules will . . . follow.

You Deserve a Break Today

[Jesus] said to them, "Come away by yourselves to a remote place and rest a while." For many people were coming and going, and they did not even have time to eat. So they went away in the boat by themselves to a remote place, but many saw them leaving and recognized them. People ran there by land from all the towns and arrived ahead of them. So as He stepped ashore, He saw a huge crowd and had compassion on them, because they were like sheep without a shepherd. Then He began to teach them many things.

When it was already late, His disciples approached Him and said, "This place is a wilderness, and it is already late! Send them away, so they can go into the surrounding countryside and villages to buy themselves something to eat."

Mark 6:31–36 HCSB

After the disciples returned from their first speaking tour, Jesus wanted to give them a break. However, when he tried to take them to a private place, crowds of people followed. Instead of a retreat, the disciples found themselves in the middle of more than five thousand hungry people.

Is that the way your day goes sometimes? You just wanted to take a short break before the evening rush of dinner, homework, baths, and bedtime. That's when the hoard descends. Your kids come home, each with a hungry friend. No rest for the weary this night.

God knows that anyone shouldering unrelenting responsibility needs some downtime. Even God reserved time to rest after creating the world. He knows the importance of rest and restoration. He calls you out of your busy day to look at a sunset, to hear a bird's song, or to see the first spring bloom—anything that will take you away from the crush of what depletes your spirit. A life without rest is unbalanced and will unravel in some way. God invites you to rest. Do you have a compelling reason to say no?

Traveling Songs

I lift up my eyes to the hills—where does my help come from? My help comes from the LORD, the Maker of heaven and earth. He will not let your foot slip—he who watches over you will not slumber; indeed, he who watches over Israel will neither slumber nor sleep.

The LORD watches over you—the LORD is your shade at your right hand; the sun will not harm you by day, nor the moon by night.

The LORD will keep you from all harm—he will watch over your life; the LORD will watch over your coming and going both now and forevermore.

Psalm 121:1–8 NIV

Psalm 121 is what is called a psalm of ascent or pilgrim psalm. People traveling through mountainous Palestine sang this type of psalm on their way to Jerusalem to celebrate religious festivals. David wrote four psalms of ascent, including this one.

Many families try singing songs together on long car trips to engage restless children. Children's camp counselors love this diversion, especially when the song has multiple verses. Singing together on the way to some anticipated destination heightens the shared experience. The journey becomes part of the destination.

God shares the same attitude toward your life. While he cares about your destination, he wants you to enjoy living the days that take you there. He invites you to contemplate the help he has to offer. His help finds the right balance between your goings and comings, your beginnings and endings, your waking and sleeping. As a mom, you may have difficulty finding good balance when you commit to a schedule that overextends in energy-robbing ways.

Where are you headed today? Find a way to slow down and enjoy the journey. You will understand how much more there is to life than just getting somewhere.

BALANCING WORDS

Be content with who you are, and don't put on airs. God's strong hand is on you; he'll promote you at the right time. Live carefree before God; he is most careful with you.

Keep a cool head. Stay alert. The Devil is poised to pounce, and would like nothing better than to catch you napping. Keep your guard up. You're not the only ones plunged into these hard times. It's the same with Christians all over the world. So keep a firm grip on the faith. The suffering won't last forever. It won't be long before this generous God who has great plans for us in Christ—eternal and glorious plans they are!—will have you put together and on your feet for good. He gets the last word; yes, he does.

1 Peter 5:6–11 MSG

What empowering words this passage contains! Look at them—*content, carefree, alert, generous*. Peter used these words to identify the important attitudes that protect community. He gave these instructions to people who experienced suffering because of their faith in Jesus. He didn't want them to lose sight of the attitudes that would keep them strong for one another.

Mothers want these words to describe their family community too. Without contentment we fall into the trap of expecting that more of something will bring satisfaction. Without carefree play and unscheduled time, nobody has fun. Without living alert to life instead of schedule, you could miss some of the most important moments of the heart. And without sharing generosity with family members, the circle of love suffers. These attitudes keep your family's life not too strict, not too loose, not too self-absorbed, and not too competitive. However, they don't come automatically. You must grow them.

God wants you to enjoy the family he has given you to mother. Look for ways to model and teach these important words of balance. They keep you focused on what enhances the circle of love you call family.

Too Good to Be Possible

A good woman is hard to find, and worth far more than diamonds. Her husband trusts her without reserve, and never has reason to regret it. Never spiteful, she treats him generously all her life long. She shops around for the best yarns and cottons, and enjoys knitting and sewing. . . . She's up before dawn, preparing breakfast for her family and organizing her day. She looks over a field and buys it, then, with money she's put aside, plants a garden. First thing in the morning, she dresses for work, rolls up her sleeves, eager to get started. She senses the worth of her work, is in no hurry to call it quits for the day.

Proverbs 31:10–13, 15–18
MSG

This passage from the Bible's classic composite picture of a woman with impeccable character shows us what a balanced life looks like in someone who knows her true worth as a woman. Written by King Solomon as an acrostic, each verse begins with a letter of the Hebrew alphabet—an alphabetical checklist to remind everyone of the ways that the life of a woman remains full and rich.

Did you notice that this woman was a mother who worked on business opportunities outside her home? That should encourage mothers who do the same. This description also emphasizes exemplary characteristics instead of perfect performance. Making perfection our goal reduces our effectiveness instead of increasing it. We can improve the efficiency of our daily routines without rendering them sterile.

God doesn't call us to be perfect mothers; he calls us to be women who learn how to raise the children he gives us. He doesn't compare you to other mothers, and you shouldn't compare yourself to others either. Let the Bible's model inspire you to growth, but never let it overwhelm you. The woman in this picture didn't become worthy of praise overnight, and neither will we.

Just Sing

Sing a new song to the Lord; sing to the Lord, all the earth. Sing to the Lord, praise His name; proclaim His salvation from day to day. Declare His glory among the nations, His wonderful works among all peoples.

For the Lord is great and is highly praised; He is feared above all gods. For all the gods of the peoples are idols, but the Lord made the heavens. Splendor and majesty are before Him; strength and beauty are in His sanctuary.

Ascribe to the Lord, you families of the peoples, ascribe to the Lord glory and strength. Ascribe to the Lord the glory of His name; bring an offering and enter His courts.

Psalm 96:1–8 HCSB

David believed that understanding new wonders about God provided good reasons for a new song. Parts of this psalm appear in the accounts of other celebrations, acknowledging God's amazing power and creativity. David wanted people to remember that God did nothing in a humdrum or dull way.

How often do you take time to contemplate the wonders of God? Worship balances who we are against who God is. Affirming God's character protects us from placing ourself at the center of our world. Look around you. That's what David did as he wrote his musical worship to God. He acknowledged that God does what no person can do. He recognized that worshipping anyone or anything else is misplaced worship. The more David absorbed God's powerful creativity in the world, the more he wanted to sing about it.

Take a walk outside or stand beside a window. Include your children when you do. Remind yourself and them of God's competency, power, and creativity. Experience his love. Pause to thank him. When you do, you will be able to return to your many mothering duties with a smile and a new song to sing.

JUST A WHISPER

"Go out and stand before me on the mountain," the Lord told him. And as Elijah stood there, the Lord passed by, and a mighty windstorm hit the mountain. It was such a terrible blast that the rocks were torn loose, but the Lord was not in the wind. After the wind there was an earthquake, but the Lord was not in the earthquake. And after the earthquake there was a fire, but the Lord was not in the fire. And after the fire there was the sound of a gentle whisper. When Elijah heard it, he wrapped his face in his cloak and went out and stood at the entrance of the cave.

And a voice said, "What are you doing here, Elijah?"

He replied again, "I have zealously served the Lord God Almighty."

1 Kings 19:11–14 NLT

God sent fire that consumed a water-soaked sacrifice and humiliated the priests of the false god Baal, who made a bigger show with no result. God's prophet Elijah left the contest as victor but raced away and retreated to a cave to hide from King Ahab's wife, Jezebel, who wanted to kill him. God brought Elijah out of hiding to learn an important lesson—how to recognize God's voice.

Is that a lesson you would like to learn? You don't have to find a mountain and experience an earthquake or fire to hear from God. This passage reminds us that God speaks more in a whisper than in a shout. Listening for a whisper is hard for moms—we live in the midst of the happy sounds of children at play, the angry sounds of children arguing, the blaring media of teens. However, the quiet we need is on the inside.

As you listen for God, start with the Bible. God will deliver the message you need. Often he begins by making sure you know how much he loves you. Today, listen carefully. God wants to tell you something you need to hear.

THE DIFFERENCE THAT YES MAKES

When Martha heard that Jesus had arrived, she went out to meet him, but Mary stayed in the house. Martha said to Jesus, "Lord, if you had been here, my brother would not have died. Yet even now I know that God will do anything you ask."

Jesus told her, "Your brother will live again!"

Martha answered, "I know that he will be raised to life on the last day, when all the dead are raised."

Jesus then said, "I am the one who raises the dead to life! Everyone who has faith in me will live, even if they die. And everyone who lives because of faith in me will never really die. Do you believe this?"

"Yes, Lord!" she replied. "I believe that you are Christ, the Son of God."

John 11:20–27 CEV

Martha and her sister sent word to Jesus when they knew their brother, Lazarus, was dying. They expected Jesus to stop what he was doing and come quickly. But he didn't, and Lazarus died. Several days later, in a patient exchange, Jesus turned Martha's if-only into an affirmation of faith that connected her to life in an unexpected way.

Sometimes moms get so preoccupied with the here and now that we can't wrap our minds around what Jesus wants us to experience. We see spilled milk, piles of laundry, too many toys, and something to clean everywhere. Jesus wants us to live without the imbalance of focusing on the wrong issues. He lifts our perspective the way he lifted Martha's.

Who do you believe Jesus is? Your healer, restorer, and always-present friend? Believing who Jesus is becomes an important step toward the life Jesus brings. When Martha took that leap of faith, Jesus brought her brother back to life. What might he restore to you? Lost belief that you are the mom your children need? Add your yes to Martha's and get ready to accept possibilities you couldn't have imagined.

Different Roles — One Goal

Brothers and sisters, I couldn't talk to you as spiritual people. . . . I didn't give you solid food because you weren't ready for it. . . .

Some of you say, "I follow Paul" and others say, "I follow Apollos." . . . Who is Apollos? Who is Paul? They are servants who helped you come to faith. Each did what the Lord gave him to do. I planted, and Apollos watered, but God made it grow. So neither the one who plants nor the one who waters is important because only God makes it grow. The one who plants and the one who waters have the same goal, and each will receive a reward for his own work. We are God's co-workers. You are God's field.

You are God's building.

1 Corinthians 3:1–2, 4–9
GOD'S WORD

Paul "planted," or began, the church at Corinth, and later Apollos "watered" what Paul had planted as he also preached to the Corinthians about Jesus. When Paul learned that some of the Corinthians were trying to divide the church between the teachings of the two, Paul wrote to remind the congregation that each minister who preached about Jesus contributed something different to their growth and understanding as Christians.

When your children try to pit your instructions against what their dad says, don't you say the same thing? Don't you remind them that everyone with authority in their lives is on the same team? Mothers and dads have different parts to play, but they have only one goal—to raise their children the best possible way.

The same is true as you learn how to make the life and teachings of Jesus your priority model for everything you do. Listen to those who are passionate about Jesus. Follow instruction that helps you apply the characteristics of Jesus to your life. Enjoy learning from teachers with different strengths. Just make sure they all have one focus—Jesus. His priority is that you grow to know him better.

LOST AND FOUND

Three days later they found Jesus sitting in the temple, listening to the teachers and asking them questions. Everyone who heard him was surprised at how much he knew and at the answers he gave.

When his parents found him, they were amazed. His mother said, "Son, why have you done this to us? Your father and I have been very worried, and we have been searching for you!"

Jesus answered, "Why did you have to look for me? Didn't you know that I would be in my Father's house?" But they did not understand what he meant.

Jesus went back to Nazareth with his parents and obeyed them. His mother kept on thinking about all that had happened.

Jesus became wise, and he grew strong. God was pleased with him and so were the people.

Luke 2:46–52 CEV

Mary, Joseph, and Jesus made the traditional journey to Jerusalem to celebrate Passover, the remembrance of God's delivering his people from slavery in Egypt. People traveled in groups, women and children setting the pace at the front and the men following behind them. When Jesus turned up missing on the return trip, Mary and Joseph became every parent as they faced another unpredictable challenge involved in raising a child. What mother hasn't panicked to discover that her child wasn't where she thought? Usually extra searching uncovers a hiding place, a lost child, or someone on an independent foray. What began as second-guessing your ability to mother ends in a warm embrace of love returned.

God announced his attitude about family when he placed Jesus in one. Just like you, Mary didn't receive an instruction manual when her baby was born. She received what God also makes available to you—his wisdom to help you grow into the mom your children need, and his support. As you think about your mothering challenges today, remember that you don't have to be the smartest mom or the most creative, just obedient. God has never asked for anything more.

A Mom's Best Invitation

One Sabbath day as Jesus was walking through some grainfields, his disciples began breaking off heads of grain to eat. But the Pharisees said to Jesus, "Look, why are they breaking the law by harvesting grain on the Sabbath?"

Jesus said to them, "Haven't you ever read in the Scriptures what David did when he and his companions were hungry? He went into the house of God (during the days when Abiathar was high priest) and broke the law by eating the sacred loaves of bread that only the priests are allowed to eat. He also gave some to his companions."

Then Jesus said to them, "The Sabbath was made to meet the needs of people, and not people to meet the requirements of the Sabbath. So the Son of Man is Lord, even over the Sabbath!"

Mark 2:23–28 NLT

The Jewish religious leaders were like vultures waiting to catch Jesus doing something wrong. When they defined handpicking wheat grains on a casual walk as work, the same thing as harvesting on the Sabbath, they accused Jesus of breaking the fourth commandment. Without flinching, Jesus reminded his accusers that God designed the Sabbath to meet the needs of people and not the other way around.

God believes in balance. The world he created is a study of balance. He wants us to learn balance so that we live with more joy, health, and peace. In a culture that uses every day as an opportunity to get too much done and push too hard and go to bed too tired, God invites us to do something different. Even medical research has confirmed that the 1:6 ratio of rest to work makes healthy sense. God wants to protect us from burnout. He asks us to stop our frantic rush one day a week. Walk more slowly, play with your kids, and give priority attention to a compassionate God who says you need rest. Don't turn down this wonderful invitation to restore and renew your spirit.

LASTING WISDOM FROM A PARENT'S HEART

Pursue righteousness and a godly life, along with faith, love, perseverance, and gentleness. Fight the good fight for the true faith. Hold tightly to the eternal life to which God has called you, which you have confessed so well before many witnesses. And I charge you before God, who gives life to all, and before Christ Jesus, who gave a good testimony before Pontius Pilate, that you obey this command without wavering. Then no one can find fault with you from now until our Lord Jesus Christ comes again. For at just the right time Christ will be revealed from heaven by the blessed and only almighty God, the King of all kings and Lord of all lords. He alone can never die, and he lives in light so brilliant that no human can approach him.

1 Timothy 6:11–16 NLT

Paul finished his mentoring letter to young Timothy with a collection of bottom-line counsel. Paul had seen great promise in Timothy ever since he accompanied Paul on a missionary trip and served as his representative. Like a grandfather sharing life wisdom with a much-loved grandson, Paul poured out his heart here in a passionate charge.

What is on your most important mentoring list? Start with Paul's if you don't have one. Plan how you will teach your children to grow faith, love, perseverance, gentleness, and other life-balancing traits. You can make every day an opportunity to raise faith awareness as you challenge your children to follow God's instruction and accept his all-knowing help. You can teach them to finish jobs so they learn how personal accomplishment links to perseverance. You can help them understand what it feels like to receive gentleness and love so they want to give it more freely. While you work with your children, don't forget to ask God to grow these characteristics in you too. Life models teach better than words. Living the characteristics you want to pass on helps everyone enjoy the balance they bring to life.

RUN THE RACE YOU CAN WIN

When I am with those who are weak, I share their weakness, for I want to bring the weak to Christ. Yes, I try to find common ground with everyone, doing everything I can to save some. I do everything to spread the Good News and share in its blessings.

Don't you realize that in a race everyone runs, but only one person gets the prize? So run to win! All athletes are disciplined in their training. They do it to win a prize that will fade away, but we do it for an eternal prize. So I run with purpose in every step. I am not just shadowboxing. I discipline my body like an athlete, training it to do what it should. Otherwise, I fear that after preaching to others I myself might be disqualified.

1 Corinthians 9:22–27 NLT

Paul often used athletic metaphors in his writing, causing many to believe that Paul had trained as an athlete. In this passage, Paul compares the rigors of living as Jesus taught to running a race. He used this illustration to encourage those who thought they weren't strong enough to live as Christians.

Some goals are worth the push. Some aren't. Balance requires knowing the difference. A lot of moms find themselves running unnecessary races. No one asked you to run the clean-house race or the perfect-family race or the well-dressed-family race. In fact, moms who run these races usually wish they could quit. Instead, God invites us to the most important race of our lives. His race takes us all the way into forever with him.

There's more than one winner in God's race. He wants you to understand how he defines winning. To win this race, just finish! Yes, this race demands training, discipline, and the perseverance of a marathoner. However, it also offers a one-of-a-kind prize to all—life with God in a place of perfect balance. Know what you're running for? Ready? Set? Go! Start running the race you *can* win.

A BALANCING ALLY

Hanani the seer came to Asa king of Judah and said to him: "Because you relied on the king of Aram and not on the LORD your God, the army of the king of Aram has escaped from your hand. Were not the Cushites and Libyans a mighty army with great numbers of chariots and horsemen? Yet when you relied on the LORD, he delivered them into your hand. For the eyes of the LORD range throughout the earth to strengthen those whose hearts are fully committed to him. You have done a foolish thing, and from now on you will be at war."

Asa was angry with the seer because of this; he was so enraged that he put him in prison. At the same time Asa brutally oppressed some of the people.

2 Chronicles 16:7–10 NIV

God reprimanded Asa, king of Judah, for political alliances he made, because God himself had promised that protection. In fact, God's messenger reminded Asa of specific times when God delivered the country from powerful enemies no other alliance could have achieved. The consequence of Asa's unnecessary treaties would be the country's entanglement in wars they never needed to fight.

Are you fighting unnecessary battles? Every mom fights a few. Sometimes you fight for clean rooms or eating vegetables or removing muddy shoes. Deciding which struggles are important and which are not takes maturity and discernment. Fighting to be right or pushing for control are struggles that create imbalance because they bring few lasting results. Without resolving the real problem, you will have to revisit the tug-of-war again.

Instead of preparing for conflict, make sure you side with your best ally. Your always-ready God will stand guard over you, fight for you, encircle you, or send in extra resources at just the right time. No one wants you to succeed more than God does. The children in your care are important to him. Align your mothering with God, and you will never lack the best help available.

It's Your Choice

The secret things belong to the Lord our God, but the things revealed belong to us and to our children forever, that we may follow all the words of this law.

When all these blessings and curses I have set before you come upon you and you take them to heart wherever the Lord your God disperses you among the nations, and when you and your children return to the Lord your God and obey him with all your heart and with all your soul according to everything I command you today, then the Lord your God will restore your fortunes and have compassion on you and gather you again from all the nations where he scattered you. Even if you have been banished to the most distant land under the heavens, from there the Lord your God will gather you and bring you back.

Deuteronomy 29:29–30:4 NIV

Moses gave the people of Israel God's last instructions before they crossed over into the land God had promised them. However, God's promise came with requirements. Wholehearted obedience would make God's promises come true. Anything less changed their circumstances enough that God's blessings could not be given. To choose God's promises meant the people chose to obey God.

Have you been the parent of a stubborn child who would not obey you and kept losing privileges as a consequence? As a mom, you want your children to enjoy special treats and fun leisure time. Does aggravation describe your response when a child's disobedience makes you look more like a mean parent than the loving, generous mom you really are? Then you can understand how God feels when his children disobey.

God loves surprising us with good things. He especially enjoys keeping his promises. Nothing pains him more than when someone loses his gifts because of disobedience. Can you see how much of your life depends on your choices? Keep God's intended balance. Obey God and enjoy his generous gifts.

More Than a Lecture

My child, pay attention to what I say. Listen carefully to my words. Don't lose sight of them. Let them penetrate deep into your heart, for they bring life to those who find them, and healing to their whole body.

Guard your heart above all else, for it determines the course of your life.

Avoid all perverse talk; stay away from corrupt speech.

Look straight ahead, and fix your eyes on what lies before you. Mark out a straight path for your feet; stay on the safe path. Don't get sidetracked; keep your feet from following evil.

Proverbs 4:20–27 NLT

Who hasn't quoted the book of Proverbs to share a pithy statement from King Solomon and others? This collection of wise counsel and commonsense reminders remains timeless in scope and wisdom. Written as passionate instructions to young listeners, Proverbs provides a balance that targets the heart of every willing learner.

Do you understand how to give instruction that targets the heart? Proverbs shares valuable insight for every mom. Notice how the author shares more do's than don'ts. The picture is not a shaking finger flung into the face of a child who has the potential to do everything wrong. The picture shows a hopeful parent dispensing loving instruction to a child who has the potential to do many things well.

Turn off your lecture mode as many times as you can. Hold a hand or put your arm around the child of your heart. Share one or two simple truths. Inspire your children to apply a lesson that will protect life as God intended. Nothing heightens your mothering mission more than the opportunity to send your children into a future you won't see, prepared to live the life God has for them.

FOUNDATION BUILDERS WANTED

According to the grace of God given to me, like a skilled master builder I laid a foundation, and someone else is building upon it. Let each one take care how he builds upon it. For no one can lay a foundation other than that which is laid, which is Jesus Christ. Now if anyone builds on the foundation with gold, silver, precious stones, wood, hay, straw—each one's work will become manifest, for the Day will disclose it, because it will be revealed by fire, and the fire will test what sort of work each one has done. If the work that anyone has built on the foundation survives, he will receive a reward. If anyone's work is burned up, he will suffer loss, though he himself will be saved, but only as through fire.

1 Corinthians 3:10–15 ESV

Foundation is everything, Paul wrote to a group of new Christians fraught with divisions and double standards. He wanted to bring these people together by common foundation. He taught that building life on who Jesus is and what he taught would restore unity and protect them from the consequences of God's judgment.

You probably don't know much about your home's foundation unless there is a problem. But a strong, level foundation built with the best materials and according to proven codes creates important balance for your house. The same is true for families. As a mom, you are a foundation builder as you raise your children. Home builders learn quickly that what you start with influences everything that follows. That's why God longs to share his experience as a loving parent with you. He suggests building codes that help your children withstand peer pressure and reject harmful experimental choices. He recommends building lives on love that welcomes boundaries and obedience for best protection. His foundation protects unity, moral purity, authentic love, and joy. Never settle for anything but the strongest foundation.

24-7 ACCESS

If you are having trouble, you should pray. And if you are feeling good, you should sing praises. If you are sick, ask the church leaders to come and pray for you. Ask them to put olive oil on you in the name of the Lord. If you have faith when you pray for sick people, they will get well. The Lord will heal them, and if they have sinned, he will forgive them.

If you have sinned, you should tell each other what you have done. Then you can pray for one another and be healed. The prayer of an innocent person is powerful, and it can help a lot. Elijah was just as human as we are, and for three and a half years his prayers kept the rain from falling.

James 5:13–17 CEV

James was a half-brother to Jesus. Even though he grew up with Jesus, he did not believe Jesus' claims until after the Resurrection. This passage about prayer shares James's straightforward teaching about the attitudes and behaviors of those who live the way Jesus taught.

How does prayer figure into your day? When the children are late for school, the dishwasher breaks down, and you have a migraine headache, what is your first reflex? Does complaint morph into whine to become a bad attitude that plagues your day? James suggests an alternative—pray.

Prayer shares a 24-7 communication line with God. Talking to God comprises only half of the conversation. The real benefit of prayer involves how God responds. God enjoys answering you with his understanding, his all-knowing perspective, his compassion and wisdom. His answers address real issues and not just symptoms. Ask God what to do about your child's insecurity or another child's learning problems. No one wants to share answers to your mothering dilemmas more than God. Talk to him early and often. Make prayer your ready access to the world's foremost child specialist and enjoy his balance-restoring answers.

No Rust Allowed

Don't store up treasures here on earth, where moths eat them and rust destroys them, and where thieves break in and steal. Store your treasures in heaven, where moths and rust cannot destroy, and thieves do not break in and steal. Wherever your treasure is, there the desires of your heart will also be.

Your eye is a lamp that provides light for your body. When your eye is good, your whole body is filled with light. But when your eye is bad, your whole body is filled with darkness. And if the light you think you have is actually darkness, how deep that darkness is!

No one can serve two masters. For you will hate one and love the other; you will be devoted to one and despise the other. You cannot serve both God and money.

Matthew 6:19–24 NLT

This passage comes near the end of Jesus' famous Sermon on the Mount, in which Jesus summarized the most important truths about living God's way. He announced radical reversals to traditional Jewish teaching. This section addresses how God treasures motives of the heart more than the destructible things money can buy. Moms know the difference between treasures you store in an attic or basement and treasures you keep in your heart. Damp basements or humid attics can destroy the first kind of treasure, but nothing robs you of the treasure you receive from watching your children grow and develop.

In the myriad of choices our culture offers, we need to listen to God's invitation to make what he treasures our first focus. He treasures kindness, reconciliation, committed love, and integrity. None of these characteristics deplete bank accounts, but each adds value that money can't buy. You can teach this same balance to your children before they experience the pain of credit card debt. Help them value heart treasures more than brand names. Not only will they save money; they'll also learn how God invests his best in what this world cannot create or destroy.

GOD LOVES A PARTY

Nehemiah the governor, Ezra the priest and scribe, and the Levites who were interpreting for the people said to them, "Don't mourn or weep on such a day as this! For today is a sacred day before the LORD your God." For the people had all been weeping as they listened to the words of the Law.

And Nehemiah continued, "Go and celebrate with a feast of rich foods and sweet drinks, and share gifts of food with people who have nothing prepared. This is a sacred day before our LORD. Don't be dejected and sad, for the joy of the Lord is your strength!" . . .

So the people went away to eat and drink at a festive meal, to share gifts of food, and to celebrate with great joy because they had heard God's words and understood them.

Nehemiah 8:9–10, 12 NLT

Ezra had returned to the ruins of Israel's homeland fourteen years earlier. He found his country's men and women living without even trying to please God. To restore God's way of living, Ezra began to read and teach God's laws regularly. As the people heard God's loving messages to warn and instruct them, they recognized the contrast between how they were living and what God wanted. In this passage, what began as remorseful confession turned into a celebration that brought balance and restoration.

Do you enjoy a party? You're in good company. God loves celebration. He loves it when we get excited about what he says is right and life balancing. Do you give your children opportunities to get excited about who God is and what he wants to do for them? Practice reading the Bible together as the most exciting story ever told. Use age-appropriate picture books to illustrate stories. Act out some scenes or listen to recorded versions. Nobody celebrates reading a rule book. Tell the stories. Pull out the lessons. Apply them in specific ways. Find out why doing what God says is always a good reason for a party.

TO BE CONTENT

Those [false teachers] . . . cause jealousy, disagreements, unkind words, evil suspicions, and nasty quarrels. They have wicked minds and have missed out on the truth.

These people think religion is supposed to make you rich. And religion does make your life rich, by making you content with what you have. We didn't bring anything into this world, and we won't take anything with us when we leave. So we should be satisfied just to have food and clothes. People who want to be rich fall into all sorts of temptations and traps. They are caught by foolish and harmful desires that drag them down and destroy them. The love of money causes all kinds of trouble. Some people want money so much that they have given up their faith and caused themselves a lot of pain.

1 Timothy 6:4–10 CEV

Paul warned Timothy about false teachers by helping him understand that sound teaching unites more than separates. He especially wanted Timothy to know that God provides contentment that would protect him from unnecessary struggle and temptation.

Paul understood that contentment is less about what we want and more about how much we already have. The get-more life philosophy creates great imbalance, scattering workaholics and burned-out moms in its path. God never intended that we live that way. He desires a more satisfying approach. Besides, if you don't enjoy contentment, neither will your children. You can't pass on what you don't have.

So how can you embrace contentment in your life and share it with your children? Reject the push to have something just because it is new or advanced. Look for ways to enjoy what you don't have to own. Parks have bigger spaces than backyards, and libraries have more books than you can buy. You don't have to buy something, enroll in something, or renovate something to enjoy what you already have. Let God show you how contentment helps you slow down and enjoy the parts of life you have been missing.

REQUIRED REST

He himself went a day's journey into the wilderness and came and sat down under a broom tree. And he asked that he might die. . . . And he lay down and slept under a broom tree. And behold, an angel touched him and said to him, "Arise and eat." And he looked, and behold, there was at his head a cake baked on hot stones and a jar of water. And he ate and drank and lay down again. And the angel of the LORD came again a second time and touched him and said, "Arise and eat, for the journey is too great for you." And he arose and ate and drank, and went in the strength of that food forty days and forty nights to Horeb, the mount of God.

1 Kings 19:4–8 ESV

Elijah enjoyed victory over King Ahab's priests on Mount Carmel. Because the victory humiliated Queen Jezebel, she threatened to kill Elijah. When Elijah learned about the death threat, he ran for his life. Drained of energy and filled with despair, Elijah discovered that God gladly gives rest to obedient servants.

Do moms ever get enough rest? Crying babies, late-night work, sick children—all of this and more rob moms of restorative sleep. And what mother ever sits down with nothing to do? Expert at multi-tasking, moms run like Energizer bunnies. Who tells moms to take a nap?

Actually, God does. Just as he provided a place for Elijah to rest and eat, God invites you to refresh. When you don't think you can, you probably need to the most. God designed your body so that rest restores physical and emotional energy. Even though your day might be spent as nonstop referee, cook, janitor, nurse, repairwoman, tutor, and more, you can't function well on less rest than God designed your body to receive. Enjoy the first four-letter word connected to God's blessing—rest. Your whole family will be glad you did!

IF YOU HAD LISTENED . . .

"Come close, listen carefully: I've never kept secrets from you. I've always been present with you."

And now, the Master, GOD, sends me and his Spirit with this Message from GOD, . . . "I am GOD, your God, who teaches you how to live right and well. I show you what to do, where to go. If you had listened all along to what I told you, your life would have flowed full like a river, blessings rolling in like waves from the sea. Children and grandchildren are like sand, your progeny like grains of sand. There would be no end of them, no danger of losing touch with me."

Isaiah 48:16–19 MSG

The prophet Isaiah delivered God's messages to the people of Judah before and during their fall to the powerful Assyrians. He spoke about the contrast between God's judgment and restoration, his punishment and blessing, and the relationship God desired with them. Isaiah wanted his countrymen to stop turning away from God's instructions and listen to him again.

Do you remember carrying your young children everywhere when they were too young to walk? Soon they toddled on their own, sometimes going where you didn't want them to go. With gentle coaxing, a few bribes, and well-placed commands, you tried to help them stay safe within their newfound freedom.

Do you understand that God does the same with you? His instructions do not restrict you; they protect you. They keep you from dead ends and unnecessary struggles. Why should you have to learn by error what God wants to teach you directly by instruction? Learn from people who found out that nothing God asked them to do was harder than what they experienced after they disobeyed. Then you won't repeat the sad words of what might have been: "If only I had listened . . ."

CHANGE

Don't run from change—embrace it! Change is uncomfortable, unsettling, sometimes even painful. However, growth requires change. When children go through their "growth spurts," everything changes—sleep patterns, appetite, clothing sizes, shoe sizes—but these are necessary changes for progress in life. When life circumstances bring change, whether natural or unexpected transitions, look for the growth to be found in it. Ruth experienced many changes when she left her homeland and family to accompany her mother-in-law to Bethlehem. Newly widowed, with no expectation for marriage in a new land, she met Boaz. Her marriage to Boaz and the son they had together gave her a place in the family tree of King David—and Jesus!

To everything there is a season, a time for every purpose under heaven.

Ecclesiastes 3:1 NKJV

Is Consistency Possible?

Oh, that my actions would consistently reflect your decrees! Then I will not be ashamed when I compare my life with your commands. As I learn your righteous regulations, I will thank you by living as I should! I will obey your decrees. Please don't give up on me!

How can a young person stay pure? By obeying your word. I have tried hard to find you—don't let me wander from your commands. I have hidden your word in my heart, that I might not sin against you. I praise you, O LORD; teach me your decrees. I have recited aloud all the regulations you have given us. I have rejoiced in your laws as much as in riches.

Psalm 119:5–14 NLT

Frustrated with his inability to apply God's ways to his life consistently, David even voiced a fear that God might give up on him. What refreshing honesty! David, who overcame a giant and won military victories against formidable enemies, had self-doubt. However, he knew where he needed consistency the most: in the way he applied what God said. He needed consistency that started in his heart.

Do you identify with David? Have you put yourself down for lack of consistency? Do you find yourself "all over the charts" as a disciplinarian? Do you want your children to follow God better than you have? Are you afraid God is going to give up on you? Take heart. He won't! It's not perfection that provides consistency; it's heart direction.

You know this from experience with your children. When they give you compliance without heart obedience, something is missing. It takes consistent nurture to turn a heart. God wants you to spend heart-to-heart time with him. Take time to read and think about what God says. Aim your heart toward his life instructions. Your attitude and actions will follow close behind.

HIDING TO BE FOUND

You are my hiding place; you will protect me from trouble and surround me with songs of deliverance.

I will instruct you and teach you in the way you should go; I will counsel you and watch over you. Do not be like the horse or the mule, which have no understanding but must be controlled by bit and bridle or they will not come to you. Many are the woes of the wicked, but the LORD's unfailing love surrounds the man who trusts in him.

Rejoice in the LORD and be glad, you righteous; sing, all you who are upright in heart!

Psalm 32:7–11 NIV

David had just confessed to God his adultery and murder. How difficult! But on the other side of confessing, he gained a new perspective. When we are forgiven, we understand how God's boundaries are for the good of his children. Before he repented (turned away from doing wrong), David tried to hide what he did *from* God. Afterward, he wanted nothing more than to hide *in* God.

How do you hide when you don't want to face something? Are you like young children, always hiding in predictable places? Just like you know your children's hiding places, God knows yours. He delights in finding you so he can bring you out of hiding into his welcoming arms. The lesson is simple. Hide *in* God, not *from* him. Hiding *in* God brings protection, deliverance, on-site instruction, and the knowledge that God is keeping watch over you.

Do you need a sanity escape? Take a hiding break. Lean into your God so that he can completely cover you. Stay until you hear his encouragement and let that silence any negative self-talk. Then, go back to your mom-work with the smile of someone who has been found.

Not Far Away

The God who made the world and all things in it, since He is Lord of heaven and earth, does not dwell in temples made with hands; nor is He served by human hands, as though He needed anything, since He Himself gives to all people life and breath and all things; and He made from one man every nation of mankind to live on all the face of the earth, having determined their appointed times and the boundaries of their habitation, that they would seek God, if perhaps they might grope for Him and find Him, though He is not far from each one of us; for in Him we live and move and exist, as even some of your own poets have said, "For we also are His children."

Acts 17:24–28 NASB

In Athens, before the apostle Paul spoke the words in this passage, he had observed the numerous statues—idols—of Greek gods and goddesses throughout the city. But the true God could not be worshipped like a statue. Paul wanted the Athenians to understand that the God who created them was closer than anything they could see or make. The God Paul talked about wanted to live in them and work through them. They'd never heard of a God like that before.

Do you know how much God wants to be involved in your life? He wants to be there for you when you have to make a tough decision for your child or when you need insight to handle a difficult relationship. God is as close as your heartbeat when you feel overwhelmed by your mothering responsibilities. He is there to give you wisdom when you are frightened for your child and don't know where to turn. When you feel alone and isolated—you're not! God is right there. Take a deep breath and realize that God is as close as the air in your lungs—and he loves you.

Please Wait . . . Quietly

I still dare to hope when I remember this:

The faithful love of the Lord never ends! His mercies never cease. Great is his faithfulness; his mercies begin afresh each morning. I say to myself, "The Lord is my inheritance; therefore, I will hope in him!"

The Lord is good to those who depend on him, to those who search for him. So it is good to wait quietly for salvation from the Lord. And it is good for people to submit at an early age to the yoke of his discipline:

Let them sit alone in silence beneath the Lord's demands. Let them lie face down in the dust, for there may be hope at last.

Lamentations 3:21–29 NLT

Jeremiah grieved the destruction of Jerusalem, especially since he knew it could have been prevented. God had used Jeremiah to sound the alarm and tell the people that if they didn't follow God's ways, they would suffer terrible consequences. The people didn't listen, and what Jeremiah predicted did happen; the people of Israel went into captivity. Jeremiah came again to the people to declare God as merciful, faithful, and loving. He urged his people, beloved Israel, to hope in their God even in their painful captivity. He asked them to wait . . . quietly . . . for their God to deliver them.

Waiting is uncomfortable enough, but waiting quietly is even more difficult, especially for children. They wiggle and squirm and keep asking questions. Maybe you can sympathize with them because you've been waiting for God to answer you about something. Even when you believe his answer will come, waiting is hard and waiting quietly can be agony. In this passage, Jeremiah reminds us that we can wait confidently because God is faithful—he will answer.

Let the certainty of this truth quiet you so that you will be ready to hear what God has to say.

Soft Hearts and Encouraging Words

My friends, watch out! Don't let evil thoughts or doubts make any of you turn from the living God. You must encourage one another each day. And you must keep on while there is still a time that can be called "today." If you don't, then sin may fool some of you and make you stubborn. We were sure about Christ when we first became his people. So let's hold tightly to our faith until the end. The Scriptures say, "If you hear his voice today, don't be stubborn like those who rebelled."

Who were those people that heard God's voice and rebelled? Weren't they the same ones that came out of Egypt with Moses? Who were the people that made God angry for forty years? Weren't they the ones that sinned and died in the desert?

Hebrews 3:12–17 CEV

No one on earth knows more about stubborn children than a mother. Pursed lips and stiffened arms and you know you're in for a push-comes-to-shove moment.

God knows about stubborn children too. When the Israelites were on the edge of entering the land God had promised them, as this passage recounts, they panicked and stubbornly refused to go on. Even though God had promised them more blessing than they could ever imagine, they demanded that Moses take them back to Egypt, where they had been slaves. But the writer of this passage reveals a surprising antidote to stubbornness. Do you know what it is? *Encouragement* literally means "to inspire courage." Encouragement can drive away panic and soften a stubborn hold on fear and insecurity.

Children are notorious for digging in their heels and refusing to do what is best for them. You've probably been there with your children more than once, throwing up your hands in frustration. But what if you offered calm encouragement the next time you find yourself in a stubborn standoff with one of your children? It just might be the breakthrough you've been looking for.

Scrapbooking

Happy is the person who trusts the Lord, who doesn't turn to those who are proud or to those who worship false gods. Lord my God, you have done many miracles. Your plans for us are many. If I tried to tell them all, there would be too many to count.

You do not want sacrifices and offerings. But you have made a hole in my ear to show that my body and life are yours. You do not ask for burnt offerings and sacrifices to take away sins. Then I said, "Look, I have come. It is written about me in the book. My God, I want to do what you want. Your teachings are in my heart."

Psalm 40:4–8 NCV

Are you a scrapbooker? Do you enjoy arranging pictures, words, and symbols on acid-free paper to protect them for the next generation? If you do, you probably don't hide your scrapbooks in a closet or drawer where nobody can see them. You look through them often instead.

In this passage, David "opens a scrapbook" to tell others about the way God provided help during a difficult time. He used his experience to encourage others that patient waiting for God pays off.

Do you have a mental scrapbook where you can review the ways God brought help or wisdom or extra strength to you at a critical time with your children? Maybe you keep a journal about the ways God has provided whatever you needed at just the right time. Records like these remind you that God is a generous God.

But remember that God prefers a relationship marked by generosity on both sides. When you look through your scrapbook, tell others where God and his unlimited resources have made a difference in your life. Explain the reasons why you say to God, like David, "I want to do what you want."

TELL YOUR CHILDREN

I will walk humbly throughout my years because of this anguish I have felt. Lord, your discipline is good, for it leads to life and health. You restore my health and allow me to live! Yes, this anguish was good for me, for you have rescued me from death and forgiven all my sins. For the dead cannot praise you; they cannot raise their voices in praise; those who go down to the grave can no longer hope in your faithfulness. Only the living can praise you as I do today. Each generation can make known your faithfulness to the next.

Isaiah 38:15–19 NLT

Hezekiah, one of the kings of Israel, became ill. Close to dying, he prayed for God to spare his life, and God did. Hezekiah wanted others to know about what God had done for him. He especially wanted children to know about God's goodness.

Have you told your children what God has done in your life? Unshared stories of what God has made possible can rob your children of reasons to follow him. Tell your children how you came to know who God is and what he can do. Recall for them the days when God helped you find a place to live or opened up the right place to work. Share stories about your struggles and their resolution, because your children need to know that God is with us in good times and bad times.

There's always a story when God does his work, and children love stories. Share your stories of faith and blessing whenever you gather for family celebrations. Share them at the dinner table or when you say good night. Make sure you tell your children about our faithful God so that the next generation will continue to praise him too.

WISDOM CALLING

Surely there is a future, and your hope will not be cut off. Listen, my son, and be wise, and direct your heart in the way. Do not be with heavy drinkers of wine, or with gluttonous eaters of meat; for the heavy drinker and the glutton will come to poverty, and drowsiness will clothe one with rags. Listen to your father who begot you, and do not despise your mother when she is old. Buy truth, and do not sell it, get wisdom and instruction and understanding. The father of the righteous will greatly rejoice, and he who sires a wise son will be glad in him. Let your father and your mother be glad, and let her rejoice who gave birth to you. Give me your heart, my son, and let your eyes delight in my ways.

Proverbs 23:18–26 NASB

Solomon, history's great wise man, wrote a lot about wisdom. He pleaded with young people to apply wisdom (knowledge and understanding) to their lives. Wisdom, he said, is a heart matter, not just head knowledge.

Solomon wanted young people to grow up with wisdom, and mothers want the same thing for their children. The first step, according to Solomon, is to get children to recognize wisdom when they hear it. The voice of wisdom and the voice of a parent should be the same. That's a big responsibility! You must recognize what wisdom looks like and sounds like so that you can share it with your children.

Mothers must be wisdom's best students. The Bible is the best place to find true wisdom. Then learn how to share wisdom without lecturing, when to allow your children to experience the consequences of their choices so that wisdom's voice will sound like a good voice to answer!

Most important, wisdom asks for your child's heart. Solomon says to all mothers, Point your child's heart in the direction of wisdom and enjoy how your children grow wiser by the day. You won't be sorry.

When Work Is Finished

Standing by the cross of Jesus were His mother, and His mother's sister, Mary the wife of Clopas, and Mary Magdalene. When Jesus then saw His mother, and the disciple whom He loved standing nearby, He said to His mother, "Woman, behold, your son!" Then He said to the disciple, "Behold, your mother!" From that hour the disciple took her into his own household.

After this, Jesus, knowing that all things had already been accomplished, to fulfill the Scripture, said, "I am thirsty." A jar full of sour wine was standing there; so they put a sponge full of the sour wine upon a branch of hyssop and brought it up to His mouth. Therefore when Jesus had received the sour wine, He said, "It is finished!" And He bowed His head and gave up His spirit.

John 19:25–30 NASB

Etched in every detail of this picture is deep pain—a grieving mother and a dying son. But this is not just the story of a mother's loss over her son's death. This is the story of Jesus' finished work for you.

The Greek language of Jesus' day used one word for "finished work." The word was written across receipts to declare a debt paid in full. Jesus used that word to say that no one needs to live with a debt to God—he had secured that debt with his life and death.

Mothers value finished work because we live so often with multiple unfinished tasks. Just say the word *finished* when you cross something off your list, and your body relaxes and celebrates. That's the message God delivered on the day Jesus died. We don't have to make ourselves good enough for God. We only need to accept his finished work. Just as Jesus wanted his disciple to take his mother in as family, God wants you to belong to him as his child too. When you believe that what Jesus did was for you, *finished* will be a word you celebrate as well.

JUST ASK

Be very happy when you are tested in different ways. You know that such testing of your faith produces endurance. Endure until your testing is over. Then you will be mature and complete, and you won't need anything.

If any of you needs wisdom to know what you should do, you should ask God, and he will give it to you. God is generous to everyone and doesn't find fault with them. When you ask for something, don't have any doubts. A person who has doubts is like a wave that is blown by the wind and tossed by the sea. A person who has doubts shouldn't expect to receive anything from the Lord. A person who has doubts is thinking about two different things at the same time and can't make up his mind about anything.

James 1:2–8 GOD'S WORD

James wrote an extremely practical letter to encourage people who were facing persecution for becoming Christ followers. He wanted them to know how to handle the difficult situations they faced.

Mothering involves hard times. If we respond to our circumstances wisely, we grow more patient and wise. And when we don't know what to do, God has wisdom to share—we just need to ask.

Have your children ever gotten into trouble because they didn't ask for help? Maybe they wanted a toy from the top shelf of the closet and tried to get it by tiptoeing precariously on a stool or chair. You've probably cleaned up plenty of messes because they didn't ask. "Next time," you tell them, "just ask."

God understands how difficult your responsibilities are. He will help by giving you all the wisdom you need, but you have to ask him for it. What difficult issue has you stumped? Don't just depend on your best idea. Stop for a moment and ask God for his wisdom. He wants to prevent a lot of unnecessary struggle. That's why he waits with an unbelievable store of ready wisdom just for you. Just ask.

Wash Day

I will wash away everything that makes you unclean, and I will remove your disgusting idols. I will take away your stubborn heart and give you a new heart and a desire to be faithful. You will have only pure thoughts, because I will put my Spirit in you and make you eager to obey my laws and teachings. You will once again live in the land I gave your ancestors; you will be my people, and I will be your God.

I will protect you from anything that makes you unclean. Your fields will overflow with grain, and no one will starve. Your trees will be filled with fruit, and crops will grow in your fields, so that you will never again feel ashamed for not having enough food.

Ezekiel 36:25–30 CEV

Ezekiel spoke to people who had disobeyed God so often and in so many ways that they felt as if they could never be right with God again. They were wrong. God prompted Ezekiel to deliver this hopeful message that no one is ever too far from God to come back to him—to be washed clean.

You probably know a lot about laundry challenges. Are you always on the lookout for a new detergent, wash booster, or stain remover to help you conquer your family's loads of dirty clothes? When you find something that really works, you won't substitute another brand just to save a few pennies. Clean, stain-free clothes are always your primary goal.

God has a laundry service, but not for grass-stained jeans and muddy socks. God launders hearts. He can take any heart and create in it a desire to follow him. When you have the desire to obey, then following God is about following his heart instead of just his rules. Besides, cleaned hearts have a new start. That's what God wants you to have. So take your heart to God's laundry service. Let him show you what clean really means.

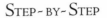

Step-by-Step

If the LORD delights in a man's way, he makes his steps firm; though he stumble, he will not fall, for the LORD upholds him with his hand.

I was young and now I am old, yet I have never seen the righteous forsaken or their children begging bread. They are always generous and lend freely; their children will be blessed.

Turn from evil and do good; then you will dwell in the land forever. For the LORD loves the just and will not forsake his faithful ones.

They will be protected forever, but the offspring of the wicked will be cut off; the righteous will inherit the land and dwell in it forever.

Psalm 37:23–29 NIV

In this psalm, David says that whoever refuses to follow God can expect unnecessary dead ends and setbacks. In contrast, those who follow God can expect directed steps, complete protection, and help to meet needs. The difference is in which steps we take.

Do you remember hovering over your children as they learned to walk? You stayed close enough to those first steps to make sure your little ones didn't stumble or fall. You were quite the cheerleader! You knew your child would learn to walk by taking one step at a time.

Step-by-step. That's how God wants to help you. He doesn't overload us with too many choices or too much to remember. If your to-do list is bigger than you think you can get done, he helps you prioritize it in a successful way. Because he sees the whole picture, he can tell you where the next best step is.

God coaches as well as celebrates every obedient step we take! Relax. Life isn't a marathon and turtles really can win a race. Just take the day one step at a time and look for your Father's hand to steady you.

Doing the Sidestep

[Jesus said,] "Isaiah was right when he prophesied about you, . . . 'Their worship is a farce, for they teach man-made ideas as commands from God.' For you ignore God's law and substitute your own tradition."

Then he said, "You skillfully sidestep God's law in order to hold on to your own tradition. For instance, Moses gave you this law from God: 'Honor your father and mother,' and 'Anyone who speaks disrespectfully of father or mother must be put to death.' But you say it is all right for people to say to their parents, 'Sorry, I can't help you. For I have vowed to give to God what I would have given to you.' In this way, you let them disregard their needy parents. And so you cancel the word of God in order to hand down your own tradition. And this is only one example among many others."

Mark 7:6–13 NLT

Jesus spoke to the religious leaders of his day with bluntness that might surprise you. He called them sidesteppers. As an example, he accused them of revising the fifth commandment so they didn't have to care for their parents if it took money they had promised to God.

Have you ever caught your children in a sidestep act? "I would have cleaned my room if I didn't have to leave for soccer practice." "I was going to feed the dog, but you told me to watch my brother and he was watching TV." Sidestepping means trying to put a believable spin on an empty excuse. When people treat God and his laws that way, he can't give them the blessings that belong to trusting, obedient children.

We can't excuse ourselves out of what God requires even if we make our excuses sound good. Excuses only prevent what God wants to do for us. Not a very good trade! God gives his laws for our protection. Sidestepping what God says cheats us out of his protection. Make sure you leave sidestepping to the dance floor and obey God's regulations the way he intended.

NEED TO KNOW

Jesus said to them, "You don't need to know the time of those events that only the Father controls. But the Holy Spirit will come upon you and give you power. Then you will tell everyone about me in Jerusalem, in all Judea, in Samaria, and everywhere in the world." After Jesus had said this and while they were watching, he was taken up into a cloud. They could not see him, but as he went up, they kept looking up into the sky.

Suddenly two men dressed in white clothes were standing there beside them. They said, "Why are you men from Galilee standing here and looking up into the sky? Jesus has been taken to heaven. But he will come back in the same way that you have seen him go."

Acts 1:7–11 CEV

This passage describes the last encounter the disciples had with Jesus on earth. They wanted to know when Jesus was going to restore a king over Israel. But instead, Jesus told them to get busy letting people everywhere know about him.

As a mom, you listen to a thousand questions from your need-to-know children. They want to know when the rain will stop or why they can't go to the store without shoes. Take a lesson from Jesus. Instead of explaining why they can't know or why they don't need to know, help them focus on something they can do.

This message isn't just for our children. How many times do you ask God for answers because you feel the need to know? Perhaps God wants to redirect your focus. Instead of stewing over an answer that isn't yours to know now, look for what you can *do*. Look for someone who needs your help or encouragement. God loves you so much that he doesn't want you to waste energy thinking about what you don't need to know. He wants you to get busy doing what you can.

Waiting for You

The other disciples stayed in the boat and dragged in the net full of fish.

When the disciples got out of the boat, they saw some bread and a charcoal fire with fish on it. Jesus told his disciples, "Bring some of the fish you just caught." Simon Peter got back into the boat and dragged the net to shore. In it were 153 large fish, but still the net did not rip.

Jesus said, "Come and eat!" But none of the disciples dared ask who he was. They knew he was the Lord. Jesus took the bread in his hands and gave some of it to his disciples. He did the same with the fish. This was the third time that Jesus appeared to his disciples after he was raised from death.

John 21:8–14 CEV

After a night spent fishing but catching nothing, in the light of dawn the disciples nearly sank their boat with a full net of fish. It didn't take them long to recognize that Jesus was the figure cooking breakfast onshore who shouted to them to put down their net on the right side of the boat. Jesus invited the successful fishermen to add their fish to the fire and eat with him. For a group still trying to understand the meaning of the Resurrection, this common meal encouraged them.

Do you love putting meals together with friends? You say something like, "You bring salad and dessert, and I'll grill chicken and bake potatoes." There's something about sharing the work that also makes sharing the meal more enjoyable. There's a message here that your loving God wants you to know. You don't have to be supermom. He wants to help you. He will suggest time-saving ways to order your agenda and make you most productive. More important, he'll wait for you with the very thing you need—comfort, peace, or rest. Whatever your harried mom heart needs, always know . . . he's waiting to give it.

IT'S WHAT'S INSIDE THAT COUNTS

Our bodies are made of clay, yet we have the treasure of the Good News in them. This shows that the superior power of this treasure belongs to God and doesn't come from us. In every way we're troubled, but we aren't crushed by our troubles. We're frustrated, but we don't give up. We're persecuted, but we're not abandoned. We're captured, but we're not killed. We always carry around the death of Jesus in our bodies so that the life of Jesus is also shown in our bodies. While we are alive, we are constantly handed over to death for Jesus' sake so that the life of Jesus is also shown in our mortal nature. Death is at work in us, but life is at work in you.

The following is written, "I believed; therefore, I spoke." We have that same spirit of faith.

2 Corinthians 4:7–13
GOD'S WORD

Do you enjoy container gardening? Then you understand that it's not the pot that grows the plant. No matter how expensive or beautiful the container, growing a plant requires more than a pot. Paul shared the same message in this passage. He wanted the readers of his letter to understand that salvation from God adds value to life—value that can't be obtained anywhere else. Paul compared his body to a clay pot that had new value because of God's treasure inside.

God wants to put his treasure inside you. He wants you to experience worth that doesn't come from physical appearance or supermom skills. After all, you can look like a great mom; talk like a great mom; discipline like a great mom, but being a great mom comes from the inside. That's why God wants to put his life inside you. All he needs from you is the container. He asks you to share your life as a container to hold his treasure. On days when your mom challenges make you feel more like a captive than a queen, offer God your clay pot and ask him for his treasure.

A Name Says It All

On the basis of faith in His name, it is the name of Jesus which has strengthened this man whom you see and know; and the faith which comes through Him has given him this perfect health in the presence of you all.

And now, brethren, I know that you acted in ignorance, just as your rulers did also. But the things which God announced beforehand by the mouth of all the prophets, that His Christ would suffer, He has thus fulfilled. Therefore repent and return, so that your sins may be wiped away, in order that times of refreshing may come from the presence of the Lord; and that He may send Jesus, the Christ appointed for you, whom heaven must receive until the period of restoration of all things about which God spoke by the mouth of His holy prophets from ancient time.

Acts 3:16–21 NASB

Peter and John met a crippled beggar outside the temple. When Peter shared healing in the name of Jesus, the crippled man walked, to the amazement of a growing crowd. Peter turned the crowd into his audience and shared who Jesus was and what his name stands for.

Do you remember how important it was to find the right names for your children? Then you watched with amazement as each child filled his name with personality and possibility. The name didn't make the child; the child made the name.

In the same way, Jesus' name is more than just a combination of letters and sounds. His name stands for who he really is. Moms need a power beyond themselves. What a relief that you can call on the name of Jesus and be connected to all the power and truth of God. When you know Jesus' name that way, you say it differently. *Jesus!* You say it with hope. You say it as a prayer.

If the name of Jesus brought healing to a crippled man, what could it bring to you today? Why don't you find out?

WHAT TIME IS IT?

There is a time for every event under heaven—a time to give birth and a time to die; a time to plant and a time to uproot what is planted. . . . A time to weep and a time to laugh; a time to mourn and a time to dance. A time to throw stones and a time to gather stones; a time to embrace and a time to shun embracing. A time to search and a time to give up as lost; a time to keep and a time to throw away. A time to tear apart and a time to sew together; a time to be silent and a time to speak.

Ecclesiastes 3:1–2, 4–7 NASB

Do you live in bondage to clocks and calendars and unbending schedules? Solomon reminds you with his wisdom that according to God's agenda, there is time for everything that needs to happen. However, while there is just enough time for the necessary, there is not time to do everything all the time. That's a hard lesson to learn, especially for moms.

This passage also reminds us that there is a rhythm to the seasons of life. We need to be seasonal in our expectations of ourselves. After a big energy push, plan downtime. Don't make your to-do list as if you will have peak energy all day. That just doesn't happen. Instead, start living by God's time clock. He wants to make sure you have time for laughter and celebration as well as work.

Even though God tells us there is a time for everything, he doesn't give us a printed schedule no matter how much you think it would help. However, we might get the closest thing to it if we start the day with a simple question: "God, what do you want me to do today?"

DEAD OR ALIVE?

Pursue the things over which Christ presides. Don't shuffle along, eyes to the ground, absorbed with the things right in front of you. Look up, and be alert to what is going on around Christ—that's where the action is. See things from *his* perspective.

Your old life is dead. Your new life, which is your *real* life—even though invisible to spectators—is with Christ in God. *He* is your life. When Christ (your real life, remember) shows up again on this earth, you'll show up, too—the real you, the glorious you. Meanwhile, be content with obscurity, like Christ.

And that means killing off everything connected with that way of death: sexual promiscuity, impurity, lust, doing whatever you feel like whenever you feel like it, and grabbing whatever attracts your fancy.

Colossians 3:1–5 MSG

Paul used the difference between being dead and alive to explain what happens when we become followers of Jesus. Old attitudes and activities have to die. Something new from God comes alive. That newness changes our life direction and attitude focus. What Jesus wants becomes what we want. No shuffling back and forth allowed.

It's just like when the family pet dies; you don't offer to keep it around for good memories. Dead animals don't belong in the house. In the same way, a woman who embraces Jesus and his ways doesn't keep around what is dead. Have you been putting up with dead dreams and unproductive attitudes? When you turn your life toward Jesus, he says, "I'll put so much of my life in you that you don't have a place for dead things anymore. You only have room for more life."

The life God gives us makes us more alive to what our families need. We become more alive to who we really are—who we were created to be. Leave dead things where they belong—buried. Let your real life, the life God gives, make you alive in every way.

JUST FOLLOW

Jesus began to preach, saying, "Change your hearts and lives, because the kingdom of heaven is near."

As Jesus was walking by Lake Galilee, he saw two brothers, Simon (called Peter) and his brother Andrew. They were throwing a net into the lake because they were fishermen. Jesus said, "Come follow me, and I will make you fish for people." So Simon and Andrew immediately left their nets and followed him.

As Jesus continued walking by Lake Galilee, he saw two other brothers, James and John, the sons of Zebedee. They were in a boat with their father Zebedee, mending their nets. Jesus told them to come with him. Immediately they left the boat and their father, and they followed Jesus.

Jesus went everywhere in Galilee, teaching in the synagogues, preaching the Good News about the kingdom of heaven.

Matthew 4:17–23 NCV

They were just doing their job when Jesus invited the fishermen to follow him. This was not just a midlife career change. This invitation would change their whole purpose for living. It would be the best adventure and most confusing work they'd ever signed up for.

Sounds like mothering, doesn't it? The desire to reproduce life and raise a child from infant dependency to adult responsibility is the hardest and best job anyone could have. Jesus knows we need all the help we can get. Perhaps that's why the invitation to follow Jesus is so appealing. In the middle of whatever mothering job you find yourself in, Jesus invites you to follow his lead. You aren't left to your own creativity or even your mother's best advice. You can link up with someone who knows your children better than you. Follow his promptings when you try to engage a child's heart in positive ways. Follow his lead to reach a child who is withdrawn or hurt. Follow the One who has been making a difference in lives for centuries. Don't go it alone. Just follow.

Even If You Weren't Raised That Way

Everyone who wants to live a godly life in Christ Jesus will suffer persecution. But evil people and impostors will flourish. They will deceive others and will themselves be deceived.

But you must remain faithful to the things you have been taught. You know they are true, for you know you can trust those who taught you. You have been taught the holy Scriptures from childhood, and they have given you the wisdom to receive the salvation that comes by trusting in Christ Jesus. All Scripture is inspired by God and is useful to teach us what is true and to make us realize what is wrong in our lives. It corrects us when we are wrong and teaches us to do what is right. God uses it to prepare and equip his people to do every good work.

2 Timothy 3:12–17 NLT

Paul mentored young Timothy with these words. He reminded Timothy that no matter how difficult it became to stay true to God, the effort to do so was worth it. Paul called him to be true to what he had already learned from Scripture.

Did you have a godly parent or grandparent who helped you know how important it is to follow the Bible's instructions? Even if you didn't, are you trying to become that parent for your children? Remember, you can't pass on what you don't have. The more you find out how the Bible applies to your life right now, the easier it will be to pass on that instruction to your children.

Look at where Paul wanted Timothy to end up—knowing how to find out what is right and what is wrong. Isn't that what you want for your children too? Point your children toward the Bible by the way you live it first. Even if you weren't raised that way, you can learn with your children how God's teachings pay off. Then one day your children will pass on the legacy they learned from you!

Pop Quiz

Examine yourselves to see whether you are still in the Christian faith. Test yourselves! Don't you recognize that you are people in whom Jesus Christ lives? . . . We pray to God that you won't do anything wrong. It's not that we want to prove that we've passed the test. Rather, we want you to do whatever is right, even if we seem to have failed. We can't do anything against the truth but only to help the truth.

We're glad when we are weak and you are strong. We are also praying for your improvement.

That's why I'm writing this letter while I'm not with you. When I am with you I don't want to be harsh by using the authority that the Lord gave me. The Lord gave us this authority to help you, not to hurt you.

2 Corinthians 13:5, 7–10
GOD'S WORD

Paul wanted to find out how serious the Corinthians were about following God, so he called for a "pop quiz." The test questions didn't come from Paul; they came from the model and teachings of Jesus. As an experienced mentor-teacher, Paul's ultimate goal was to make sure everyone passed the test.

Nobody likes pop quizzes. And yet they are a good way to see if a student is learning anything or just sloughing off. Did you catch that Paul wanted his students to score better than he did? That's a parent's heart, isn't it? We moms want our children to do better in life than we did. It's more than selfish pride. We want to spare our children unnecessary struggle. That's the motivation behind every act of discipline, every word of instruction, and every rule.

That same love that prompts your parenting describes the love God uses to shape you. He wants to prepare you for any test that comes your way. Get to know him as a loving teacher. Hang on his every word. He's ready to give you all the study guides you need, because he wants you to pass the test.

IF I JUST WEREN'T SO WEAK

I won't [boast], because I don't want anyone to give me credit beyond what they can see in my life or hear in my message, even though I have received such wonderful revelations from God. So to keep me from becoming proud, I was given a thorn in my flesh, a messenger from Satan to torment me and keep me from becoming proud.

Three different times I begged the Lord to take it away.

Each time he said, "My grace is all you need. My power works best in weakness." So now I am glad to boast about my weaknesses, so that the power of Christ can work through me. That's why I take pleasure in my weaknesses, and in the insults, hardships, persecutions, and troubles that I suffer for Christ. For when I am weak, then I am strong.

2 Corinthians 12:6–10 NLT

Paul was a strong spokesman for God, but he struggled with a challenge that he called a thorn. Some think it was failing eyesight or a speech impediment. Paul asked God to remove it in order to make him more effective, but God helped Paul understand that God's grace uses our weaknesses to show God's strength.

What's your thorn? What personal weakness do you wish you could get rid of? Impatience? Insecurity? Maybe you fight energy drains or some health issue. You know you could be a better mother without some identified challenge. Here's the good news: God wants you to be the best mother you can be, so he empowers you to live *with* your weakness but not *in* weakness.

The only way you can do that is with his power. When you ask him, God fills your place of weakness with his strength. When you experience God's power in spite of a weakness, it makes you want to share what God did for you. God loves to do this for moms and everyone else. God calls it grace, and you'll call it amazing.

DON'T SETTLE FOR SECONDHAND

When Jesus came to the region of Caesarea Philippi, he asked his disciples, "Who do people say the Son of Man is?"

They answered, "Some say you are John the Baptizer, others Elijah, still others Jeremiah or one of the prophets."

He asked them, "But who do you say I am?"

Simon Peter answered, "You are the Messiah, the Son of the living God!"

Jesus replied, "Simon, son of Jonah, you are blessed! No human revealed this to you, but my Father in heaven revealed it to you. You are Peter, and I can guarantee that on this rock I will build my church. And the gates of hell will not overpower it. I will give you the keys of the kingdom of heaven. Whatever you imprison, God will imprison. And whatever you set free, God will set free."

Matthew 16:13–19
GOD'S WORD

Jesus gave his disciples time to find out for themselves who he really was. What they learned came from personal encounters. They witnessed his miracles; they heard his authoritative teaching; they watched his day-to-day life. Peter took what he saw and heard and shared the testimony that God would use to influence his church forever—"You are the Messiah."

Secondhand information is never as good as a firsthand report. You know that principle as you work with your children. Your daughter rejects another girl because everybody says she's mean. You steer her away from what everybody else says in favor of what she knows for herself. You want her to depend on the truth, firsthand truth.

Firsthand truth is especially important when reviewing what you believe about Jesus. It is possible to let secondhand information color your understanding and push you to believe something that isn't true. Do you want to know who Jesus really is? Read what he says for yourself. Apply his teaching to your life. See what happens. God wants to know who *you* say Jesus is. The answer is a first-person encounter that influences your whole life.

When the Alarm Sounds

Two people will not walk together unless they have agreed to do so. A lion in the forest does not roar unless it has caught an animal; it does not growl in its den when it has caught nothing. A bird will not fall into a trap where there is no bait; the trap will not spring shut if there is nothing to catch. When a trumpet blows a warning in a city, the people tremble. When trouble comes to a city, the Lord has caused it. Before the Lord God does anything, he tells his plans to his servants the prophets. The lion has roared! Who wouldn't be afraid? The Lord God has spoken.

Amos 3:3–8 NCV

God sent Amos to deliver special messages to God's people about the consequences of perpetuating social and economic injustices. It's not surprising that Amos, a shepherd, used scenes from nature to make his point. In this passage, using several cause-and-effect illustrations, Amos told the nation of Israel that God's warning emphasized that trouble awaited.

We warn our children about cause and effect all the time. We teach them that hot things burn. We remind them that busy streets are dangerous. We don't say such things to be obnoxious or just to hear ourselves talk. We warn our children because we love them and want to protect them.

God feels the same way about you. His warnings don't bring the disaster. His warnings alert you so that you can prevent trouble or prepare yourself for it. Whether it is a warning about wrong priorities or moral boundaries or relationship issues, ignoring the alarm is what can bring disaster.

So the next time you read one of God's warnings, feel the love. There's no reason to warn someone you don't want to protect. God's warnings are always about love.

WITHOUT THE VEIL

The people's minds were hardened, and to this day whenever the old covenant is being read, the same veil covers their minds so they cannot understand the truth. And this veil can be removed only by believing in Christ. Yes, even today when they read Moses' writings, their hearts are covered with that veil, and they do not understand.

But whenever someone turns to the Lord, the veil is taken away. For the Lord is the Spirit, and wherever the Spirit of the Lord is, there is freedom. So all of us who have had that veil removed can see and reflect the glory of the Lord. And the Lord—who is the Spirit—makes us more and more like him as we are changed into his glorious image.

2 Corinthians 3:14–18 NLT

Different cultures use veils in interesting ways. Some cover for modesty. Some cover for mystery. All keep something hidden. Paul wanted his readers to allow Jesus to remove anything that kept them from knowing and being known by God so that they could enjoy true freedom.

A lot of moms cover up who they really are. Maybe that's what you do. If so, you probably don't intend to be deceptive but are looking for a way to protect yourself from something. In the same way that you don't want your children to hide things from you, however, God doesn't want you to hide anything from him. He already knows all about you anyway.

God says we don't need to wear a veil with him. In fact, if we do, it will be difficult for us to understand what is true about God. God wants you to know his complete acceptance. He takes great joy in your existence. He wants you to experience his delight in who you are. Don't let anything separate you from experiencing that joy. Receive Paul's counsel. Turn to know Jesus. The veil will come off and you will start enjoying freedom.

LINE BY LINE

"Whom will he teach knowledge? And whom will he make to understand the message? Those just weaned from milk? Those just drawn from the breasts? For precept must be upon precept, precept upon precept, line upon line, line upon line, here a little, there a little."

For with stammering lips and another tongue He will speak to this people, . . . yet they would not hear. But the word of the LORD was to them, "Precept upon precept, precept upon precept, line upon line, line upon line, here a little, there a little," that they might go and fall backward, and be broken and snared and caught.

Isaiah 28:9–13 NKJV

It's one thing to speak baby talk to your newborn, but if you're still talking baby talk to your teenager, something is wrong! That's what Isaiah was trying to get Israel's priests and religious teachers to understand. They had accused Isaiah of treating them like babies, and they repeated a singsong verse to mock him. Isaiah repeated the verse to them to underline the importance of listening to God's simple messages principle by principle and line by line.

As a mom, you try to simplify your instructions to your young children. You know they can't process and obey multiple steps all at once, so you try to give them one instruction at a time. Your Creator God treats you the same way. The Bible records his instructions principle by principle and line by line. They are simple—but that doesn't make them easy.

God is a patient teacher. He knows that if you receive his principles slowly, you are more likely to apply them to life in lasting ways. So take your time with the Bible. While you read it line by line, make sure you are learning about God, principle by principle.

KINDLY CONSIDER THE INVITATION

God judges those who do wrong things, and we know that his judging is right. You judge those who do wrong, but you do wrong yourselves. Do you think you will be able to escape the judgment of God? He has been very kind and patient, waiting for you to change, but you think nothing of his kindness. Perhaps you do not understand that God is kind to you so you will change your hearts and lives. But you are stubborn and refuse to change, so you are making your own punishment even greater on the day he shows his anger. On that day everyone will see God's right judgments. God will reward or punish every person for what that person has done. Some people, by always continuing to do good, live for God's glory, for honor, and for life that has no end.

Romans 2:2–7 NCV

Before his visit to Rome, Paul reminded those with a Jewish background that they were just as accountable to God's judgment as those who had turned to Jesus from idol worship and false religions. He told them that God expected them to conform to his teachings just like everyone else.

How do you get your children to change an attitude or action that could hurt them or someone else? Simply saying that they need to change doesn't get the job done. And if they don't want to change, you know they make everything harder, not easier.

Think of God as your loving parent who wants only good things to happen to you. He invites you to change for your own good. He's not waiting to pounce on you for doing the wrong thing. He knows that wrong attitudes and actions bring their own punishment. He kindly invites you to change, giving you freedom to accept or reject his invitation.

Where could a change make a difference in your life? In your parenting, marriage, or how you view yourself? Is it possible that the more kindly you understand God's invitation, the more receptive you'll be to change?

PRESCRIPTION POWER

Naaman came with his horses and chariot and stopped at the entrance to Elisha's home. Elisha sent a messenger to him. He said, "Wash yourself seven times in the Jordan River, and your skin will be healthy and clean."

But Naaman became angry and left. He said, "I thought he would at least come out of his house, stand somewhere, call on the name of the LORD his God, wave his hand over the infected place, and heal the skin disease. The Abana and Pharpar Rivers in Damascus have better water than any of the rivers in Israel. Couldn't I wash in them and be clean?" So he turned around and left in anger.

But Naaman's servants went to him and said, "Master, if the prophet had asked you to do some extraordinary act, wouldn't you have done it?"

2 Kings 5:9–13 GOD'S WORD

Naaman, a military commander, was accustomed to giving orders that his soldiers had to follow immediately. When he contracted the dreaded disease of leprosy, his wife's Jewish slave girl suggested that he go to God's messenger Elisha and ask for healing. At first, Naaman's pride kept him from following Elisha's instructions, and he placed his healing in jeopardy.

When you get a prescription from the doctor, do you read the directions only to decide how you want to change them? If taking the medication is inconvenient, would you take it every other day instead of daily? Probably not. If you trust the doctor, you follow the directions.

The same is true with prescriptions that our loving God dispenses. They might sound inconvenient or difficult. God's prescriptions for healing might require us to address motives we didn't want anyone to know about or to learn how to forgive a person who wronged us. Or God might prescribe reaching out for help by joining a support group or seeing a counselor. No matter what God asks you to do, do what he asks. His prescriptions don't fail—just follow his directions.

A New-Heart Day

"When you arrive at Gibeah of God, where the garrison of the Philistines is located, you will meet a band of prophets coming down from the place of worship. They will be playing a harp, a tambourine, a flute, and a lyre, and they will be prophesying. At that time the Spirit of the LORD will come powerfully upon you, and you will prophesy with them. You will be changed into a different person. After these signs take place, do what must be done, for God is with you. Then go down to Gilgal ahead of me. I will join you there to sacrifice burnt offerings and peace offerings. You must wait for seven days until I arrive and give you further instructions."

As Saul turned and started to leave, God gave him a new heart, and all Samuel's signs were fulfilled that day.

1 Samuel 10:5–9 NLT

The people of Israel wanted a human king. Although this wasn't God's will for them, at their insistence he allowed it. God wanted Saul to know that it would take more than popular approval for him to succeed as the first king of Israel. Saul realized that even special signs from God weren't as important as receiving a new heart from God for this new assignment.

Making a heart change is more than making a behavior change. How many times have you thought it was *your* child in time-out who inspired the punch line "I may be sitting down on the outside, but I'm standing up on the inside"? True spiritual change allows God to work from the inside out.

How do you help your children cooperate with God's heart work? Explain how God helps us become better people than we can be without him. Compare God's work to a heart transplant. God shares his heart so that we will want what God wants and love as God loves. Ask God to help you see how he is shaping your children's hearts so that you can share in the celebration too.

Loving Obedience More Than Rules

What actually took place is this: I tried keeping rules and working my head off to please God, and it didn't work. So I quit being a "law man" so that I could be *God's* man. Christ's life showed me how, and enabled me to do it. I identified myself completely with him. Indeed, I have been crucified with Christ. My ego is no longer central. It is no longer important that I appear righteous before you or have your good opinion, and I am no longer driven to impress God. Christ lives in me. The life you see me living is not "mine," but it is lived by faith in the Son of God, who loved me and gave himself for me. I am not going to go back on that.

Galatians 2:19–21 MSG

Early in his life, Paul thought pleasing God directly connected to keeping religious rules. With unreserved zeal he persecuted Christians because they didn't follow the Jewish traditions he had been taught. Paul came to understand that pleasing God is about accepting who Jesus is and what he taught. Embracing Jesus' life keeps first things first.

Mothers have to make a lot of rules to keep a family running smoothly. While you want your children to obey you, you don't want to raise rule keepers. You hope your children will follow your rules because of who you are—the mother who loves them and wants what is best for them. God wants the same kind of loving obedience from you.

Starting with rules is harsh and impersonal. Starting with a person makes all the difference. God sent Jesus so that we could identify with a person who lived the life God wants us to live. Get to know who Jesus is, how he loves, and how he forgives. Make his life your first focus. When you do, his teachings will make sense and they'll be a lot easier to obey.

JUST BREATHE

I felt the power of the LORD on me, and he brought me out by the Spirit of the LORD and put me down in the middle of a valley. It was full of bones. He led me around among the bones, and I saw that there were many bones in the valley and that they were very dry. Then he asked me, "Human, can these bones live?"

I answered, "Lord GOD, only you know."

He said to me, "Prophesy to these bones and say to them, 'Dry bones, hear the word of the LORD. This is what the Lord GOD says to the bones: I will cause breath to enter you so you will come to life. I will put muscles on you and flesh on you and cover you with skin. Then I will put breath in you so you will come to life.'"

Ezekiel 37:1–6 NCV

God gave Ezekiel a chance to see what happened to Israel from God's perspective. The people of Israel had let their desire to obey God die. God reminded Ezekiel that this desire could live again with the creative, empowering breath of God.

Breath is life. We watch our sleeping children; their chests rise and fall and the rhythm reassures us. We live with the same oxygen and carbon dioxide exchange in our own bodies and never think about the process unless something compromises our ability to breathe.

Has something sucked the life out of you? Are you juggling too many family responsibilities? Are you pushing yourself to the end of your energy? God wants to give you breathing room. He wants you to recognize that his expectations will not overwhelm you and his life can renew you. Don't settle for dry-bones living. Look for a way to stop and breathe. Inhale God's love, his purpose, his compassion. Receive his empowerment for the most important responsibility of your life—mothering. Then let the dry bones of your life come together again to live the way God says you can.

Hope & Peace

The responsibility of mothering would be overwhelming were it not for what we see when we look into the faces of our children—*hope*, that God-inspired ingredient that makes all the difference. Our mother hearts are fueled by hope. Hope is God's gift to us, and it does more than make us good mothers. In a world of disappointments, confusion, and ever-present evil, hope opens our eyes of faith and makes it possible for us to take hold of God's promises.

Having hope brings us peace. Have you ever tried hiding in the bathroom for a little peace and quiet? You don't have to play hide-and-seek with peace, sneaking just a moment here and there. A warm bubble bath might settle your mind and body briefly, but peace is a condition of the spirit, and God will give you peace freely when you seek him in every situation you face.

> May the Lord of peace himself give you peace at all times and in every way.
>
> 2 Thessalonians 3:16 NIV

DELIGHTED

Delight yourself in the LORD; and He will give you the desires of your heart. Commit your way to the LORD, trust also in Him, and He will do it. He will bring forth your righteousness as the light and your judgment as the noonday.

Rest in the LORD and wait patiently for Him; do not fret because of him who prospers in his way, because of the man who carries out wicked schemes. Cease from anger and forsake wrath; do not fret; it leads only to evildoing. For evildoers will be cut off, but those who wait for the LORD, they will inherit the land. Yet a little while and the wicked man will be no more; and you will look carefully for his place and he will not be there. But the humble will inherit the land.

Psalm 37:4–11 NASB

In this psalm David shares a refreshing plan for living God's way. He suggests that we start with delight and end with rest. How does that sound? Just what every mother needs!

Begin by making everything that pleases God your delight. Find joy in what brings joy to God. When you do this, something amazing happens: you want what God wants, and that enables him to give you your true heart desires. More than the simple wants and wishes that you think about throughout the day, these heart desires make a lasting differences. As a mom you want to give your children the best. You don't expect that your children will know what *best* means. That's why you choose for them. You give them boundaries and responsibility and healthy food even when they wish for something else. God has the same parent heart. When you recognize God's desires as your very own, you can experience contentment you would not know any other way. You realize that your best hope lies in what God desires for you. Keep asking for God's desires and find out why they put your heart at rest.

BE PREPARED

I don't think, friends, that I need to deal with the question of when all this is going to happen. You know as well as I that the day of the Master's coming can't be posted on our calendars. He won't call ahead and make an appointment any more than a burglar would. About the time everybody's walking around complacently, congratulating each other— "We've sure got it made! Now we can take it easy!"—suddenly everything will fall apart. It's going to come as suddenly and inescapably as birth pangs to a pregnant woman.

But friends, you're not in the dark, so how could you be taken off guard by any of this? You're sons of Light, daughters of Day. We live under wide open skies and know where we stand. So let's not sleepwalk through life like those others.

1 Thessalonians 5:1–6 MSG

Paul wrote hopeful instruction to the Thessalonian Christians about how to live until Jesus returns. He was concerned about the careless living that the Thessalonians had reverted to because they didn't know an exact date for this event. Paul reminded them that God didn't share dates because God wanted them to live prepared.

Do you act like Chicken Little when you hear predictions about the end of the world, afraid of what you don't know? God wants you to enjoy a hopeful confidence in a world where everything that happens doesn't appear on a calendar. "Just be ready," he says.

Moms understand that raising children is full of unpredictability. You probably carry extra clothes, snacks, toys, or CDs to meet a variety of crises. Just because you can't know everything that might happen doesn't prevent you from preparing for it. God applauds the same readiness as it applies to living your life according to what he has told you. In all the upredictabilities life hands you, live with the confidence that what you really need to know, God is willing to tell you, so that you can be prepared.

LOOKING FOR SOMETHING NEW?

"I am the LORD, your Holy One, the Creator of Israel, your King."

This is what the LORD says. He is the one who made a road through the sea and a path through rough waters. He is the one who defeated the chariots and horses and the mighty armies. They fell together and will never rise again. They were destroyed as a flame is put out. The LORD says, "Forget what happened before, and do not think about the past. Look at the new thing I am going to do. It is already happening. Don't you see it? I will make a road in the desert and rivers in the dry land."

Isaiah 43:15–19 NCV

The nation of Israel knew that God had performed miracles that helped the people out of some dead-end circumstances. The Red Sea miracle topped a list that included many military victories as well. But God didn't want his people to overemphasize what he had done; he also wanted them to know that he could bring protection and deliverance in new ways.

The tendency to expect God to do something he has done before can prevent us from perceiving his new work. God has more creativity than anyone you know. He can open opportunities that didn't exist before, send people to you with resources you need, or show you a new perspective that changes your approach. What's your biggest challenge today? Are you concerned that the meeting with your child's teacher won't make the difference your child needs? Do you want to know how to build your son's confidence after his experience with bullies at school? Nothing challenges God's way-making ability. While you may run out of ideas to apply to a difficulty, God never will. Give him a chance to show you his best work. He is anxious to do something new just for you.

Saved from Uselessness

All your hope should be for the gift of grace that will be yours when Jesus Christ is shown to you. Now that you are obedient children of God do not live as you did in the past. You did not understand, so you did the evil things you wanted. But be holy in all you do, just as God, the One who called you, is holy. It is written in the Scriptures: "You must be holy, because I am holy."

You pray to God and call him Father, and he judges each person's work equally. So while you are here on earth, you should live with respect for God. You know that in the past you were living in a worthless way, a way passed down from the people who lived before you. But you were saved from that useless life.

1 Peter 1:13–18 NCV

Peter wrote to Christians experiencing many kinds of persecution. He wanted to encourage them to remain faithful to how Jesus asked them to live. He called them to a life that persecution couldn't silence. Only God's holy life could make that difference.

Does God's standard of holy living, or "set-apart" living, seem impossible to you? Do you think that holy living is for people who isolate themselves and pray all day? God says no. Holy living influences everything you do, because God shares his priorities and character with you. God says that holy living prevents uselessness. Your life becomes holy and useful not because of what you do but because of what God does in you. Holy living rejects a try-to-be-better lifestyle. God helps you point your heart toward him, because the direction of your heart impacts how you think and what you do.

In a world filled with unholy chaos, the possibility of something holy brings a refreshing change. God invites you to share *his* holiness as you respond to the needs of your children and those around you. Nothing you do from God's prompting will ever be useless.

Keep Growing

I do not mean that I am already as God wants me to be. I have not yet reached that goal, but I continue trying to reach it and to make it mine. Christ wants me to do that, which is the reason he made me his. Brothers and sisters, I know that I have not yet reached that goal, but there is one thing I always do. Forgetting the past and straining toward what is ahead, I keep trying to reach the goal and get the prize for which God called me through Christ to the life above.

All of us who are spiritually mature should think this way, too. And if there are things you do not agree with, God will make them clear to you. But we should continue following the truth we already have.

Philippians 3:12–16 NCV

Thirty years had passed since Paul made Jesus' way of living his priority. However, he still expressed his need to become more like Jesus by deliberate growth. Paul wanted the Philippian Christians, and us, to understand that no matter how long we have been Christians, there is always more growing to do.

Do you fill your mothering role with too many ought-to's? Do you think you *ought to* parent better or organize time better? God wants you to know that he does not point his finger at what you could do better. He invites you to keep growing by increasing your focus on becoming more like Jesus. He knows that if you take this attitude toward yourself, you will be able to help your children develop in ways that please Jesus too.

Take God's growth-coaching approach with your children. Keep their focus on Jesus' life and character. Affirm their progress often. Share positive reminders and helpful hints that keep them headed toward the goal. God says that this kind of growth helps you and your children mature. He celebrates growth wherever it happens. Make it your goal too. Keep growing.

Don't Give Up

Everything in creation is being more or less held back. God reins it in until both creation and all the creatures are ready and can be released at the same moment into the glorious times ahead. Meanwhile, the joyful anticipation deepens.

All around us we observe a pregnant creation. The difficult times of pain throughout the world are simply birth pangs. But it's not only around us; it's *within* us. The Spirit of God is arousing us within. We're also feeling the birth pangs. These sterile and barren bodies of ours are yearning for full deliverance. That is why waiting does not diminish us, any more than waiting diminishes a pregnant mother. We are enlarged in the waiting. We, of course, don't see what is enlarging us. But the longer we wait, the larger we become, and the more joyful our expectancy.

Romans 8:20–25 MSG

How are you at waiting? Waiting for hard times to end is like waiting for a baby to be born—the pregnancy isn't fun and the labor is painful, but holding that new life in your arms is so worth the wait for that child! That's the message in this Scripture: don't give up hope when you live through difficult times. Keep the same heightened anticipation that you had during pregnancy. Wait with the end result in mind.

God doesn't want us to get discouraged during waiting times. He wants us to trust that what he is working to give us is so wonderful that we won't give up waiting for it. It's the old "no pain, no gain" script; however, God isn't telling us to enjoy the pain. This passage says, Don't lose sight of the gain.

What are you tired of waiting for? A family issue to resolve? A child to have a better day at school? An answer to a health challenge? Don't give up. God is working even when you don't see the results. Keep focused on what is ahead. You don't want to miss what God is preparing just for you.

HONEST TALK

LORD, hear me when I call; have mercy and answer me. My heart said of you, "Go, worship him." So I come to worship you, LORD. Do not turn away from me. Do not turn your servant away in anger; you have helped me. Do not push me away or leave me alone, God, my Savior. If my father and mother leave me, the LORD will take me in. LORD, teach me your ways, and guide me to do what is right because I have enemies. Do not hand me over to my enemies, because they tell lies about me and say they will hurt me.

I truly believe I will live to see the LORD's goodness.

Psalm 27:7–13 NCV

David was the people's poet. He knew how to communicate what everyone was thinking but didn't always talk about. In this psalm he shared honestly about feeling desperate to hear from God. He voiced fears that God might not help him. But David didn't stop with a tirade of raw emotion. In the end, he submitted that trust in God's goodness would give him exactly what he needed.

Are you honest with God? You can be. You can talk to God about anything. You can tell him your biggest fear as well as your most important dream. You can even express your anger to him. On a day when you are afraid everybody and everything is against you, you will find out that God is never against you. He's always on your side, preparing exactly what will make the biggest difference at the best time. Talk to him as you would a friend. Turn self-talk into a conversation with God, and keep it going throughout the day. Take a tip from David, though. You haven't finished the conversation until you end with confidence in the good things God is preparing.

TIME TO PARTY

When the LORD brought back the captives to Zion, we were like men who dreamed. Our mouths were filled with laughter, our tongues with songs of joy. Then it was said among the nations, "The LORD has done great things for them." The LORD has done great things for us, and we are filled with joy.

Restore our fortunes, O LORD, like streams in the Negev. Those who sow in tears will reap with songs of joy. He who goes out weeping, carrying seed to sow, will return with songs of joy, carrying sheaves with him.

Psalm 126:1–6 NIV

A dream came true when the exiled people of Israel returned to their homeland. However, backbreaking work would be needed to once again plant the deserted land. Even as the people dropped seeds into the ground, they began to visualize the celebration that harvest would bring. More than that, they celebrated what God had done for them.

Everybody likes a party. But even parties take hard work. Nothing good comes without a little effort. You want your children to catch this idea when you try to get them to finish chores so the family can do something fun together. But in the middle of a long period of time when nothing but trouble hits, how hard is it to believe that something good will ever happen again!

God says it will. Don't give up. Just because you can't see a change coming doesn't mean that it isn't on the way. Besides, there's always a reason to celebrate what God has already done or what you know he can do. Can you think of something like this in your own life? Then your heart has a good reason to plan a party too!

GOT HOPE?

I will always have hope and will praise you more and more. I will tell how you do what is right. I will tell about your salvation all day long, even though it is more than I can tell. I will come and tell about your powerful works, Lord GOD. I will remind people that only you do what is right.

God, you have taught me since I was young. To this day I tell about the miracles you do. Even though I am old and gray, do not leave me, God. I will tell the children about your power; I will tell those who live after me about your might.

Psalm 71:14–18 NCV

This passage gives the life testimony of an aging psalmist. He makes a very bold statement about hope—there's always a reason to hope. He comes to that belief as he reviews what God has done in his life. Then with new determination he promises to share that hope with others.

Do you *always* have hope? Or do you stand in line with countless other moms who run out of hope on a regular basis? You wonder if family economics will get easier or the day's responsibilities will lessen. Usually, you know the answer to both. Hoping for something different is useless when your hope depends on circumstances that might or might not change. The writer of this psalm had learned something different: he anchored his hope on God, whose track record for doing the right thing at the right time is completely reliable.

Have you lost hope somewhere in the mothering chaos of laundry and sickness and messes and schedule? Take a hope break today. Sit with the God of all hope. Ask him to help you find your hope again. He will.

SOMETHING INDESTRUCTIBLE

God is so good, and by raising Jesus from death, he has given us new life and a hope that lives on. God has something stored up for you in heaven, where it will never decay or be ruined or disappear.

You have faith in God, whose power will protect you until the last day. Then he will save you, just as he has always planned to do. On that day you will be glad, even if you have to go through many hard trials for a while. Your faith will be like gold that has been tested in a fire. And these trials will prove that your faith is worth much more than gold that can be destroyed. They will show that you will be given praise and honor and glory when Jesus Christ returns.

1 Peter 1:3–7 CEV

People throw the word *faith* around in a lot of ways. Most of the time they make faith sound like something we must try harder to get. Peter wrote to give good news to believers living with the threat of persecution: faith *isn't* something *we* create; faith is our confident response to what is absolutely true. The word *faith* comes from verbs that mean to be true, solid, and firm. Our faith can only be as solid as its source.

How strong is your faith? This passage says that the resurrection of Jesus proves how much God can do. What kind of power do you need in your life today? If your faith has its source in God, you connect to his power. Faith rooted in God doesn't depend on circumstances or another person's choice or even on what you can do. When God is the source of our faith, God sustains us, and our faith endures because God endures.

As moms, we frequently encounter things that don't last: clothes, appliances, patience. God suggests we need a faith that nothing can destroy. Faith that finds its source in God is indestructible. That's a faith worth having!

Don't Keep It a Secret

I, Paul, am a prisoner of Christ Jesus for you who are not Jews. Surely you have heard that God gave me this work to tell you about his grace. He let me know his secret by showing it to me. I have already written a little about this. If you read what I wrote then, you can see that I truly understand the secret about the Christ. People who lived in other times were not told that secret. But now, through the Spirit, God has shown that secret to his holy apostles and prophets. This is that secret: that through the Good News those who are not Jews will share with the Jews in God's blessing. They belong to the same body, and they share together in the promise that God made in Christ Jesus.

Ephesians 3:1–6 NCV

Paul wrote the Ephesians from prison about the mission God had given him. Paul had learned that God's plan to deliver the news about Jesus included the Gentiles—non-Jewish people like the Ephesians. Some Christians thought that the Messiah had been sent only to the Jews. Paul wanted the Ephesians to accept God's heart on this matter and understand clearly that the good news was for them too.

Moms share all kinds of mothering secrets with one another, not the kind of secret you aren't supposed to tell anyone but secret because the information hadn't been passed on to you earlier. Paul says that the news about Jesus being for all people was a secret that had now been revealed.

How can you share the secret? Why Jesus came, what he taught, and how he lives today is the kind of information that should be passed on, especially to your family. Consider sharing the life of Jesus with your children as you would tell a secret. Share it in the spirit of passing on something valuable that you don't want your children to live without. Don't keep God's secret to yourself. Share it!

An Energy Boost

Israel, why do you say, "My way is hidden from the LORD, and my rights are ignored by my God"? Don't you know? Haven't you heard? The eternal God, the LORD, the Creator of the ends of the earth, doesn't grow tired or become weary. His understanding is beyond reach. He gives strength to those who grow tired and increases the strength of those who are weak. Even young people grow tired and become weary, and young men will stumble and fall. Yet, the strength of those who wait with hope in the LORD will be renewed. They will soar on wings like eagles. They will run and won't become weary. They will walk and won't grow tired.

Isaiah 40:27–31 GOD'S WORD

Israel faced the possibility of attack by a powerful enemy. Fatigued by the never-ending stress, they felt that God wasn't paying attention to them. In this passage, the prophet Isaiah encouraged the people by reminding them that because God never gets tired, he always has energy to share.

Fatigue is an occupational hazard of motherhood. Moms might be the most sleep-deprived people around. How many days do you long for body-restoring, mind-easing, motivation-renewing rest? You hope no one notices your dark circles and half-closed eyes. But someone does—God notices. Not only does he notice, but he wants to give you his special energy boost. He wants you to stop acting as if everything depends on you. He reminds you that he is on duty 24-7 so you don't have to be. Sometimes God renews you through restful sleep—but you have to go to bed to enjoy it. Sometimes he renews your perspective. He meets all your dwindling reserves with his never-ending supplies.

Don't let an energy drain keep you from enjoying your motherhood. You need more than a vacation. You need God's energy boost, and he's anxiously waiting to share it with you.

NOT FORGOTTEN

Zion said, "The LORD has forsaken me, the Lord has forgotten me."

"Can a mother forget the baby at her breast and have no compassion on the child she has borne? Though she may forget, I will not forget you! See, I have engraved you on the palms of my hands; your walls are ever before me. Your sons hasten back, and those who laid you waste depart from you. Lift up your eyes and look around; all your sons gather and come to you. As surely as I live," declares the LORD, "you will wear them all as ornaments; you will put them on, like a bride."

Isaiah 49:14–19 NIV

The nation of Israel had been captured and taken to a foreign land. They felt alone and forgotten. In this passage, one of the Bible's most poignant reminders of God's love, Isaiah used the bond a mother has for her child to say that God never forgets his children. Isaiah reassured the Israelites that God's promise to restore would still come true.

How many times have you replayed that first moment when you held your child? Do you remember feeling ready to give your life away for this bundle of need and innocence? Even when your toddler—or your teenager—pushed you away in early attempts at independence, you didn't turn in your mother credentials. Nothing takes away your love, although many experiences may threaten your joy for a time. God says that he has something in common with you. The love you have for your child, God has for you. Nothing prevents his love for you. Nothing lessens his love for you. On that day when you feel unappreciated and maybe a little forgotten, remember that nothing makes God forget about you. And nothing ever will.

REACHING OUT FOR HOPE

If you devote your heart to him and stretch out your hands to him, if you put away the sin that is in your hand and allow no evil to dwell in your tent, then you will lift up your face without shame; you will stand firm and without fear. You will surely forget your trouble, recalling it only as waters gone by. Life will be brighter than noonday, and darkness will become like morning. You will be secure, because there is hope; you will look about you and take your rest in safety. You will lie down, with no one to make you afraid, and many will court your favor.

Job 11:13–19 NIV

If anyone needed hope, it was Job. He had lost family, wealth, and even health. In this passage a friend of Job's, named Zophar, counsels him about his need to recover good standing with God. But Zophar was misinformed. Suffering is not necessarily a sign of God's displeasure. Job sifted through what was true in Zophar's words and what was not to find God's hope within his reach.

When young children stretch their hands out to their mother, something stirs her heart to respond as quickly as possible. Reaching out to God is a good thing too, because God wants to give you hope. While you might face difficult times, you can experience a companionship with God that assures you that you're not alone, that someone cares for you.

God wants you to know that you can survive a crisis and persevere on a rough day. He especially wants you to know that whatever lowers your confidence gets his attention. Your loving, faithful God performs sentry duty just for you. Never forget that God plans to give you hope. Reach out to him today, and his hope will be within your reach.

LET IT OVERFLOW

May God, the source of hope, fill you with joy and peace through your faith in him. Then you will overflow with hope by the power of the Holy Spirit.

I'm convinced, brothers and sisters, that you, too, are filled with goodness. I'm also convinced that you have all the knowledge you need and that you are able to instruct each other. However, I've written you a letter, parts of which are rather bold, as a reminder to you. I'm doing this because God gave me the gift to be a servant of Christ Jesus to people who are not Jewish. I serve as a priest by spreading the Good News of God. I do this in order that I might bring the nations to God as an acceptable offering, made holy by the Holy Spirit.

Romans 15:13–16 GOD'S WORD

Moms always need hope. We need it for ourselves and for our children. Running out of hope can be worse than running out of energy, because hope fuels the motivation to keep going in the face of ups and downs. In this passage, Paul prays that we will know more than just-enough hope; he prays that we will have hope that overflows.

Is it possible that you miss the signs of hope God sends your way? Hope exists in a child's compassionate act toward a friend, because you can encourage more compassion. Hope surfaces when a child masters a difficult skill, because new learning brings the possibility of more learning. When you look for hope in this way, you understand that hope is more than wishful or optimistic thinking. Hope springs from God through the possibilities he helps you recognize.

Like a fountain you can't turn off, hope begins to bubble up. Where hope flows, joy, peace, and power follow close behind. Who needs hope in your circle of care? Ask God to help you find where your fountain of hope begins and let hope overflow.

When "Try Harder" Doesn't Work

He said to me, "This is the word of the LORD to Zerubbabel: Not by might, nor by power, but by my Spirit, says the LORD of hosts. Who are you, O great mountain? Before Zerubbabel you shall become a plain. And he shall bring forward the top stone amid shouts of 'Grace, grace to it!'"

Then the word of the LORD came to me, saying, "The hands of Zerubbabel have laid the foundation of this house; his hands shall also complete it. Then you will know that the LORD of hosts has sent me to you. For whoever has despised the day of small things shall rejoice, and shall see the plumb line in the hand of Zerubbabel.

"These seven are the eyes of the LORD, which range through the whole earth."

Zechariah 4:6–10 ESV

Overwhelming jobs require more than a try-harder work ethic. That's what Zerubbabel found out as he brought the first group of exiled Jews back to their homeland to rebuild it. God wanted him to know that armed with God's power, even small beginning steps would lead to success.

You know about overwhelming jobs. On some days, laundry. On other days, a child's illness. Perhaps you struggle with a child whose behavior you don't understand. You wonder if discipline will do any good, and if so, what should you try? God knows about big jobs too. He wants to help you with your most daunting task—growing a life.

Don't think you can handle this important responsibility just by trying harder. God wants to share his power with you. His power added to your parenting is an unbeatable partnership. He empowers you to be the parent he knows you can be. He empowers grace, forgiveness, patience, self-control—everything that makes a difference. So don't just try harder, let God help you try differently—with his power. No one wants your parenting to succeed more than God does.

Labor Pains and Mothering Gains

Some of His disciples then said to one another, . . . "What is this that He says, 'A little while'? We do not know what He is talking about." Jesus knew that they wished to question Him, and He said to them, "Are you deliberating together about this, that I said, 'A little while, and you will not see Me, and again a little while, and you will see Me'? Truly, truly, I say to you, that you will weep and lament, but the world will rejoice; you will grieve, but your grief will be turned into joy.

"Whenever a woman is in labor she has pain, because her hour has come; but when she gives birth to the child, she no longer remembers the anguish because of the joy that a child has been born into the world."

John 16:17–21 NASB

Have you noticed how many times the Bible uses a mothering image to deliver a message? Jesus did it here as he tried to prepare his disciples for his coming death and resurrection. He compared the pain of separation to labor pains that come before celebrating a new birth.

One writer quipped, "If mothering was going to be easy, it never would have started with something called labor." On most days you say your pain during labor was worth it. That wide-eyed wonderer made you forget all the pain when you first held him or her. Wouldn't it be great if labor pains were the last pain a mother experienced in raising a child? But they're not. Labor pains continue in a different way as you watch your children grow through rejection or struggle with school. At these times, remember that some pain is necessary to bring about something new. Without it, you will short-circuit your children's learning experience.

What's the hardest mothering task you face today? Think about it as something good that needs to be born. Focus on the gain, not the pain, and enjoy the fruit of your labor.

DRY TIMES AND WATERING HOLES

You will rejoice in the LORD. You will glory in the Holy One of Israel.

When the poor and needy search for water and there is none, and their tongues are parched from thirst, then I, the LORD, will answer them. I, the God of Israel, will never abandon them. I will open up rivers for them on the high plateaus. I will give them fountains of water in the valleys. I will fill the desert with pools of water. Rivers fed by springs will flow across the parched ground. I will plant trees in the barren desert—cedar, acacia, myrtle, olive, cypress, fir, and pine. I am doing this so all who see this miracle will understand what it means—that it is the LORD who has done this, the Holy One of Israel who created it.

Isaiah 41:16–20 NLT

This passage served like a review lesson for the people of Israel, who had seen these miracles when they traveled through dry land. They had learned that God could make things happen that could come about no other way. Do you believe that? It doesn't mean he will miraculously resupply what you keep in the fridge for your kids to drink. But it does mean that God matches his compassionate resources to your greatest need.

Mothers struggle with desert times without ever visiting a cactus-prickled part of the country. We go without sleep, money, or down-time as a regular part of the mothering geography. Are you that needy mom? Which of God's mighty acts do you need? Maybe it's reassurance that no matter what happens, God will never leave you helpless. Or maybe you need a new perspective that enables you to see possibilities where you didn't think they existed. God will show you what only he can do so you know whom to thank for it. Even when you don't even know what you need, just leave it to him. Your faithful God has already figured it out.

Help Is on the Way

Brothers and sisters, we don't want you to be ignorant about the suffering we experienced in the province of Asia. It was so extreme that it was beyond our ability to endure. We even wondered if we could go on living. In fact, we still feel as if we're under a death sentence. But we suffered so that we would stop trusting ourselves and learn to trust God, who brings the dead back to life. He has rescued us from a terrible death, and he will rescue us in the future. We are confident that he will continue to rescue us, since you are also joining to help us when you pray for us. Then many people will thank God for the favor he will show us because many people prayed for us.

2 Corinthians 1:8–11
GOD'S WORD

Paul encountered an angry riot in Ephesus that could have cost him his life. Paul knew that people prayed for him and it made a difference. Since he knew that God delivered special help when people prayed, he understood that more prayer delivered more power.

Who prays for you? Your mother? Your grandmother? Someone from a church you attended? Then you've got powerful help on the way. God never wastes a single prayer. Mothers need those prayers. We're always finding ourselves at the end of our energy and ideas. We need the answers God wants to give. God loves when moms pray because prayer gives him an invitation to participate in someone's life. Invited, God shows up.

If people praying for you make a difference, then think about how your prayers for others can also make a difference. Pray for your children as they leave the house or as you drive them to school. Pray for them as you do their laundry. Pray for them when you see one of their pictures. Prayer sends help where you can't go. Don't underestimate the power God delivers when people pray.

A Song Just for You

The Lord your God is with you, he is mighty to save. He will take great delight in you, he will quiet you with his love, he will rejoice over you with singing. The sorrows for the appointed feasts I will remove from you; they are a burden and a reproach to you.

At that time I will deal with all who oppressed you; I will rescue the lame and gather those who have been scattered. I will give them praise and honor in every land where they were put to shame. At that time I will gather you; at that time I will bring you home.

Zephaniah 3:17–20 NIV

Zephaniah shared encouragement with the people of Judah who had continued to obey God. Even though they would have to endure a time of judgment because of others' disobedience, God didn't want them to lose hope that the good things he had promised would happen. The heartwarming predictions in this passage are a hopeful song that God offers to anyone who needs a reminder that times of difficulty don't have to predict the future.

Did you ever sing to calm a crying child? Your child cried as if nothing would ever be better again. You soothed with a gentleness your baby trusted. The tune didn't matter. Your pitch didn't matter. You sang your belief that something would be better.

God wants to renew your hope in the same way, with a song only he knows how to share. He sings the song of a new day over you. He sings the song of new possibility. He sings the song of unfailing love. He wants you to share his belief that good things will happen again. He makes promises that only he can keep. Let his song of promise give you new reasons for hope.

An Energy Boost

O God, You are my God; early will I seek You; my soul thirsts for You; my flesh longs for You in a dry and thirsty land where there is no water. . . .

Because Your lovingkindness is better than life, my lips shall praise You. Thus I will bless You while I live; I will lift up my hands in Your name. My soul shall be satisfied as with marrow and fatness, and my mouth shall praise You with joyful lips.

When I remember You on my bed, I meditate on You in the night watches. Because You have been my help, therefore in the shadow of Your wings I will rejoice. My soul follows close behind You; Your right hand upholds me.

Psalm 63:1, 3–8 NKJV

As a former shepherd, David knew about thirst in a hot, dry land. He compared this desire for water with how desperately he wanted God. The more he thought about God's love and availability, the more he knew that a relationship with God would satisfy his deepest longing and restore hope.

What is the first thing you long for in the morning? More sleep? A cup of coffee? An uninterrupted run? David wanted to experience God's love first thing. He knew that if he immersed himself in the love God offered him, he could confront the challenges of his day. In fact, this would give him more than enough reasons to thank God by the end of the day.

Every mom needs a jump start to her day; there's much to do and much that can make you feel incompetent or insecure. You need an energy source you can depend on. God offers to renew your hope, completely love you, and help you become the best mom he knows you can be. Start your day with an energy boost from God, and you'll be thanking him by the time your head hits your pillow.

On Guard

I will stand at my guard post. I will station myself on the wall. I will watch to see what he will say to me and what answer I will get to my complaint.

Then the LORD answered me, "Write the vision. Make it clear on tablets so that anyone can read it quickly. The vision will still happen at the appointed time. It hurries toward its goal. It won't be a lie. If it's delayed, wait for it. It will certainly happen. It won't be late.

"Look at the proud person. He is not right in himself. . . . He has a large appetite like the grave. He is like death—never satisfied. He gathers all the nations to himself. He collects all the people to himself."

Habakkuk 2:1–5 GOD'S WORD

Habakkuk asked why God didn't prevent bad things from happening. He was at the end of his hope as he contemplated the wickedness that went unpunished around him. With new resolve Habakkuk decided to wait until God answered him. God rewarded his perseverance with a peek into the future and new reasons for hope.

Do you have questions you wish God would answer? Do you wonder why diabetes made the genetic jump to your child? Or why your sister's child has autism? Or why one of your children struggles in school and another breezes by? When you tie your hope to an answer that doesn't come, hopelessness lurks nearby. Habakkuk learned a different model. He found out that asking questions didn't frustrate God. Then he discovered that faithful listening brought answers he could live with, even when they weren't the answers he expected.

God knows the answers that will make the biggest difference for you today. Whether they are about parenting or budgeting or future planning, he makes your questions his personal project. So take your sentry position. God wants to send you one of his answers. Are you listening?

DOUBLY BLESSED

When Job prayed for his friends, the LORD restored his fortunes. In fact, the LORD gave him twice as much as before! Then all his brothers, sisters, and former friends came and feasted with him in his home. And they consoled him and comforted him because of all the trials the LORD had brought against him. And each of them brought him a gift of money and a gold ring.

So the LORD blessed Job in the second half of his life even more than in the beginning. For now he had 14,000 sheep, 6,000 camels, 1,000 teams of oxen, and 1,000 female donkeys. He also gave Job seven more sons and three more daughters. He named his first daughter Jemimah, the second Keziah, and the third Keren-happuch. In all the land no women were as lovely.

Job 42:10–15 NLT

Job tells a powerful story of hope in God in spite of unimaginable loss. Even friends who came to comfort Job assumed that God had punished him for wrongdoing. But God had the last word. He doubled Job's resources. God demonstrated to everyone that Job knew where to place his hope—in God.

Was it coincidence that God doubled Job's resources after he began praying for his unhelpful friends? Probably not. Praying for anyone who has hurt us or made our lives more difficult creates an opening where love can work. When your heart holds more forgiveness than revenge, you can more easily recognize God's blessings to receive them.

Your role as a mother places you in a position where many people want to tell you what they think. Some of their advice helps. Some doesn't. Like Job, you need to pray for your unhelpful helpers. Pray that God treats them with as much mercy as you want him to have toward you. Then anchor your hope in God and his resources to help. He may not double your income, but he generously doubles his help.

HE PRAYS FOR YOU

There were many priests under the old system, for death prevented them from remaining in office. But because Jesus lives forever, his priesthood lasts forever. Therefore he is able, once and forever, to save those who come to God through him. He lives forever to intercede with God on their behalf.

He is the kind of high priest we need because he is holy and blameless, unstained by sin. He has been set apart from sinners and has been given the highest place of honor in heaven. Unlike those other high priests, he does not need to offer sacrifices every day. They did this for their own sins first and then for the sins of the people. But Jesus did this once for all when he offered himself as the sacrifice for the people's sins.

Hebrews 7:23–27 NLT

The Hebrew people (the Israelites) understood the role of priests in worship. God had established very specific requirements for the sacrifices and prayers that the priests offered to him on behalf of the people. The writer of the book of Hebrews wanted his readers to understand how Jesus performed every priestly function in a more lasting and complete way.

Did you catch the encouraging information that this passage offers you? Jesus prays for you! Long ago Jesus accepted his role as your advocate before God. Since he knows what it means to be human, he can represent your deepest needs in order to connect you to your best help—God.

If anyone needs an advocate, mothers do. We need someone to advocate for our children when our own emotional involvement skews our perspective. We need an advocate to articulate issues we don't have the words to speak. Jesus himself offers to be that advocate. Whatever prayer is on your heart, Jesus helps you focus that prayer toward God's will. He prays for God's best for you. Team up with Jesus on any prayer project; you won't find a better prayer partner.

ASK FOR ANYTHING

Later I will see you, and you will be so happy that no one will be able to change the way you feel. When that time comes, you won't have to ask me about anything. I tell you for certain that the Father will give you whatever you ask for in my name. You have not asked for anything in this way before, but now you must ask in my name. Then it will be given to you, so that you will be completely happy.

I have used examples to explain to you what I have been talking about. But the time will come when I will speak to you plainly about the Father and will no longer use examples like these. You will ask the Father in my name, and I won't have to ask him for you.

John 16:22–26 CEV

Jesus shared key summary lessons during his last days with his disciples. He wanted to teach his followers how to ask for what they needed after he was no longer with them face-to-face. Using the name of Jesus means to shape our requests to God's will. God always granted Jesus' request because his requests always matched God's will. God would do the same for the disciples—and for you.

Moms get a thousand or more questions in a day. A lot of the questions can be answered with a simple yes or no. Others require instructions or explanations. Whatever the issue, mothers want to give their children the best answers, wisdom, or boundaries they can. They answer yes to what is best.

God answers the same way. He already sent Jesus to let us know how much he wants to give us his best. When we pray in Jesus' name, we pray in ways that reflect Jesus' life and teaching, asking for what he would approve. When we pray for God's will, God answers us in the same way he answered Jesus' prayer for God's will; he says yes. Much hope exists when God says yes!

When a Progress Report Is Due

I have brought glory to you here on earth by doing everything you gave me to do. Now, Father, give me back the glory that I had with you before the world was created.

You have given me some followers from this world, and I have shown them what you are like. They were yours, but you gave them to me, and they have obeyed you. They know that you gave me everything I have. I told my followers what you told me, and they accepted it. They know that I came from you, and they believe that you are the one who sent me. I am praying for them, but not for those who belong to this world. My followers belong to you, and I am praying for them.

John 17:4–9 CEV

This honest and hope-filled exchange between Jesus and his Father, recorded by John, shows Jesus' passion for his disciples as well as how much he trusted God. At a time when Jesus knew that religious leaders plotted to kill him, he also knew that he had little time left with his disciples. Jesus needed the help and hope of his Father to keep him focused on his mission.

You have a big job too. God has given you the responsibility of teaching your children the most important lessons that will help them develop into responsible and healthy adults. On some days this seems next to impossible as you repeat the same lectures over and over. On other days you see progress. If Jesus couldn't fulfill his mission without regular conversations with God, do you really think you can? Take some time to make a progress report to God today. Tell him where you see good things happening in your children's lives and where you still need help. Thank him that he trusts you with these children. Then keep praying for them the way Jesus earnestly prayed for those he loved.

No More Tears

I heard a loud voice shout from the throne: God's home is now with his people. He will live with them, and they will be his own. Yes, God will make his home among his people. He will wipe all tears from their eyes, and there will be no more death, suffering, crying, or pain. These things of the past are gone forever.

Then the one sitting on the throne said: I am making everything new. Write down what I have said. My words are true and can be trusted. Everything is finished! I am Alpha and Omega, the beginning and the end. I will freely give water from the life-giving fountain to everyone who is thirsty. All who win the victory will be given these blessings. I will be their God, and they will be my people.

Revelation 21:3–7 CEV

John's revelation from God talks about a time when the world as we know it is finished and the world as God wants it begins in a brand-new way. God raises everyone's hope that whatever creates pain, suffering, and death will be over. No more tears, God says. This gives all who live by God's priorities new reasons to celebrate with hope.

Are there days when you wish that a no-tears shampoo would put a stop to other kinds of tears around your house? Are you tired of sibling-rivalry tears? Have you had enough of hurt-feelings tears? What about the I-don't-want-to tears? Sometimes you probably think you should buy stock in a tissue company because you use so many.

What about you? Do you need a no-tears hope of your own? Without warning, stress builds up and the dam breaks. To think about a world where there will be no reason for tears challenges the imagination. Do you realize that you can experience this hope by living God's priorities now? He makes something new every time you do. Then you will have new reasons to thank him.

WHEN YOU NEED A FRIEND

If it were I, I would appeal to God; I would lay my cause before him. He performs wonders that cannot be fathomed, miracles that cannot be counted. He bestows rain on the earth; he sends water upon the countryside. The lowly he sets on high, and those who mourn are lifted to safety. He thwarts the plans of the crafty, so that their hands achieve no success. He catches the wise in their craftiness, and the schemes of the wily are swept away. Darkness comes upon them in the daytime; at noon they grope as in the night. He saves the needy from the sword in their mouth; he saves them from the clutches of the powerful.

Job 5:8–15 NIV

Job's friend Eliphaz counseled Job to appeal his predicament before God. Eliphaz tried to use this eloquent, hope-filled summary of God's resourceful power to pressure Job into confessing what he had done wrong that caused his trouble. While Job believed that everything Eliphaz said about God was true, Job maintained his innocence before God.

Nothing fills a day with more hope than a review of God's creative power. Stand by a window on a stormy day and watch God's power at work. See how God made trees to take the fury of wind and rain without always incurring damage. Such an examination helps you submit yourself to God's authority and expect his help to make a difference no one else could make. When your mothering responsibilities place you in a storm, remember that the God who made this world for endurance knows how to help you survive too. When you feel at the mercy of someone's sharp words or insensitive actions, plead your case to your powerful God, who is ready to protect you. Don't try to make it alone. God wants to be the friend you can count on. Will you let him?

THE TRADE OF YOUR LIFE

Jesus said to his followers, "If people want to follow me, they must give up the things they want. They must be willing even to give up their lives to follow me. Those who want to save their lives will give up true life, and those who give up their lives for me will have true life. It is worthless to have the whole world if they lose their souls. They could never pay enough to buy back their souls. The Son of Man will come again with his Father's glory and with his angels. At that time, he will reward them for what they have done. I tell you the truth, some people standing here will see the Son of Man coming with his kingdom before they die."

Matthew 16:24–28 NCV

Tell a child to give up a toy in order to get something else and you're in for anything from a whine to a struggle. Even to receive what someone else says is better, children don't like giving up what they like. Jesus knew that children aren't the only ones reluctant to make this exchange, but he taught his followers to give up control of their lives and submit to his authority. He said that this kind of submission creates a quality of life that only God makes possible.

You gave up a lot to be a mother. You are always putting your child's needs over your wants. Most of the time you make this submission willingly, as the natural reflex of a mother. Even when you have to give up something you want, you say it is worth it.

Jesus doesn't ask you to give up everything without receiving something in return. He wants to share his best plans for you. But they materialize only when your life is under his control. If your best hope depended on Jesus' best plan, would you make the trade? Have you? If not, why not do it now?

POSITIONED FOR BLESSINGS

Jesus looked at them and said, "For people this is impossible, but for God all things are possible."

Peter said to Jesus, "Look, we have left everything and followed you. So what will we have?"

Jesus said to them, "I tell you the truth, when the age to come has arrived, the Son of Man will sit on his great throne. All of you who followed me will also sit on twelve thrones, judging the twelve tribes of Israel. And all those who have left houses, brothers, sisters, father, mother, children, or farms to follow me will get much more than they left, and they will have life forever. Many who are first now will be last in the future. And many who are last now will be first in the future."

Matthew 19:26–30 NCV

Jesus had just told a rich man he needed to give away his wealth in order to become his follower. This bothered Peter, because Jewish teachers taught that wealth was a sign of God's approval. Jesus encouraged Peter by sharing astounding news about a special place in heaven for the disciples. However, it would mean accepting a servant's last-place role now.

How many times have you refereed an argument about taking the first turn in a game or choosing the first dessert? Getting children, even older ones, to understand the importance of giving up first place takes a lot of persuasion. Something in all of us pushes us toward the front. Accepting last place as a way of life doesn't sound pleasant. However, Jesus said that last place positions us for God's blessings.

God needs a large army of last-place servants. He has a lot of people who need to be loved, helped, and encouraged. Mothers have a lot of experience as last-place servants. Let God enlarge the family you serve by showing you some of his children with needs. Then enjoy God's many blessings from your new last-place perspective.

You Don't Need a Number

Thank the LORD because he is good. His love continues forever. Let the people of Israel say, "His love continues forever." Let the family of Aaron say, "His love continues forever." Let those who respect the LORD say, "His love continues forever."

I was in trouble, so I called to the LORD. The LORD answered me and set me free. I will not be afraid, because the LORD is with me. People can't do anything to me. The LORD is with me to help me, so I will see my enemies defeated. It is better to trust the LORD than to trust people. It is better to trust the LORD than to trust princes.

Psalm 118:1–9 NCV

This praise psalm contains a victory song about God's forever love and goodness. The psalmist reminds us of the hopeful truth that trusting God makes more sense than trusting people with political or social power.

When you first became a mother, did you have any idea how hard mothering could be? Each stage of childhood has its challenges, from a baby's total dependence to an adolescent's frustrating push for independence. And the challenges don't stop with the teen years. Once a mother, always a mother. You probably have a whole shelf of books and several websites you regularly peruse to find help for each new issue. Wouldn't you like to know where the most reliable, up-to-date, perfectly matched help is available 24-7 in one place? God offers himself as that source of help for you. You can still get growth charts and home-organization tips from books and websites, but you will never find better counsel about discipline, character development, or moral boundaries. And do you know what the best news is? You never have to take a number. God remains always available for a free private consultation. Where else can you find help like that?

FAMILY MAKES A DIFFERENCE

This resurrection life you received from God is not a timid, grave-tending life. It's adventurously expectant, greeting God with a childlike "What's next, Papa?" God's Spirit touches our spirits and confirms who we really are. We know who he is, and we know who we are: Father and children. And we know we are going to get what's coming to us—an unbelievable inheritance! We go through exactly what Christ goes through. If we go through the hard times with him, then we're certainly going to go through the good times with him!

That's why I don't think there's any comparison between the present hard times and the coming good times. The created world itself can hardly wait for what's coming next. Everything in creation is being more or less held back.

Romans 8:15–20 MSG

Paul's letter to the Romans doesn't skimp on hope. With bold abandon, Paul announced how anticipation for our future with God empowers us to live well in the context we find ourselves.

Do your children wake you up on Saturdays wanting to go somewhere or do something special together? Sometimes coming up with an agenda that interests, excites, and doesn't cost much can be a challenge. The joy comes from the joint experience and not just the activity. God wants you to enjoy your place in his family just as much. God wants to treat us as family, with privileges that only family members can share. As children of God we become his heirs, to inherit what hardship or death cannot take away. He doesn't want you to wallow in yesterday's mistakes or borrow tomorrow's stress. Like excited children on a family outing, God wants us to enjoy unparalleled hope in a family relationship with him.

Where have you been living below the family privilege God offers? God desires that no one in his family suffer or celebrate alone. Take your family standing with God very seriously and keep asking, "What's next?"

HEALING AND RELEASE

"Certainly the day is coming! It will burn like a furnace. All arrogant people and evildoers will be like straw. . . .

"The Sun of Righteousness will rise with healing in his wings for you people who fear my name. You will go out and leap like calves let out of a stall. You will trample on wicked people, because on the day I act they will be ashes under the soles of your feet," says the LORD of Armies.

"Remember the teachings of my servant Moses, the rules and regulations that I gave to him at Horeb for all Israel.

"I'm going to send you the prophet Elijah before that very terrifying day of the LORD comes. He will change parents' attitudes toward their children and children's attitudes toward their parents."

Malachi 4:1–6 GOD'S WORD

Malachi lived during a difficult time of transition for the Jews. Some rebuilding had taken place after their exile but much still needed completion. Hopes dimmed as they compared their lives to former times. Malachi reminded them that living God's promise required faithfulness to his instructions. Malachi's message warned as well as encouraged, depending on how each responded to God's ways.

When you read this passage, did you put yourself into any of Malachi's word pictures? Leaping out of a cow stall probably doesn't conjure up the picture of grace and femininity you like to reflect, and trampling sounds more like an after-Christmas sale gone bad. But take another look at Malachi's intended message from these scenes. What does God want to bring? Release and healing. Does that sound like something moms need? Maybe it's release from the impossible expectations you hold for yourself. Maybe it's healing from the fear that you will never be a good-enough mom. Look for God to make a special appearance in your day as surely as the sun rises. Find new encouragement as you live the way he instructs. God has always been your best help and never-failing hope.

A BIG-PICTURE GOD

That night the secret was revealed to Daniel in a vision. Then Daniel praised the God of heaven. He said, "Praise the name of God forever and ever, for he has all wisdom and power. He controls the course of world events; he removes kings and sets up other kings. He gives wisdom to the wise and knowledge to the scholars. He reveals deep and mysterious things and knows what lies hidden in darkness, though he is surrounded by light. I thank and praise you, God of my ancestors, for you have given me wisdom and strength. You have told me what we asked of you and revealed to us what the king demanded."

Daniel 2:19–23 NLT

When King Nebuchadnezzar had a dream that no one in his court could interpret, Daniel, an exiled Jew living in Persia, interpreted its meaning. Daniel credited God for giving him interpretive ability and explained that only a big-picture God could accomplish such a revelation.

On most days, mothers don't think big-picture. By the nature of our multiple responsibilities, it is all we can do to keep focused on the day's schedule and be ready for it. However, big-picture thinking makes a critical contribution to keeping us pointed in the right direction for the right reasons.

Consider God's big-picture knowledge. He knows everything about everything. Nothing happens without his knowledge or understanding. In other words, God can handle the world today. Does that give you pause for relief? And if he can handle the whole world, he can also help you handle your little piece of it. Do you need extra wisdom to help your child have more self-confidence? Do you need him to show you some fear or motive your child won't talk about? Let God share with you his big-picture knowledge. You'll be singing God's praises just as Daniel did.

311

NEED SOME GOOD NEWS?

"This has happened so my people will know who I am, and so, on that future day, they will know that I am the one speaking to them. It will really be me."

How beautiful is the person who comes over the mountains to bring good news, who announces peace and brings good news, who announces salvation and says to Jerusalem, "Your God is King." . . .

They all will see with their own eyes when the LORD returns to Jerusalem. Jerusalem, your buildings are destroyed now, but shout and rejoice together, because the LORD has comforted his people. The LORD will show his holy power to all the nations. Then everyone on earth will see the salvation of our God.

Isaiah 52:6–10 NCV

In this prophetic passage, Isaiah told two reasons why the people of Israel had reason to hope. He predicted the return to their homeland after years of exile, but he also wrote of the day when God himself would return and bring with him a rule of peace the world had not known. Both messages celebrated God's good news.

What would be good news for you today? Free babysitting? A child who comes home from school happy? An all-expenses-paid vacation? Or maybe just a quiet night at home without a child's meltdown would be enough for you. What God wants to do for you today and in the future has front-page importance. God shares a quality of peace that doesn't come from a quiet house or napping children. His peace comes from a quieted heart. When you trust what God is doing for you *before* you see it arrive, you have the best kind of good news—hope. You know that your resourceful God continues to look for creative ways to bring good things into your life.

Do you need some good news today? God says good news is on the way.

Know Any New Songs?

God, I will sing a new song to you; I will play to you on the ten-stringed harp. You give victory to kings. You save your servant David from cruel swords. Save me, rescue me from these foreigners. They are liars; they are dishonest.

Let our sons in their youth grow like plants. Let our daughters be like the decorated stones in the Temple. Let our barns be filled with crops of all kinds. Let our sheep in the fields have thousands and tens of thousands of lambs. . . . Let no one break in. Let there be no war. . . Happy are those who are like this; happy are the people whose God is the LORD.

Psalm 144:9–15 NCV

David was a harpist, poet, lyricist, and composer. He wrote seventy-three of the psalms in the Bible. He composed his psalms, or songs, to tell how God delivered him from difficult people and predicaments and to summarize and praise the power and creativity of God. David never ran out of new songs because he sang about the God who never runs out of new ways to help.

Young children make up songs all the time. They don't have to know anything about music or rhythm to create them. They sing about toys and pets, stories and memories. They sing whether they have an audience or not. For them ordinary life becomes a good reason for a new song.

Do you need a new song for your day? Do you need a new way to put your life events together to recognize the melody God wants you to create? Look for the times where your mothering made a difference. When did you encourage a child to try again? When did unconditional love wrap you in your child's hug? When did you watch innocence sleep? Those are new songs for your day.

THE HUMBLE HERO

As holy people whom God has chosen and loved, be sympathetic, kind, humble, gentle, and patient. Put up with each other, and forgive each other if anyone has a complaint. Forgive as the Lord forgave you. Above all, be loving. This ties everything together perfectly. Also, let Christ's peace control you. God has called you into this peace by bringing you into one body. Be thankful. Let Christ's word with all its wisdom and richness live in you. Use psalms, hymns, and spiritual songs to teach and instruct yourselves about God's kindness. Sing to God in your hearts. Everything you say or do should be done in the name of the Lord Jesus, giving thanks to God the Father through him.

Wives, place yourselves under your husbands' authority. This is appropriate behavior for the Lord's people. Husbands, love your wives.

Colossians 3:12–19
GOD'S WORD

Family relationships do not always feel like a blessing, although we want them to be. Whether young children are arguing over whose turn it is or you're engaged in a much more serious disagreement with extended relatives, every family must learn to deal with conflict. In any group of people, especially if they're close, disagreements occur. The difference with family is that we can't just get away from the problems; we eventually have to face the family again.

All families have their challenges. Some are more serious than others, but all families have something in common—the need for forgiveness and reconciliation. Forgiveness always requires someone to take the first step. It is important to try to live in peace with everyone. If you are willing to let Christ's peace control what you say and do, you will be able to express love above all else. When you have the occasional (or frequent) disagreement, be the bigger person and extend an apology or forgiveness, even if it isn't deserved. After all, that is the example set for us by God himself. Family is worth the humility required to be at peace.

Bridge over Troubled Waters

In the past we thought of Christ as the world thinks, but we no longer think of him in that way. If anyone belongs to Christ, there is a new creation. The old things have gone; everything is made new! All this is from God. Through Christ, God made peace between us and himself, and God gave us the work of telling everyone about the peace we can have with him. God was in Christ, making peace between the world and himself. In Christ, God did not hold the world guilty of its sins. And he gave us this message of peace.

So we have been sent to speak for Christ. It is as if God is calling to you through us. We speak for Christ when we beg you to be at peace with God.

2 Corinthians 5:16–20 NCV

Suppose one of your children grows up with a rebellious streak. As the years go by, the rift between you widens. One day your child turns his back on you altogether, convinced he knows what's best and that you don't have a clue. That's exactly what God's children have done to him. Even if we haven't outwardly rebelled, inwardly we know how much we want things *our* way. But just like wayward children, as time goes by we realize we really don't know what's best. We can't seem to make life work out on our own.

That's where Jesus comes in. When the apostle Paul wrote to the church at Corinth, he used a word for *peace* that can also be translated "reconciliation." Jesus reconciles us with God, mending our broken relationship through the gift of his death on the cross. If you and your rebellious child reconciled, you'd want to tell everyone the good news. In the same way, knowing Jesus has set things right between you and God is something too wonderful to keep to yourself. One way to share God's peace is to share with others what God has done for you.

NIGHTY NIGHT, SLEEP TIGHT

Make things easier for me when I am in trouble. Have mercy on me and hear my prayer. . . .

You know that the LORD has chosen for himself those who are loyal to him. The LORD listens when I pray to him. When you are angry, do not sin. Think about these things quietly as you go to bed. Do what is right as a sacrifice to the LORD and trust the LORD.

Many people ask, "Who will give us anything good?" LORD, be kind to us. But you have made me very happy, happier than they are, even with all their grain and new wine. I go to bed and sleep in peace, because, LORD, only you keep me safe.

Psalm 4:1, 3–8 NCV

What mom hasn't wished for a peaceful night's sleep? Motherhood invites predawn feedings, quieting bad dreams, and soothing a sick child in the middle of the night. But there are some nocturnal events in your control—such as choosing where you will bed down your mind for the night.

Right before you fall asleep, it's easy to replay the day's events on the movie screen of your mind. Unfortunately anger, trouble, and discontent seem to demand the most screen time. In this psalm, David offers some wise words on this matter: disagreements need to be resolved, not left to fester. Nursing a grudge is the same as nursing an infant—it helps it grow. But how is it possible to be angry and yet not sin?

When God's children disobey, he doesn't sit and stew about it. He gives clear direction on how to make things right, freely offers forgiveness, and leaves the incident in the past once it's resolved. Tonight, attend to anything that's upset you during the day. Then choose to rest your mind on the good things God has brought your way. That's the secret to sleeping in heavenly peace.

Stop and Think about It

Many are saying of my soul, "There is no deliverance for him in God." *Selah*.

But You, O Lord, are a shield about me, my glory, and the One who lifts my head. I was crying to the Lord with my voice, and He answered me from His holy mountain. *Selah*.

I lay down and slept; I awoke, for the Lord sustains me. I will not be afraid of ten thousands of people who have set themselves against me round about.

Arise, O Lord; save me, O my God! For You have smitten all my enemies on the cheek; You have shattered the teeth of the wicked. Salvation belongs to the Lord; Your blessing be upon Your people! *Selah*.

Psalm 3:2–8 NASB

Psalm 3 contains a lot of firsts. It's the first prayer in the psalms. It's the first psalm attributed to David. And it's the first psalm to use the word *selah*. *Selah* gave musical direction to those who performed the psalms as songs. However, its meaning is still under debate. Bible scholars believe it means either "to pause and reflect" or "to lift up and praise loudly." David does both in this psalm.

Like you, David was a parent. When he wrote this psalm, he was fleeing from his son Absalom, who'd stolen his throne. David's kingdom was divided, his life was in danger, and his relationship with his son seemed beyond repair. In the midst of this chaos, David still slept peacefully and awoke praising God. David may have been forced from his throne, but he knew God was still on his.

Like David, why not begin your morning by sharing with your heavenly Father any fears or worries you have? Pause to reflect on how God has come through for you in the past. Thank God for who he is and what he's done. Then move forward with a peaceful, confident heart.

Power for the Impossible

You rule the oceans. You subdue their storm-tossed waves. . . . The heavens are yours, and the earth is yours; everything in the world is yours—you created it all. . . . Powerful is your arm! Strong is your hand! Your right hand is lifted high in glorious strength. Righteousness and justice are the foundation of your throne. Unfailing love and truth walk before you as attendants. Happy are those who hear the joyful call to worship, for they will walk in the light of your presence, LORD. They rejoice all day long in your wonderful reputation. They exult in your righteousness.

You are their glorious strength. It pleases you to make us strong.

Psalm 89:9, 11, 13–17 NLT

Little kids believe mom can do the impossible. She's an all-powerful superhero, able to fix any toy that breaks or heal any scrape with a kiss. You know the truth—a mother's power is limited. But that doesn't mean you're powerless. God, the only One who truly can do anything and everything, enjoys making you strong.

God is almighty. That means his power has no limits. It takes that kind of power to rule the sea or to create the universe and everything in it. The thought of limitless power can be frightening to consider, but God is loving and faithful as well as powerful. If this were not true, there would be nothing to keep him from wielding his power in chaotic, unpredictable ways.

We have the peace of knowing that love is behind everything our all-powerful God does. You have a direct connection to that love and power. You have God's Spirit living inside you, helping you be the mom your kids need. When you feel you don't have the strength to handle what you know you need to do, call on God. He's the only parent who truly can do the impossible.

CHAIN REACTION

Since we have been made right with God by our faith, we have peace with God. This happened through our Lord Jesus Christ, who through our faith has brought us into that blessing of God's grace that we now enjoy. And we are happy because of the hope we have of sharing God's glory. We also have joy with our troubles, because we know that these troubles produce patience. And patience produces character, and character produces hope. And this hope will never disappoint us, because God has poured out his love to fill our hearts. He gave us his love through the Holy Spirit, whom God has given to us.

When we were unable to help ourselves, at the right time, Christ died for us, although we were living against God.

Romans 5:1–6 NCV

Babies are helpless without someone to care for them. They cannot fix themselves something to eat, change their own diapers, or open the door to come in from the rain. That's how helpless we are trying to make peace with God on our own. No matter how sorry we are or how many good deeds we do to try to make things right, reconciliation with God remains out of our reach—without Jesus' help.

Finding peace with God through Jesus is what the book of Romans is all about. But with this peace we receive much more. One gift we receive is the ability to find joy in the midst of trouble. Trouble is often referred to as tribulation in the Bible. *Tribulation* comes from the Latin word *tribulum*, the name of a Roman farming tool. This heavy piece of metal-spiked lumber was pulled over grain to separate the wheat from the chaff. In the same way, God uses hard things in our lives to help us sift out what is useful. As we persevere, we uncover treasures like patience, character, and hope. Thanks to Jesus, we're no longer helpless, but hopeful and filled with peace.

PLEASINGLY PEACEFUL LIVES

God called us to be holy and does not want us to live in sin. So the person who refuses to obey this teaching is disobeying God, not simply a human teaching. And God is the One who gives us his Holy Spirit.

We do not need to write you about having love for your Christian family, because God has already taught you to love each other. And truly you do love the Christians in all of Macedonia. Brothers and sisters, now we encourage you to love them even more.

Do all you can to live a peaceful life. Take care of your own business, and do your own work as we have already told you. If you do, then people who are not believers will respect you, and you will not have to depend on others for what you need.

1 Thessalonians 4:7–12 NCV

Living a peaceful life doesn't necessarily mean you live in a peaceful household. Any home where children live is bound to be loud, messy, busy, and bursting with energy at times. When the Bible talks about a peaceful life, picture the eye of a storm instead of the stacks of a library.

Three things that can help us find this place of peace—even when winds of chaos howl all around us—are leaning, loving, and diligence.

In his letters to the Thessalonians, Paul encouraged God's people to come together as a family. Drawing close to your own church family can help you the way it helped Paul's original readers. When God's people lean on one another for support, encouragement, and prayer, we put love into action. We also learn how to forgive and resolve conflict, which is as beneficial in a church family as it is in our own homes.

As for diligence, it helps you accomplish what needs to be done. Consistently fulfilling the responsibilities God has entrusted to you will help life feel less chaotic. By leaning, loving, and working diligently you can live peacefully, regardless of what's going on around you.

Choose to Love Life

"Whoever would love life and see good days must keep his tongue from evil and his lips from deceitful speech. He must turn from evil and do good; he must seek peace and pursue it. For the eyes of the Lord are on the righteous and his ears are attentive to their prayer, but the face of the Lord is against those who do evil."

Who is going to harm you if you are eager to do good? But even if you should suffer for what is right, you are blessed. "Do not fear what they fear; do not be frightened." But in your hearts set apart Christ as Lord. Always be prepared to give an answer to everyone who asks you to give the reason for the hope that you have.

1 Peter 3:10–15 NIV

Loving life is a choice, especially when the "good days" you're experiencing aren't easy ones. Maybe you were up all night with a newborn. Perhaps you canceled highly anticipated plans after picking your sick child up from school. The apostle Peter was not a mother, but he certainly faced his fair share of tough "good days." Bible scholars believe Peter wrote this letter from Rome, where he would eventually be martyred for his faith. Yet Peter talks about loving life, pursuing peace, and banishing fear.

In this passage, Peter uses the words of King David and the prophet Isaiah, as well as his own. David wrote the first section, quoted from the Psalms, while running for his life from his enemies. The second quote is Isaiah's warning to King Ahaz not to form alliances with his enemies out of fear but to trust wholeheartedly in God.

Peter's timeless message applies to mothers, kings, prophets, and apostles: Don't let fear prevent you from loving life or pursuing peace. Look to God first, do what you know is right, and watch fear flee from your life. Just don't be surprised when others ask, "How'd you do that?"

Puzzle Peace

I urge you who have been chosen by God to live up to the life to which God called you. Always be humble, gentle, and patient, accepting each other in love. You are joined together with peace through the Spirit, so make every effort to continue together in this way. There is one body and one Spirit, and God called you to have one hope. There is one Lord, one faith, and one baptism. There is one God and Father of everything. He rules everything and is everywhere and is in everything.

Christ gave each one of us the special gift of grace, showing how generous he is. That is why it says in the Scriptures, "When he went up to the heights, he led a parade of captives, and he gave gifts to people."

Ephesians 4:1–8 NCV

Keeping peace within your family takes work. Personalities clash. The lines of communication get tangled. Adults as well as kids can get cranky, act selfishly, and speak thoughtlessly.

What's true within your nuclear family is also true within your spiritual family. Like your own children, God's children are all individuals. This means they won't always see eye to eye. When the apostle Paul wrote to the church of Ephesus, he explained that God's Spirit joins God's children together with peace. Though this bond of peace is God's gift to us, keeping that peace is an act of will.

Working together as a spiritual family is a little like putting together a jigsaw puzzle. No two pieces are alike, but all are designed to fit together to form a single image. Different personalities, experiences, and God-given gifts shape each unique piece. Trying to cram a piece into a spot it wasn't designed to fit is an exercise in frustration, but with patience and gentleness diverse individuals discover where they fit and how they can work peacefully with one another. By the power of God's Spirit, unity without uniformity reveals a marvelous portrait of love in action.

HEADS UP, SHEEP!

The LORD is my shepherd. I am never in need. He makes me lie down in green pastures. He leads me beside peaceful waters. He renews my soul. He guides me along the paths of righteousness for the sake of his name. Even though I walk through the dark valley of death, because you are with me, I fear no harm. Your rod and your staff give me courage.

You prepare a banquet for me while my enemies watch. You anoint my head with oil. My cup overflows.

Certainly, goodness and mercy will stay close to me all the days of my life, and I will remain in the LORD's house for days without end.

Psalm 23:1–6 GOD'S WORD

It's a harried mom's dream come true—being led to a quiet meadow beside a bubbling stream and then encouraged to lie down and rest. God will provide these moments of peace, but for God to be our Shepherd, we need to be attentive sheep. That means we need to listen for the Shepherd's voice and follow where he leads.

You'll notice in this psalm that God not only leads his sheep to peaceful waters but through dark valleys. When hard times come, don't set up camp and stay there. Draw close to God. Listen and follow. Keep moving forward, persevering through fear, confusion, sorrow, or pain. The journey might be difficult and you might find yourself moving slowly—but you never travel alone. God is right there, protecting you, comforting you, and guiding you out of the dark valley toward a banquet table full of blessings.

Regardless of where you are right now—beside the stream or in the valley—you can trust that God is near. Stop and listen for his voice throughout the day. Allow him to lead. Draw close like a sheep, keeping the Shepherd in sight.

WHO'S ON FIRST?

We who are strong in faith should help the weak with their weaknesses, and not please only ourselves. Let each of us please our neighbors for their good, to help them be stronger in faith. Even Christ did not live to please himself. It was as the Scriptures said: "When people insult you, it hurts me." Everything that was written in the past was written to teach us. The Scriptures give us patience and encouragement so that we can have hope. May the patience and encouragement that come from God allow you to live in harmony with each other the way Christ Jesus wants. Then you will all be joined together, and you will give glory to God the Father of our Lord Jesus Christ. Christ accepted you, so you should accept each other, which will bring glory to God.

Romans 15:1–7 NCV

Share. Play nice. Watch out for your younger sister. These wise words have been repeated by moms since the dawn of time. What's good advice for kids on the playground is also sound counsel for moms building godly relationships—or for the church of Rome in the first century.

We've all felt that urge to push toward the head of the line, to do things our way, to nab the biggest piece of cake, to hang out exclusively with friends of our choosing. But what sounds like a surefire way to secure personal satisfaction is actually selfish and divisive, and Jesus showed us a better way through his words and example—how to stop acting like toddlers and start living like good neighbors. Jesus lived a you-first life in a me-first world. So can we. If we act on what we read in the Bible, accept one another just as God has accepted us, reach out to help those who are struggling with their faith, and pray for the wisdom and patience we need to truly love those around us, God will transform our hearts and our communities. We'll help promote peace wherever we are.

A Peaceful Harvest

Remember this saying, "A few seeds make a small harvest, but a lot of seeds make a big harvest."

Each of you must make up your own mind about how much to give. . . . God can bless you with everything you need, and you will always have more than enough to do all kinds of good things for others. The Scriptures say, "God freely gives his gifts to the poor, and always does right."

God gives seed to farmers and provides everyone with food. He will increase what you have, so that you can give even more to those in need. You will be blessed in every way, and you will be able to keep on being generous.

2 Corinthians 9:6–11 CEV

If you help your kids plant a garden, one lesson they'll learn is that the more seeds they plant, the more fruits and vegetables they'll have to harvest. The Bible uses this same principle to illustrate that the more generous we are, the more generous God is with us. However, it can feel risky to give of your time and resources, especially during the mom stage when your schedule is often filled to capacity and your bank account never seems to be. Doing what God asks is what faith is all about. The more you risk doing the right thing, the more you'll experience firsthand how faithful God is to his promises—and the more you'll feel at peace about trusting God to supply what you need financially, physically, and spiritually.

God's generosity to you is part of his cycle of giving. The more you give, the more you receive, and the more you then have to give. Just don't be surprised if you find your kids following your example. A generous parent fosters generous children. Just look at how God is nurturing a more generous heart in you.

Consolation Gift

I'm telling you these things while I'm still living with you. The Friend, the Holy Spirit whom the Father will send at my request, will make everything plain to you. He will remind you of all the things I have told you. I'm leaving you well and whole. That's my parting gift to you. Peace. I don't leave you the way you're used to being left—feeling abandoned, bereft. So don't be upset. Don't be distraught.

You've heard me tell you, "I'm going away, and I'm coming back." If you loved me, you would be glad that I'm on my way to the Father because the Father is the goal and purpose of my life.

I've told you this ahead of time, before it happens, so that when it does happen, the confirmation will deepen your belief in me.

John 14:25–29 MSG

Picture dropping your kids off at summer camp for the very first time. You've explained there are good things ahead, adventures they wouldn't experience if they never left home. You've assured them there's a counselor nearby who will guide and care for them. You've promised you'll be back to pick them up—and that your love for them won't ever change, whether you're physically with them or not. Now, put yourself in their shoes. How do you feel?

When Jesus told his disciples he was going away, he knew worry would set in. So Jesus left his beloved friends with a priceless parting gift—peace. Jesus offers this gift to us as well. This kind of peace isn't a promise for a problem-free life; it's an assurance that no matter what happens, you can rest in God's sovereignty and love.

Like at camp, you also have a Counselor who guides and cares for you. *Counselor* is one of the names the Bible uses to describe God's Spirit. This Counselor promotes peace by reminding us of God's promises. When worry strikes, be still, and rest in the Counselor's reminder that God is in control.

Hold On to Hope

The time will come when I will heal Jerusalem's wounds and give it prosperity and true peace. I will restore the fortunes of Judah and Israel and rebuild their towns. I will cleanse them of their sins against me and forgive all their sins of rebellion. Then this city will bring me joy, glory, and honor before all the nations of the earth! The people of the world will see all the good I do for my people, and they will tremble with awe at the peace and prosperity I provide for them.

This is what the Lord says: You have said, "This is a desolate land where people and animals have all disappeared." Yet in the empty streets of Jerusalem and Judah's other towns, there will be heard once more the sounds of joy and laughter.

Jeremiah 33:6–11 NLT

Peace was a distant memory during the time of the prophet Jeremiah. God's people, including their priests and kings, had turned their backs on God and worshipped idols. They fought among themselves and adopted the customs of foreign faiths. Through the prophets, God warned his people what would happen if they didn't follow him, but they refused to listen. So God sent his people into exile to live as captives in the land of Babylon.

Yet God remained a loving parent. He set limits for his children, grieved when they breached those limits, and continued to offer forgiveness to those who rebelled against him. God also promised his people that one day their homeland and the city of Jerusalem would be fully restored to places of peace.

If your own home feels far from peaceful right now, don't give up hope. God has the power to restore your family just as surely as the city of Jerusalem. But you're part of that restoration plan. Daily share your struggles with him, asking for wisdom and strength. Be consistent in setting limits. Then give your children the same opportunity God gives us—the chance to start again, fully forgiven.

Peace of Your Mind

Open the gates that the righteous nation may enter, the nation that keeps faith. You will keep in perfect peace him whose mind is steadfast, because he trusts in you. Trust in the Lord forever, for the Lord, the Lord, is the Rock eternal. He humbles those who dwell on high, he lays the lofty city low; he levels it to the ground and casts it down to the dust. . . .

The path of the righteous is level; O upright One, you make the way of the righteous smooth. Yes, Lord, walking in the way of your laws, we wait for you; your name and renown are the desire of our hearts.

Isaiah 26:2–5, 7–8 NIV

In the Old Testament the Hebrew word for *peace* is *shalom*, a common Jewish greeting for centuries. Bidding someone shalom is more than wishing that person a peaceful life—it's a prayer for wholeness, health, and security.

This passage from the prophet Isaiah teaches that setting your mind on God and then doing what you know is right are two things that nurture shalom in your life. When you feel at odds during the day as a mom, if disciplining a child leaves you feeling inadequate or you find yourself overwhelmed at how little protection you can really offer your children in this world, refocus your thoughts on God. Cling to the power of his promises. Rest in the fact that he fulfills each one. Recall how you've seen God come through in the past. God's own steadfastness toward you and your children will help steady your own mind and emotions.

But don't stop there. Walk the path of the righteous—do what you know is right. Worry, regret, and fear will fall by the wayside. Life can't help but feel more peaceful. A home filled with shalom blesses God and those who live there.

328

SIDE BY SIDE

Jesus declared, "I thank you, Father, Lord of heaven and earth, that you have hidden these things from the wise and understanding and revealed them to little children; yes, Father, for such was your gracious will. All things have been handed over to me by my Father, and no one knows the Son except the Father, and no one knows the Father except the Son and anyone to whom the Son chooses to reveal him. Come to me, all who labor and are heavy laden, and I will give you rest. Take my yoke upon you, and learn from me, for I am gentle and lowly in heart, and you will find rest for your souls. For my yoke is easy, and my burden is light."

Matthew 11:25–30 ESV

Do it myself!" These words are familiar in the realm of motherhood, but it's not only children who utter them. Some moms try to live out this sentiment in their own lives. They do all the household chores themselves in an attempt to keep their children happy or maintain their own impossibly high standards. They help friends in need but never let friends know when they need help. They wake up too early and work too late. They feel guilty allowing themselves a time-out. They believe the words *rest* and *peace* should apply only at the end of life.

Jesus spoke of a better way. In New Testament times, yokes were designed to fit on the shoulders of a pair of oxen. The animals walked side by side, working together to pull heavy farm equipment across a field. In the same way, Jesus wants to walk beside you, to help you carry whatever is weighing you down. When Jesus speaks of his yoke being *easy*, that literally means "well-fitting." The work of motherhood God has chosen for you will fit you well if you allow him to help you carry the load.

PUT ON YOUR PARTY CLOTHES

Weeping may tarry for the night, but joy comes with the morning. . . .

To you, O LORD, I cry, and to the Lord I plead for mercy: "What profit is there in my death, if I go down to the pit? Will the dust praise you? Will it tell of your faithfulness? Hear, O LORD, and be merciful to me! O LORD, be my helper!"

You have turned for me my mourning into dancing; you have loosed my sackcloth and clothed me with gladness, that my glory may sing your praise and not be silent. O LORD my God, I will give thanks to you forever!

Psalm 30:5, 8–12 ESV

What do your clothes say about you? In the Bible a change of clothes often signifies an important change in someone's life. People worthy of great honor were given a new robe. Changing into clean clothes was required before entering the temple. Donning dark, rough sackcloth made from goat's hair signaled that a person was in mourning.

In this psalm, David rejoices over how God changed his clothes *and* his heart. God transformed David's time of sorrow into a time of rejoicing. This change was so significant that it was as different to David as night and day.

If you feel as though sackcloth would be appropriate attire for what you're currently facing, hold on to hope and peace. Thanks to God, change is in the air. In the same way that a baby brings pain to its mother during the labor necessary for its birth and then great joy when it enters the world, God can—and will—transform your pain and sorrows into celebration. As you get dressed each morning, use that time as a reminder—a change of clothes, and heart, is coming. It's simply a matter of time, perseverance, perspective, and prayer.

A PEBBLE FOR YOUR THOUGHTS

[Jesus said,] "Is not life more than food, and the body more than clothing? Look at the birds of the air, that they do not sow, nor reap nor gather into barns, and yet your heavenly Father feeds them. Are you not worth much more than they? And who of you by being worried can add a single hour to his life? And why are you worried about clothing?

"Observe how the lilies of the field grow; they do not toil nor do they spin, yet I say to you that not even Solomon in all his glory clothed himself like one of these. But if God so clothes the grass of the field, which is alive today and tomorrow is thrown into the furnace, will He not much more clothe you? You of little faith!"

Matthew 6:25–30 NASB

Worry, like a pebble dropped into a still pond, creates far-reaching ripples that disturb the peace of everything around it. Are there any pebbles you're nervously letting fall? Perhaps you're worried about how your children are doing in school. Anxious over the weight you haven't lost since the birth of your child. Concerned about layoffs at work. Even something as insignificant as being stressed about what to make for dinner can rob you of the peace God offers in this life.

That's because worry doesn't take God into account. Instead of trusting in God's love and power, worry clings to the hope that good luck, hard work, or a big enough bank account will meet all of your needs.

Only God has the power to provide what you need when you need it. Worry doesn't have the power to do anything—other than stress you out and disturb your peace. In this passage Jesus reminds us that his Father is both powerful and loving. God cares for his creation, from the tiniest wildflower to the busiest mom. So don't let pebbles of worry unsettle your mind. Place each one in your Father's capable hands.

NEITHER STIRRED NOR SHAKEN

Be careful and do not refuse to listen when God speaks. Others refused to listen to him when he warned them on earth, and they did not escape. So it will be worse for us if we refuse to listen to God who warns us from heaven. When he spoke before, his voice shook the earth, but now he has promised, "Once again I will shake not only the earth but also the heavens." The words "once again" clearly show us that everything that was made—things that can be shaken—will be destroyed. Only the things that cannot be shaken will remain.

So let us be thankful, because we have a kingdom that cannot be shaken. We should worship God in a way that pleases him with respect and fear, because our God is like a fire that burns things up.

Hebrews 12:25–29 NCV

Earthquakes, tornadoes, tsunamis . . . Raising children in a world of so many disasters can heighten feelings of anxiety. How can we find peace in the midst of potential chaos? By holding on to what cannot be shaken.

Our almighty God deserves awe. Awe carries with it an element of fear. That's because we recognize we are in the presence of something stronger and greater than ourselves. In the Old Testament the sound of God speaking to Moses was powerful enough to shake Mount Sinai. In the book of Haggai, which is quoted in this passage, the author refers to another time the earth will shake—when Jesus returns to take God's children with him to heaven.

At that time this earth will come to an end. But the story of God's children will not. Regardless of whether this event happens in our lifetime, our children's lifetime, or many centuries from now, we need not fear. Earthquakes, tornadoes, tsunamis—even the end of the world—cannot change our destiny. Our future is secure in God's promise of eternal life. Don't be frightened or distracted by disasters. Remember, God is as loving as he is powerful.

SAFE PLACE TO HIDE

I will say to the LORD, "You are my place of safety and protection. You are my God and I trust you."

God will save you from hidden traps and from deadly diseases. He will cover you with his feathers, and under his wings you can hide. His truth will be your shield and protection. . . . You will not be afraid of diseases that come in the dark or sickness that strikes at noon. . . .

The LORD is your protection; you have made God Most High your place of safety. . . . He has put his angels in charge of you to watch over you wherever you go.

Psalm 91:2–4, 6, 9, 11 NCV

When your children play hide-and-seek, it's all in good fun. But when you're frightened, when you long for protection and a renewed sense of peace, you're not playing around. Neither is God.

When the Bible talks about finding shelter beneath the protection of God's wings, it's referring to a very specific hiding place called the mercy seat. This seat was the lid of the ark of the covenant, a gold-covered acacia-wood chest where God's presence dwelled in Old Testament times. Above the seat two large golden angels stood facing each other, their wingtips touching.

Today, God's presence surrounds us no matter where we are. Thanks to Jesus, we no longer need a priest to make sacrifices for us to gain mercy from God. Jesus' sacrifice on the cross secured God's mercy once and for all. But God still invites you to curl up in the shelter of his protection and power. When fears for your own safety or that of your children threaten your peace of mind, don't wing it on your own. Trust in God. Draw close to your loving Father in prayer. Clinging to God's truth offers both peace and protection.

STRESSED TO IMPRESS

Walk into the fields and look at the wildflowers. They don't fuss with their appearance—but have you ever seen color and design quite like it? The ten best-dressed men and women in the country look shabby alongside them. If God gives such attention to the wildflowers, most of them never even seen, don't you think he'll attend to you, take pride in you, do his best for you?

What I'm trying to do here is get you to relax, not be so preoccupied with *getting* so you can respond to God's *giving*. People who don't know God and the way he works fuss over these things, but you know both God and how he works. Steep yourself in God-reality, God-initiative, God-provisions. You'll find all your everyday human concerns will be met. Don't be afraid of missing out.

Luke 12:27–32 MSG

Moms love to brag about their kids. How cute they are! How smart they are! What amazing things they've accomplished! Being proud of your kids isn't wrong. But if you find yourself working hard to keep up appearances—to make sure your kids have just the right clothes, education, and opportunities so they'll succeed in life—it's time to stop and smell the flowers. Better yet, instead of simply smelling them, try learning from them.

Flowers don't stress. They simply do what they were created to do: grow, provide pollen, and look pretty. God takes care of the soil, the rain, and the bees flowers need to thrive. God also cares for you and your family. When you focus on God and how good he has been to you instead of focusing on what you and your children do or do not have, you find your perspective changes. You go from feeling stressed to feeling blessed.

As you freely talk to God about your concerns, he'll help you sort your wants from your needs. Then keep your eyes and heart open as you watch for the amazing ways he provides what truly matters.

What's in a Name?

I will ask the Father, and He will give you another Helper, that He may be with you forever; that is the Spirit of truth, whom the world cannot receive, because it does not see Him or know Him, but you know Him because He abides with you and will be in you.

I will not leave you as orphans; I will come to you. After a little while the world will no longer see Me, but you will see Me; because I live, you will live also. In that day you will know that I am in My Father, and you in Me, and I in you. He who has My commandments and keeps them is the one who loves Me; and he who loves Me will be loved by My Father, and I will love him and will disclose Myself to him.

John 14:16–21 NASB

A mother is a priceless gift. You help your children accomplish what's too difficult for them to handle on their own. You console them when they're hurting or frightened. You teach them right from wrong. You provide for their needs.

In many ways, the Holy Spirit mothers each of us. When Jesus rose from the dead and returned to heaven, he was absent from his disciples physically. But Jesus promised he wouldn't abandon his followers, leaving them orphans. The Greek word for *orphan* used in this passage means "comfortless." That word certainly describes a motherless child. But to comfort someone means more than just to soothe or console. It literally means "to impart strength."

The Holy Spirit has many names throughout the Bible. Comforter and Helper are two of the most common. In the Old Testament, God's Spirit stayed with people for a season, until they filled a specific task or role on God's behalf. But thanks to Jesus' sacrifice, the Comforter now remains with God's children straight through to eternity. No matter what you face today, God's Spirit within you will provide the peace and strength you need to do whatever needs to be done.

Sticks and Stones

You have tested my heart; You have visited by night; You have tried me and found nothing [evil]; I have determined that my mouth will not sin. Concerning what people do: by the word of Your lips I have avoided the ways of the violent. My steps are on Your paths; my feet have not slipped.

I call on You, God, because You will answer me; listen closely to me; hear what I say. Display the wonders of Your faithful love. . . . Guard me as the apple of Your eye; hide me in the shadow of Your wings from the wicked who treat me violently, my deadly enemies who surround me.

Psalm 17:3–9 HCSB

David wrote this prayer during a turbulent season in his life. King Saul, who at one time had been a friend and a role model, wanted David dead. Frustrated by God's continued protection and favor of David, Saul tried to verbally assassinate his rival by spreading lies about David's character.

Situations like this don't happen just in the Bible. Undoubtedly you've experienced times in life when people said things about you or your children that weren't true. Whether jealousy, misinformation, neighborhood gossip, or genuine malice spawned the lies doesn't matter. You know the truth. And so does God. You can't always quiet a rumor. But God can quiet your heart in the face of false accusations as you simply continue to do what you know is right.

The next time you're struggling under the shadow of a wrong impression, ask God to reveal any truth that may be hiding there. If there's anything you need to make right, do so. Cling to the truth of what God says about you. Pray for the strength to forgive your accuser. Then continue to walk the path God has set before you, regardless of what others say.

Controlling Factor

Speak to the earth, and it will teach you, or let the fish of the sea tell you. Every one of these knows that the hand of the LORD has done this. The life of every creature and the breath of all people are in God's hand. The ear tests words as the tongue tastes food. Older people are wise, and long life brings understanding.

But only God has wisdom and power, good advice and understanding. What he tears down cannot be rebuilt; anyone he puts in prison cannot be let out. If God holds back the waters, there is no rain; if he lets the waters go, they flood the land. He is strong and victorious; both the one who fools others and the one who is fooled belong to him.

Job 12:8–16 NCV

Job had good reason for distress. Invaders carried off his livestock. Fire burned his sheep and servants to death. Next, a hurricane leveled his home, killing all of his children. Then Job's skin broke out with festering sores, leaving him in constant pain. Instead of comforting him, Job's so-called friends then proceeded to accuse this righteous man of hidden sin.

But Job wouldn't back down. He rebutted his accusers, reminding them that all of creation is under God's control. What God says goes, even if we don't understand the whys and wherefores.

Job's lesson is difficult to take to heart. It's reassuring to know that when bad things happen, we're not being punished for some unknown sins in our lives. Still, we're left to ponder how a loving God can allow the things we treasure most to be taken away—financial security, health, even the life of a child. We wish we could control God, but we're also fully aware of what fickle, fallible gods we'd make. Like Job, only by drawing closer to God can we learn to trust him, even though he'll always be too big for us to fully understand.

Influence & Love

Have you ever watched your children play follow the leader? How about Simon says? Most children want to be in charge of these games, deciding who gets to be "it" and often wanting that for themselves. Somehow, though, fear often sets in as we get older. Following becomes more comfortable than leading. But it's important to engage your power of influence to help others around you make better decisions.

The most powerful influence is always love. The ultimate romance is with the One who first loved you—God. Love is simply action with someone else's best interest as the goal. A bride delights in telling and showing her new groom how much she loves him by her words and deeds, and he responds. Whether you are a newlywed, a single mom, or a grandmother, romance is in the air—God sought you because of his great love.

We love because he first loved us.

1 John 4:19 NIV

THE POWER OF INFLUENCE

We belong to the day, so we should control ourselves. We should wear faith and love to protect us, and the hope of salvation should be our helmet. God did not choose us to suffer his anger but to have salvation through our Lord Jesus Christ. Jesus died for us so that we can live together with him, whether we are alive or dead when he comes. So encourage each other and give each other strength, just as you are doing now.

Now, brothers and sisters, we ask you to appreciate those who work hard among you, who lead you in the Lord and teach you. Respect them with a very special love because of the work they do.

Live in peace with each other. We ask you, brothers and sisters, to warn those who do not work. Encourage the people who are afraid. Help those who are weak. Be patient with everyone.

1 Thessalonians 5:8–14 NCV

Paul instructed the Thessalonian Christians as a parent counsels children. His influence followed his reputation as someone committed to helping others adopt Jesus' way of living. Paul was an influential teacher because he lived what he taught.

Influence is power, according to a dictionary definition. Influence wields subtle authority to effect change. However, influence without integrity can become manipulation. All mothers have influence. The important questions are, What kind of influence do you have? And what will you do with it?

Your influence has the possibility to shape your children and their future. The scary truth about influence is that you can't turn it on and off at convenient times. Children are always watching. They catch as many not-so-good things you do as good things. What can you do about that? Own your imperfections and inconsistencies but don't ever use them as excuses. Model what to do when your attitude is less than kind or helpful. Your influence will increase in proportion to the way you learn and grow. Live what you teach before you teach it. Then watch for the power of influence to do its best work.

PLEASING GOD, NOT PEOPLE

We speak the Good News because God tested us and trusted us to do it. When we speak, we are not trying to please people, but God, who tests our hearts. You know that we never tried to influence you by saying nice things about you. We were not trying to get your money; we had no selfishness to hide from you. God knows that this is true. We were not looking for human praise, from you or anyone else, even though as apostles of Christ we could have used our authority over you.

But we were very gentle with you, like a mother caring for her little children. Because we loved you, we were happy to share not only God's Good News with you, but even our own lives. You had become so dear to us!

1 Thessalonians 2:4–8 NCV

Philosophers traveled throughout the Roman Empire hoping to collect crowds of followers. The number of followers affected the philosophers' reputation. Because of this, some philosophers catered to what the people wanted to hear to increase the money in their pockets. Paul didn't follow this practice. He wanted only to please God.

People pleasers have a hard life because no two people want the same thing! And when you give to another person what that person wants but not what you want to give, you prevent authenticity in the relationship. You trade your identity to make someone else happy. People pleasers have little influence because their lives have little to no consistency.

As a committed mother, you want to please your children. That's why you fix their favorite foods and take them to their favorite places. However, if you make their happiness your number one goal, you might be in danger of giving them what they want over what they need. Paul says to please God first. Ask God what your children need and how to provide it. Don't compromise your influence by overpleasing. Please God and learn how his requirements protect your true identity and empowering influence.

A Kind Influence

Boaz said, "The Lord bless you, my daughter. This act of kindness is greater than the kindness you showed to Naomi in the beginning. You didn't look for a young man to marry, either rich or poor. Now, my daughter, don't be afraid. I will do everything you ask, because all the people in our town know you are a good woman. It is true that I am a relative who is to take care of you, but you have a closer relative than I. Stay here tonight, and in the morning we will see if he will take care of you. If he decides to take care of you, that is fine. But if he refuses, I will take care of you myself, as surely as the Lord lives. So stay here until morning."

Ruth 3:10–13 NCV

Ruth, a Moabite widow, chose to move to Bethlehem, the hometown of her mother-in-law, Naomi. Boaz, a relative of Naomi, owned a field where he allowed Ruth to gather leftover grain. When Boaz noticed Ruth's uncommon kindness to her mother-in-law, that prompted kindness from Boaz, and a beautiful love story began to unfold.

Kindness is contagious. One kind act often encourages many others. Unfortunately, the reverse is also true. Selfishness encourages more selfishness. What mother doesn't want to help her children practice kindness? Yet children are not born to be kind. Their "me-Me-ME" grows in volume and consequences without deliberate influence from you. So what encourages children to adopt kind attitudes and actions? Sometimes a gentle prompt helps. Or you can suggest kind actions and let your children choose one. You can adopt a family project to be kind to someone and talk about the results. Affirm kindness when children initiate it.

Commit to model kindness. Speak difficult warnings and discipline in a kind, respectful way so that children always hear the love in your voice. When you make kindness a family standard, you will enjoy watching its ripples enlarge.

SEASONED WORDS

Continue earnestly in prayer, being vigilant in it with thanksgiving; meanwhile praying also for us, that God would open to us a door for the word, to speak the mystery of Christ, for which I am also in chains, that I may make it manifest, as I ought to speak. Walk in wisdom toward those who are outside, redeeming the time.

Let your speech always be with grace, seasoned with salt, that you may know how you ought to answer each one.

Colossians 4:2–6 NKJV

Paul was imprisoned in Rome when he wrote this letter to the Colossians. His confinement gave him plenty of opportunities to understand how much help prayer could be. It also heightened his perspective about the importance of using opportunities to share truth about Jesus in a way that others would receive the message.

While it's a fact that what we say doesn't influence as much as what we do, what we say still matters. *How* we say things matters even more. Whom would you rather listen to—the one who criticizes your work with a lecture about what you should have done or someone who affirms your desire to learn and shares instruction to help you? Affirmation plus instruction goes a lot farther than criticism. You don't have to change the message your children need to hear, just the way you deliver it.

Did you know that it takes seven positive words to cancel the impact of one negative word? That places a big responsibility on moms as we instruct, discipline, remind, and discuss. Season your words with love, respect, encouragement, and affirmation. Besides keeping you proactive, your seasoned speech will accomplish more.

NEVER STOP PRAYING

Since the day we heard about you, we have not stopped praying for you and asking God to fill you with the knowledge of his will through all spiritual wisdom and understanding. And we pray this in order that you may live a life worthy of the Lord and may please him in every way: bearing fruit in every good work, growing in the knowledge of God, being strengthened with all power according to his glorious might so that you may have great endurance and patience, and joyfully giving thanks to the Father, who has qualified you to share in the inheritance of the saints in the kingdom of light. For he has rescued us from the dominion of darkness and brought us into the kingdom of the Son he loves, in whom we have redemption, the forgiveness of sins.

Colossians 1:9–14 NIV

Epaphras, a member of the Colossian church, gave Paul a good report about how the people were doing. This positive news encouraged Paul to share how he had been praying for them. Paul wanted the Colossians to continue to develop every God-pleasing characteristic that would increase their influence in a world that desperately needed it.

How do you pray for your children? Do you slip into crisis prayers that have more to do with circumstances than character building? Consider a different approach. Use Paul's summary about how he wanted God to mature the Colossians. Pray that your children grow a stronger desire for God's wisdom. Pray that they learn why living to please God protects them from a lot of unnecessary consequences. Pray for their endurance when they confront peer pressure to conform in destructive ways. Then tell your children what you are praying and why! Often the difference your prayers make begins when a child knows you are praying. Model prayer as a connection to God's wisdom your children can access whether you are with them or not. Make prayer your first offense and your best defense. Never stop praying.

THE BEST IMITATION

Imitate God, therefore, in everything you do, because you are his dear children. Live a life filled with love, following the example of Christ. He loved us and offered himself as a sacrifice for us, a pleasing aroma to God.

Let there be no sexual immorality, impurity, or greed among you. Such sins have no place among God's people. Obscene stories, foolish talk, and coarse jokes—these are not for you. Instead, let there be thankfulness to God. . . .

Don't be fooled by those who try to excuse these sins, for the anger of God will fall on all who disobey him. Don't participate in the things these people do. For once you were full of darkness, but now you have light from the Lord. So live as people of light!

Ephesians 5:1–4, 6–8 NLT

In Paul's day Ephesus was the fourth largest city in the Roman Empire, a religious center for the Asian province with the great temple of Artemis located there. Paul spent three years with the church in Ephesus on his third missionary tour. He earned the right to lovingly remind these believers that they could not adopt ungodly behavior *and* reflect the model of Jesus.

Children are great imitators. They imitate sounds and words and expressions, often to the great embarrassment of their parents. Since this seems to be a natural ability, why not give them a great model to copy? Help them imitate God. Lift up God's model of love, relationship, and morality. Help your children establish a relationship with the God who loves them so they can understand the wisdom of his boundaries. Love empowers what rules cannot. Of course *you* have to imitate God too. You are his best advertisement.

Children are going to face pressure to conform to attitudes and behavior that do not reflect God's character. You won't always be there to caution them. But God can. Teach them to depend on his guidance. They will never find anyone better to imitate.

AN IMPORTANT MATH LESSON

Do not add to what I command you and do not subtract from it, but keep the commands of the LORD your God that I give you.

You saw with your own eyes what the LORD did at Baal Peor. The LORD your God destroyed from among you everyone who followed the Baal of Peor, but all of you who held fast to the LORD your God are still alive today.

See, I have taught you decrees and laws as the LORD my God commanded me, so that you may follow them in the land you are entering to take possession of it. Observe them carefully, for this will show your wisdom and understanding to the nations, who will hear about all these decrees and say, "Surely this great nation is a wise and understanding people."

Deuteronomy 4:2–6 NIV

Events at Baal Peor before the Israelites entered the Promised Land demonstrated the disastrous results of adding to or subtracting from God's instructions. Thousands died after repeated actions of sexual immorality, adultery, and sacrificing to foreign gods. Moses used the memory of this horrible time to remind the people about the importance of living God's instructions exactly as he gave them.

God desires obedience from us not because he wants to be an authoritative controller but because he gives only instructions that will protect us and give us the best possible life. Adding or subtracting to what God says weakens what God wants his instructions to do in our lives. Have you ever added too much water to soup or left out a key ingredient? Changing the recipe changes the end result every time. If your children make lunch without cleaning up their mess as you told them to, do you still call that obedience? Probably not. Careful obedience reproduces the instructions as given. Help your children understand the value of obedience—to you as well as to God. Never ask more from them than God would but never ask less from them either.

Enough Strength to Say No

The things that happened to those people . . . were written down to teach us, because we live in a time when all these things of the past have reached their goal. If you think you are strong, you should be careful not to fall. The only temptation that has come to you is that which everyone has. But you can trust God, who will not permit you to be tempted more than you can stand. But when you are tempted, he will also give you a way to escape so that you will be able to stand it.

So, my dear friends, run away from the worship of idols. I am speaking to you as to reasonable people; judge for yourselves what I say. We give thanks for the cup of blessing . . . [and] the bread that we break.

1 Corinthians 10:11–16 NCV

Paul spent a year and a half with the Corinthians. After moving on, he received a report that they had returned to lifestyle practices that did not reflect who Jesus was. Paul used this first letter to share pastoral guidance in a way that would help them overcome temptation and choose obedience.

Temptation shows up when we least expect it, making us feel weaker than we really are. That's the bad news. The good news is that God also shows up to provide a way through the temptation. The dilemma every mother faces is how to get her children to choose the good news.

If another child tries to entice your child to watch something or try something that you would never condone, how will your child respond? Rules might build a protective fence, but they don't make it electric. The decision to say no has to be your child's choice, but the strength to make it comes from God. Teach your children to ask for and receive God's help. Encourage them to learn many ways to say no to temptations and yes to God. Then you can influence many more good choices.

To Tell the Truth

If I had not come and spoken to them, they would not be guilty of sin. Now, however, they have no excuse for their sin. He who hates me hates my Father as well. If I had not done among them what no one else did, they would not be guilty of sin. But now they have seen these miracles, and yet they have hated both me and my Father. But this is to fulfill what is written in their Law: "They hated me without reason."

When the Counselor comes, whom I will send to you from the Father, the Spirit of truth who goes out from the Father, he will testify about me. And you also must testify, for you have been with me from the beginning.

John 15:22–27 NIV

In Jesus' last teaching time before his death and resurrection, he shared with his disciples that he would send help when he was separated from them. The word Jesus used for *Counselor* is the word that means "someone to come alongside to help." This Counselor would share the complete essence of Jesus in a way that memory could not. The Holy Spirit would always bring the truth.

You usually know when your children are not telling the truth. Eye contact suffers. The children squirm in total discomfort. You can tell that someone knows the truth but will not tell it.

The helper Jesus promised comes alongside of us to tell us the truth, without delay or mistake. No person or perspective holds truth like God's Spirit of truth. We need that truth to discern the source of behavior problems in our children. We need that truth to examine our own motives when responding to relationship issues. This truth goes beyond our best idea or collected facts. This is truth that influences for the good of everyone.

What situation confuses you with too many perspectives? Welcome the Spirit of truth as your best helper today.

Make Music Together

I always thank my God for you and for the gracious gifts he has given you, now that you belong to Christ Jesus. Through him, God has enriched your church in every way—with all of your eloquent words and all of your knowledge. This confirms that what I told you about Christ is true. Now you have every spiritual gift you need as you eagerly wait for the return of our Lord Jesus Christ. He will keep you strong to the end so that you will be free from all blame on the day when our Lord Jesus Christ returns. God will do this, for he is faithful to do what he says, and he has invited you into partnership with his Son, Jesus Christ our Lord.

I appeal to you . . . to live in harmony with each other.

1 Corinthians 1:4–10 NLT

The church at Corinth began to reflect the surrounding immoral city more than the exemplary life of Jesus. Paul wrote the church to address the ways their disobedience affected their unity. Without heavy-handed scolding, Paul affirmed their good traits and called them to use their differences to create harmony.

For moms who deal with sibling rivalry every day, unity may sound like a faraway goal. Strong wills clash often. Me-first egos trample others. Car rides become war zones. Harmony may sound like a good goal, but you wonder if your family will ever be able to make good music together.

God understands your plight because he continues to bring his broken-apart family together to teach us what unity looks like. He wants us to remember that harmony depends on using differences in pleasing ways. God applauds differences. He created each person with a unique personality and unique abilities. Differences don't have to divide; they can make a family stronger as you learn to make use of each person's strength to benefit the family. Let God help you influence harmony. Make unity a more important goal than unison.

A Change of Heart

Paul called out in a loud voice, "Don't harm yourself, because all of us are here!"

Then the jailer called for lights, rushed in, and fell down trembling before Paul and Silas. Then he escorted them out and said, "Sirs, what must I do to be saved?"

So they said, "Believe on the Lord Jesus, and you will be saved—you and your household." Then they spoke the message of the Lord to him along with everyone in his house. He took them the same hour of the night and washed their wounds. Right away he and all his family were baptized. He brought them up into his house, set a meal before them, and rejoiced because he had believed God with his entire household.

When daylight came, the chief magistrates sent the police to say, "Release those men!"

Acts 16:28–35 HCSB

From where he stood, the jailer couldn't see into the dark prison cell. But from inside, where the prisoners were, his silhouette was framed clearly in the dimly lit doorway. Holding his dagger to his chest, thinking everyone had escaped when the earthquake rattled the doors off their hinges, he reasoned that he would be better off dead than caught sleeping on the job.

The striking irony of this story is that although Paul suffered severe abuse at times, his compassionate concern for the prison guard led to an immediate reversal in the man's calloused heart, resulting in a radical act of obedience and mercy.

As a mother, you have frequent opportunities to influence the heart of your child, particularly when your child has shown disrespect or inconsiderate behavior. Not by sweeping the unacceptable behavior under the rug and acting as if it didn't happen—notice Paul told the jailer and his family the truth they needed to hear—but by modeling with genuine compassion the character you want your child to develop.

Obedience that finds its inspiration in the heart is much more effective than that which comes by force.

FOCUS AND FORMATION

We tell the truth before God, and all who are honest know this.

If the Good News we preach is hidden behind a veil, it is hidden only from people who are perishing. Satan, who is the god of this world, has blinded the minds of those who don't believe. They are unable to see the glorious light of the Good News. They don't understand this message about the glory of Christ, who is the exact likeness of God.

You see, we don't go around preaching about ourselves. We preach that Jesus Christ is Lord, and we ourselves are your servants for Jesus' sake. For God, who said, "Let there be light in the darkness," has made this light shine in our hearts so we could know the glory of God that is seen in the face of Jesus Christ.

2 Corinthians 4:2–6 NLT

This passage gives us a glimpse into a profound mystery far beyond our imagination or experience. What is it, and what does it have to do with being a mom?

In the original creation humankind was remarkably like God—a glorious race, living in a face-to-face relationship with the Creator. That all changed when Satan enticed Adam and Eve into rebellion against God. Humanity lost touch not only with who God is but who we were supposed to be. The situation worsened with time until Jesus came—a fresh specimen of humanity—like the very first human, radiant in the image of God. He came to restore our vision. By looking at Jesus in the Gospels, we are able to "see" God again.

The "hiddenness" of God confronts everyone and can have disastrous results. We mothers have daily opportunities to influence our children's impressions of God, not by calling attention to ourselves but by consistently reflecting on and demonstrating the unique characteristics of Jesus in our own lives—particularly in the way we treat people, love people, and serve people . . . all people . . . of every sort . . . and everywhere.

Wisdom Is Power

The Spirit will make you wise and let you understand what it means to know God. My prayer is that light will flood your hearts and that you will understand the hope that was given to you when God chose you. Then you will discover the glorious blessings that will be yours together with all of God's people.

I want you to know about the great and mighty power that God has for us followers. It is the same wonderful power he used when he raised Christ from death and let him sit at his right side in heaven. There Christ rules over all forces, authorities, powers, and rulers. He rules over all beings in this world and will rule in the future world as well. God has put all things under the power of Christ, and . . . made him the head of everything.

Ephesians 1:17–22 CEV

This passage from Paul's letter to the church at Ephesus makes a very bold promise: we are not on our own! For mothers these are comforting words. It means we are not left to depend upon our own wisdom or to operate on our own power.

But where does a mother access the wisdom that comes from the Spirit? Wisdom is derived by considering the self-disclosure God has provided in the Bible. With God in view we can contemplate our role as parents from his "parental" perspective.

And how do you tap into the "mighty power" about which Paul speaks when you are feeling weak and frustrated? As we become aware of Jesus' authority—an authority derived from his devoted love for God and for all humanity—we begin to grasp the power that God has delegated to us. It is the power to put his wisdom to good use.

With an enlightened understanding we have the power to influence our children's understanding of the world and their place in it. Teaching our children to love God and to love like God will make them wise and powerful both now and in the future.

Content or Contentious?

God is working in you to make you willing and able to obey him.

Do everything without grumbling or arguing. Then you will be the pure and innocent children of God. You live among people who are crooked and evil, but you must not do anything that they can say is wrong. Try to shine as lights among the people of this world, as you hold firmly to the message that gives life. Then on the day when Christ returns, I can take pride in you. I can also know that my work and efforts were not useless. Your faith in the Lord and your service are like a sacrifice offered to him. And my own blood may have to be poured out with the sacrifice. If this happens, I will be glad and rejoice with you.

Philippians 2:13–17 CEV

A child's earliest habits and behaviors are mere imitations of what he has observed in his parents. As a mother, your attitude toward life is the grid through which your child develops his perspective and disposition. Perhaps it is one of the reasons that Paul advised his readers in this important passage to be aware of their tendency to grumble and argue when things don't go their way. It isn't an effective response to life's trials; therefore, it isn't a good example either.

Paul acknowledged that his readers were surrounded by people opposed to God. That's enough to cause any believer to feel contentious and out of sorts much of the time. Yet Paul says that we have been called to stand against the status quo and do just the opposite—instead of grumbling and arguing, be content and cooperative. This is particularly important for mothers because we have more inconveniences and stresses to deal with than anyone. We also have more influence.

Choosing the higher ground is a powerful alternative by which your children will learn authentic joy, the meaning of community, and a deep sense of responsibility—character traits from which leaders are forged.

THE JOURNEY TO WISDOM

My father taught me, . . . "Get wisdom; develop good judgment. Don't forget my words or turn away from them. Don't turn your back on wisdom, for she will protect you. Love her, and she will guard you. Getting wisdom is the wisest thing you can do! And whatever else you do, develop good judgment. If you prize wisdom, she will make you great. Embrace her, and she will honor you. She will place a lovely wreath on your head; she will present you with a beautiful crown."

My child, listen to me and do as I say, and you will have a long, good life. I will teach you wisdom's ways and lead you in straight paths. When you walk, you won't be held back; when you run, you won't stumble.

Proverbs 4:4–12 NLT

If you're typical, you probably feel that you often come up short on wisdom. You might also assume that the older your children get, the more wisdom will be required. Intrigued by the first words of this proverb, you might be wondering, "Where do I go to get this wisdom and understanding?"

When we pray for wisdom, we typically are praying for an answer to some kind of trial or decision we face. The peculiar truth revealed here is that wisdom doesn't come as an all-inclusive, one-time resource. For the key to accessing wisdom, look at the very end of the passage. Wisdom is the destination of an entire journey . . . a journey with God throughout life.

The wisdom and understanding you need to effectively parent your children is available to you if you seek it where it can be found . . . in God. This will require of you a deeper level of persistence and commitment than you might have experienced and possibly a complete readjustment of your values. But be encouraged by the last words of the passage—though the pace will seem slow at first, you'll be sprinting in no time!

Obedience as Influence

The glory of the Lord appeared to them, and the Lord spoke to Moses, saying, "Take the staff, and assemble the congregation, you and Aaron your brother, and tell the rock before their eyes to yield its water." . . .

Then Moses and Aaron gathered the assembly together before the rock, and he said to them, "Hear now, you rebels: shall we bring water for you out of this rock?" And Moses lifted up his hand and struck the rock with his staff twice, and water came out abundantly, and the congregation drank, and their livestock. And the Lord said to Moses and Aaron, "Because you did not believe in me, to uphold me as holy in the eyes of the people of Israel, therefore you shall not bring this assembly into the land that I have given them."

Numbers 20:6–8, 10–12 ESV

Frustrated, you ask yourself, "How are my children ever going to learn obedience?" This critical passage holds forth an answer.

Moses had been selected by God to deliver Israel—a nation of slaves—out from under the tyranny of Egypt, to lead the newly liberated people through a vast wilderness, and finally to take them victoriously into the land God had promised them.

With this new beginning, it was important that Moses teach the Israelites who their new king was and with what kind of government he would reign. Moses was a living illustration of what their relationship to God should look like. His respect for God's authority, his submission to God's will, and his obedience to God's commands demonstrated to the people of Israel how to live and thrive in their newfound freedom.

On this one occasion—a very important occasion—Moses stumbled in front of the whole nation: instead of telling the rock to surrender the bountiful spring gushing beneath its surface, he lashed out in anger. Striking the rock, he broke the heart of his God.

Your child will be influenced to obey you by witnessing your obedience to God.

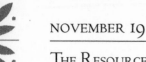

THE RESOURCEFULNESS OF GOD

"For some time now," [Abner] told them, "you have wanted to make David your king. Now is the time! For the LORD has said, 'I have chosen David to save my people Israel from the hands of the Philistines and from all their other enemies.'" Abner also spoke with the men of Benjamin. Then he went to Hebron to tell David that all the people of Israel and Benjamin had agreed to support him.

When Abner and twenty of his men came to Hebron, David entertained them with a great feast. Then Abner said to David, "Let me go and call an assembly of all Israel to support my lord the king. They will make a covenant with you to make you their king, and you will rule over everything your heart desires."

2 Samuel 3:17–21 NLT

Only one of the twelve tribes of Israel recognized that David was God's anointed king now that Saul had been killed in battle. The other eleven tribes—the overwhelming majority—believed that Saul's son Ishbosheth was heir to the throne. A civil war broke out in Israel over who would be king.

Abner was a relative and commander in chief of David's rival, his right-hand man and his trusted adviser. Ironically, Abner was the very man God used—eventually—to influence the remaining eleven tribes to accept David as king, restoring peace to Israel. Abner's loyalties turned toward David because of a misunderstanding between Abner and Ishbosheth. Abner exclaimed, "What the Lord has sworn to David, I will accomplish for him, to transfer the kingdom from the house of Saul, and set up the throne of David."

As strange as it may seem, you can take great comfort in knowing that God is so resourceful and powerful he can turn a threatening situation into a source of good influence over his people. As a mother, be confident that if you are seeking God's will for your children's lives, God has the resources to support you.

Tough Mothering

This is how the LORD responds:

"If you return to me, I will restore you so you can continue to serve me. If you speak good words rather than worthless ones, you will be my spokesman. You must influence them; do not let them influence you! They will fight against you like an attacking army, but I will make you as secure as a fortified wall of bronze. They will not conquer you, for I am with you to protect and rescue you. I, the LORD, have spoken! Yes, I will certainly keep you safe from these wicked men. I will rescue you from their cruel hands."

Jeremiah 15:19–21 NLT

In faithfulness to God and to Israel, Jeremiah often had to speak words of warning that the people didn't want to hear. As a result, he was perceived as a traitor.

Does that sound familiar? Mothers often find themselves in similar straits. Trying to do what is best for your child, you speak words that upset your child. The next thing you know, you receive a barrage of accusations: "You just don't understand me!" "You're mean!" This passage is critical to a mother's survival in times like these.

God counseled Jeremiah to resist the temptation to collapse into self-pity—a passive form of rebellion—and trust that God would sustain him in his role. God then cautioned Jeremiah not to let the people influence his thinking but to keep speaking words of truth and wise counsel: "You must influence them; do not let them influence you!"

Finally, God warned Jeremiah that the situation could get worse before it got better. He encouraged Jeremiah to persevere and promised him that the outcome would be rewarding. Take God's words of counsel to heart as a mother. Your child will thank you . . . some day.

THE INFLUENCE OF INTERPRETATION

His parents said this because they were afraid of the elders, who had already decided that anyone who said Jesus was the Christ would be avoided. That is why his parents said, "He is old enough. Ask him."

So for the second time, they called the man who had been blind. They said, "You should give God the glory by telling the truth. We know that this man is a sinner."

He answered, "I don't know if he is a sinner. One thing I do know: I was blind, and now I see."

They asked, "What did he do to you? How did he make you see again?"

He answered, "I already told you, and you didn't listen. Why do you want to hear it again? Do you want to become his followers, too?"

John 9:22–27 NCV

Why was healing a blind man such a crime? God's laws stated that it was wrong to work on the Sabbath, but the laws didn't include the long list of things that the Jewish religious leaders claimed constituted work. Spitting on the ground, for example, was outlawed on the Sabbath by these leaders because saliva and dirt make mud, which can be used as mortar, which could produce work. Jesus had done that very thing, and as a result a man was healed!

You might ask, "Why didn't Jesus heal the blind man some other way, instead of upsetting the powers that be?" The leaders of Israel had reduced God's law—designed to enhance Israel's freedom—to a long, petty list of prohibited activities, which kept the people in bondage. By defying their misinterpretation of God's law, Jesus influenced many Israelites to reconsider God's intent and readjust their faith.

Mothers have the difficult job of interpreting the commands of God and the laws of the land to their children. The greatest challenge you face is conveying what is behind civil law—concern for community—as well as what is behind biblical commands—God's compassionate heart.

WORDS AS WITNESS

Anyone who speaks against the Son of Man can be forgiven, but anyone who speaks against the Holy Spirit will never be forgiven, either in this world or in the world to come.

A tree is identified by its fruit. If a tree is good, its fruit will be good. If a tree is bad, its fruit will be bad. You brood of snakes! How could evil men like you speak what is good and right? For whatever is in your heart determines what you say.

A good person produces good things from the treasury of a good heart, and an evil person produces evil things from the treasury of an evil heart. And I tell you this, you must give an account on judgment day for every idle word you speak. The words you say will either acquit you or condemn you.

Matthew 12:32–37 NLT

One of the most sobering things about being a mother is the sheer volume of your words. Throughout the formative years of your child's development, your words carry more influence than anyone else's. Is it any wonder, then, that Jesus said we'll give an account for all the empty words we speak?

It sounds as if there is some kind of word-ledger kept for review at the end of one's life. More likely, our effectiveness or ineffectiveness will go on record in terms of actual results. It isn't our words but their effect on our children's attitudes and actions that tells the story, and character development is the measure.

Notice that the tree in Jesus' illustration isn't stripped of its bark and then dissected and inspected. The tree is examined by the fruit that it bears. Fruit is an extension of the tree but not the tree itself. Furthermore, the fruit is the part that benefits the rest of creation. It's a source of health, nutrition, and pleasure, not to mention that it is the casing in which the seed for propagation is hidden.

A mother's words need to be timely, wise, tasteful, and life-giving.

ADVOCATING MERCY

You are a chosen people, a royal priesthood, a holy nation, a people belonging to God, that you may declare the praises of him who called you out of darkness into his wonderful light. Once you were not a people, but now you are the people of God; once you had not received mercy, but now you have received mercy.

Dear friends, I urge you, as aliens and strangers in the world, to abstain from sinful desires, which war against your soul. Live such good lives among the pagans that, though they accuse you of doing wrong, they may see your good deeds and glorify God on the day he visits us.

Submit yourselves for the Lord's sake to every authority instituted among men: whether to the king, as the supreme authority, or to governors.

1 Peter 2:9–14 NIV

In this intriguing passage, Peter has drawn together some intense symbolism from within the ancient faith of the Israelites and given it meaning within the contemporary society of the early church and for us today.

First, he claimed that those who had received the mercy of God were now considered set apart from the status quo. On the issue of giving versus receiving, remember that the mercy, or undeserved forgiveness, that God is willing to give is not always received. His lavish generosity isn't welcomed by all. Being receptive is commendable.

Second, being set apart from the status quo doesn't imply an elitist community, particularly when we consider that we have been chosen to turn around and extend mercy as advocates for the sake of others. That is what a priest does.

You have been chosen to receive God's mercy and to be the merciful mother of children. You're set apart for the task. Your responsibility is to "live such a good life" that your children will recognize that God has motivated and empowered you to be who you are. In this way, you positively influence your children's impressions of who God is.

PARENT, NOT POLITICIAN

The mother of James and John, the sons of Zebedee, came to Jesus with her sons. She knelt respectfully to ask a favor. "What is your request?" he asked.

She replied, "In your Kingdom, please let my two sons sit in places of honor next to you, one on your right and the other on your left."

But Jesus answered by saying to them, "You don't know what you are asking! Are you able to drink from the bitter cup of suffering I am about to drink?"

"Oh yes," they replied, "we are able!"

Jesus told them, "You will indeed drink from my bitter cup. But I have no right to say who will sit on my right or my left. My Father has prepared those places for the ones he has chosen."

Matthew 20:20–23 NLT

Are you surprised that James and John had such ambitious aspirations? However noble someone's motivation is, at least a grain of personal gain lies within any move toward power. What really might surprise us is that the mother of these two was willing to represent their ambitions, attempting to leverage her influence for their sake. If you haven't faced this temptation as a mother already, be prepared that you probably will. It might be at cheerleading tryouts or the youth league baseball draft; it could be your motivation to run for PTO president or to sign up as a room mother.

The teaching in the passage pivots on Jesus' response. Peculiarly, he didn't answer the mother of James and John. He spoke directly to the men, holding them accountable for the request and its implications. Jesus' implied message to their mother was very clear: "Don't try to run interference and hope to gain an unfair advantage for your sons. That will not accomplish the will of God." It might even put their integrity at risk.

Your children need a mother for a parent—a wise, loving, and fully committed nurturer—not a politician.

THE INFLUENCE OF IDENTITY

How great is the love the Father has lavished on us, that we should be called children of God! And that is what we are! The reason the world does not know us is that it did not know him. Dear friends, now we are children of God, and what we will be has not yet been made known. But we know that when he appears, we shall be like him, for we shall see him as he is. Everyone who has this hope in him purifies himself, just as he is pure.

Everyone who sins breaks the law; in fact, sin is lawlessness. But you know that he appeared so that he might take away our sins. And in him is no sin. No one who lives in him keeps on sinning.

1 John 3:1–6 NIV

In an outburst of gratitude, John exclaimed with wonder that we are not merely called the children of God but are in reality God's cherished family. The problem is, those who refuse to become part of the family of God do not understand why we are who we are—or why we do what we do, creating the potential for conflict.

It is critical that mothers teach their children the contrast between being a child of God and not being one. A child's identity is forged by his relational bearings as well as by the influence of his role models. Being in relationship with God provides mothers a handle with which to explain why our children are to live above compromise with our culture.

For instance, in dealing with the issue of gossip, you might counsel your child: "The reason we don't say harmful words is because our God is a loving God who doesn't hurt people with his words. As his children we follow his example, causing us to become more like him. One day we'll get to see him face-to-face, and he'll rejoice at how much like him we've become."

INFLUENCE IN ADVERSITY

They told the officials, "These Jews are upsetting our city! They are telling us to do things we Romans are not allowed to do."

The crowd joined in the attack on Paul and Silas. Then the officials tore the clothes off the two men and ordered them to be beaten with a whip. After they had been badly beaten, they were put in jail, and the jailer was told to guard them carefully. The jailer did as he was told. He put them deep inside the jail and chained their feet to heavy blocks of wood.

About midnight Paul and Silas were praying and singing praises to God, while the other prisoners listened. Suddenly a strong earthquake shook the jail to its foundations. The doors opened, and the chains fell from all the prisoners.

Acts 16:20–26 CEV

What did Paul tell the Romans to do that was against their law? He told them to confess Jesus as King of kings. Roman citizens believed that Caesar was lord—that Roman government would always prevail.

For a mother, the importance of this story pivots on the influence Paul and Silas had on their fellow prisoners. Remarkably, the prisoners didn't run away when their chains fell off. They recognized that the One to whom Paul and Silas had been praying and singing was a power greater than Caesar. What had gripped their attention, initially, was that Paul and Silas were not negatively affected by the flogging or imprisonment to begin with. Their devotion to Jesus in the midst of severe trial was a powerful witness to the unbelievers.

What will your children do when confronted with the question, Who is really my master? Will they understand that Jesus has more authority than those who try to convince them that they should compromise their beliefs, their values, or their dignity? Their answer could depend on how they saw their mom handle adversity. The God of your trials will likely become the God of theirs.

IMPRESSIONS OF THE HEART

Hear, O Israel, and be careful to obey so that it may go well with you and that you may increase greatly in a land flowing with milk and honey, just as the LORD, the God of your fathers, promised you.

Hear, O Israel: The LORD our God, the LORD is one. Love the LORD your God with all your heart and with all your soul and with all your strength. These commandments that I give you today are to be upon your hearts. Impress them on your children. Talk about them when you sit at home and when you walk along the road, when you lie down and when you get up. Tie them as symbols on your hands and bind them on your foreheads. Write them on the doorframes of your houses and on your gates.

Deuteronomy 6:3–9 NIV

According to Moses, God's instructions for living were never meant to be a rigid piece of legislation by which his people were hemmed in and kept under restraint. Instead, God's law represented a wise way of being in the world, grounded in genuine love and promoting authentic compassion. It was a template for being human that would become a source of freedom, joy, and abundance for all of creation.

This wisdom finds its foundation in learning to love God with every dimension of our lives. To love God with heart, soul, and strength means submitting every aspect of our lives to his good counsel. As a mother, you are commissioned in this passage to impress God's instructions for life upon your child's heart. Moses makes it clear that the most effective place to do that is not in a classroom or lab. The best teaching context puts God's wisdom into practice in your everyday life—when you're sitting around at home, as you go about your routine business, and even when you lie down to sleep.

Any learning that begins with impressions upon the heart finds its truest expression coming from the heart.

THE COMPOSITION OF A CHILD

Your lives are a letter written in our hearts; everyone can read it and recognize our good work among you. Clearly, you are a letter from Christ showing the result of our ministry among you. This "letter" is written not with pen and ink, but with the Spirit of the living God. It is carved not on tablets of stone, but on human hearts.

We are confident of all this because of our great trust in God through Christ. It is not that we think we are qualified to do anything on our own. Our qualification comes from God. He has enabled us to be ministers of his new covenant. This is a covenant not of written laws, but of the Spirit. The old written covenant ends in death; but under the new covenant, the Spirit gives life.

2 Corinthians 3:2–6 NLT

Has it ever occurred to you that the role you play in your child's life is much like that of an author? Your child is the blank page upon which you are to compose something worthy of publishing to the world.

This passage makes the important point that the formation of a child's character is accomplished from within the heart of the child, never by force, manipulation, or logic. It could be interpreted to mean that as a mother, you must find your way into the deep recesses of your children's existence: their fears, hopes, resentments, desires, and joys. From that spot, a mom can influence a child's responses to almost anything the child encounters and nurture a healthy perspective with diligent care.

But how does a mom gain access to her child's heart? The same way God's Spirit gains ground within her own. The Spirit inspires a quality of togetherness in relationships . . . a vibrancy in community. Think of high school students cheering about school spirit; the term signifies a student body that is powerfully alive as one. And fully alive to your child—engaged and enthusiastic—you'll find profound influence.

WATCH YOUR STEP

Whoever receives one such child in my name receives me, but whoever causes one of these little ones who believe in me to sin, it would be better for him to have a great millstone fastened around his neck and to be drowned in the depth of the sea.

Woe to the world for temptations to sin! For it is necessary that temptations come, but woe to the one by whom the temptation comes! And if your hand or your foot causes you to sin, cut it off and throw it away. It is better for you to enter life crippled or lame than with two hands or two feet to be thrown into the eternal fire. And if your eye causes you to sin, tear it out and throw it away.

Matthew 18:5–9 ESV

An accomplished teacher knows the effective use of *hyperbole*, intentional exaggeration. Jesus was a very accomplished teacher and used hyperbole effectively in this passage. The point of his exaggeration in this passage is clear: you never want to be the source of temptation that causes someone, particularly a child, to sin. God is displeased when indifference and negligence in our actions lead another person to stumble. Obviously, this passage holds important implications, especially for mothers.

As a mom you must influence your children intentionally and consistently, and not only your own children but all with whom they associate. Your ability to influence the lives of children—rightly or wrongly—reaches far beyond the four walls in which you live. The temptation to sin is much stronger in groups and among peers and particularly with the young. Being genuinely invested and concerned about the people with whom your children "hang out" will ensure your influence among them, safeguarding your own children's attitudes and actions.

Young people gravitate toward those who genuinely care about what's going on in their lives, and you have the opportunity to be one of the people to whom they turn when they need someone.

BODY LIFE

Our bodies have many parts, and God has put each part just where he wants it. How strange a body would be if it had only one part! . . .

In fact, some parts of the body that seem weakest and least important are actually the most necessary. And the parts we regard as less honorable are those we clothe with the greatest care. So we carefully protect those parts that should not be seen, while the more honorable parts do not require this special care. So God has put the body together such that extra honor and care are given to those parts that have less dignity. This makes for harmony among the members, so that all the members care for each other. If one part suffers, all the parts suffer with it, and if one part is honored, all the parts are glad.

1 Corinthians 12:18–19, 22–26 NLT

The metaphor of the body is one of the most powerful visual images in the Bible. Consider how a painfully abscessed tooth can interrupt your productivity in every aspect of life. On the other hand, when healing in your mouth takes place, your whole life begins to function normally again. What better illustration could there be concerning how deeply we should impact—or be impacted—by one another?

As a mother, you will probably recognize your children's propensities and talents long before anyone else. You have the opportunity to speculate with each child over what he or she will be as an adult. Imagine the impact you can have concerning the unique part that your children play in your family, among friends, and even in the larger community.

Engaging in imaginative conversation with your children over their roles in life can play a powerful part in laying a foundation for their future, helping them develop healthy aspirations and goals. Not only will this exercise give your children something at which to aim, but it also will teach them how to value and respect others no matter how different their interests and abilities may be.

THE UPSIDE OF DISCIPLINE

My son, do not despise the LORD's discipline and do not resent his rebuke, because the LORD disciplines those he loves, as a father the son he delights in.

Blessed is the man who finds wisdom, the man who gains understanding, for she is more profitable than silver and yields better returns than gold. She is more precious than rubies; nothing you desire can compare with her. Long life is in her right hand; in her left hand are riches and honor. Her ways are pleasant ways, and all her paths are peace. She is a tree of life to those who embrace her; those who lay hold of her will be blessed.

Proverbs 3:11–18 NIV

All discipline doesn't have to be negative. There's more to effective discipline than a good scolding and a time-out. Discipline also has a positive aspect that allows a child to accumulate wisdom and life skills without tears.

The mom teaching her two-year-old how to eat with a fork is engaged in a necessary act of discipline that will affect the remainder of the child's life. The mother teaching her five-year-old how to say thank you is also engaged in discipline. Learning to ride a bike, to brush one's hair, to ice-skate, or to write a letter . . . All of these are forms of discipline.

Wise mothers capitalize on opportunities to engage in positive discipline in order to avoid the unnecessarily negative, but it requires *self*-discipline on our part. For example, when toilet training, taking the initiative to escort your two-year-old to the "potty" as soon as naptime is over will end in success, but procrastinating about this will end in frustration and failure.

This important Bible passage accentuates the place of wisdom in discipline: on the part of the child being trained, and on the part of the parent doing the discipline.

SIMPLICITY IN SPEECH

When I first came to you, dear brothers and sisters, I didn't use lofty words and impressive wisdom to tell you God's secret plan. For I decided that while I was with you I would forget everything except Jesus Christ, the one who was crucified. I came to you in weakness—timid and trembling. And my message and my preaching were very plain. Rather than using clever and persuasive speeches, I relied only on the power of the Holy Spirit. I did this so you would trust not in human wisdom but in the power of God.

Yet when I am among mature believers, I do speak with words of wisdom, but not the kind of wisdom that belongs to this world or to the rulers of this world, who are soon forgotten.

1 Corinthians 2:1–6 NLT

Although Paul could speak before thousands, he assumed a humble posture when teaching new believers. The method he used proves to be effective for mothers as well.

First, Paul addressed his audience with words of deep affection. Your children will listen more attentively to the language of love. Next, Paul filtered out what wasn't necessary. Moms who know to keep from cluttering their communication with too many words are more likely to experience some success in getting their point across.

Paul then focused diligently on the central point of his teaching. Don't allow your child's response, or lack of response, to get you off track. Stay on task and follow through with your thoughts. Next, Paul used plain speech when he was instructing others. Speaking over your child's head won't get the job done. Simplify your words. Use vocabulary the child can understand. Use voice inflection and body language to reinforce your message.

Finally, Paul relied upon his intuitive powers to discern the needs of others. This is the most crucial point of all. The more attuned you are to the hearts of your children, the more powerful will be your influence.

NURTURING STRATEGIES

The baby's sister stood at a distance to see what would happen to him.

While Pharaoh's daughter came to the Nile to take a bath, her servants walked along the bank of the river. She saw the basket among the papyrus plants and sent her slave girl to get it. Pharaoh's daughter . . . looked at the baby. . . . He was crying, and she felt sorry for him. She said, "This is one of the Hebrew children."

Then the baby's sister asked Pharaoh's daughter, "Should I go and get one of the Hebrew women to nurse the baby for you?"

She answered, "Yes!" So the girl brought the baby's mother.

Pharaoh's daughter said to the woman, "Take this child, nurse him for me, and I will pay you."

Exodus 2:4–9 GOD'S WORD

Moses' mother, Jochebed, was a slave in Egypt under a cruel tyrant who felt threatened by the unusual expansion of the Hebrew nation. God was blessing the Hebrews (the Israelites) by multiplying them, just as he had promised Abraham. In an attempt to curtail the growth, the Egyptian pharaoh ordered all Hebrew baby boys to be thrown into the Nile.

Jochebed refused to surrender her child. Knowing she couldn't keep Moses concealed any longer, she placed her son afloat in a basket at the place where Pharaoh's daughter habitually bathed. Moses' sister, Miriam, stood watch nearby in order to capitalize on the compassion of the Egyptian princess and return the child to his mother for continued nurture—physically and spiritually—only this time under imperial sanction. His mother's continued influence laid the foundation for Moses' development into one of the most powerful leaders Israel would ever know.

There will be times as a mother when you will need to develop creative strategies for nurturing your children in life and in faith. Never surrender your children to seemingly inevitable evils. God will help you find ways to keep them safe and on track with his purpose.

INSIDE-OUT PERSPECTIVE

When many of his disciples heard it, they said, "This is a hard saying; who can listen to it?" But Jesus, knowing in himself that his disciples were grumbling about this, said to them, "Do you take offense at this? . . . It is the Spirit who gives life; the flesh is of no avail. The words that I have spoken to you are spirit and life." . . .

After this many of his disciples turned back and no longer walked with him. So Jesus said to the Twelve, "Do you want to go away as well?" Simon Peter answered him, "Lord, to whom shall we go? You have the words of eternal life, and we have believed, and have come to know, that you are the Holy One of God." Jesus answered them, "Did I not choose you, the Twelve?"

John 6:60–61, 63, 66–70 ESV

Jesus' teachings often seemed cryptic to those listening. As in this passage, his words sometimes produced adverse reactions. Was he trying to confuse or repulse his followers? No, Jesus was actually training them to seek understanding from a different perspective. Instead of interpreting life from a superficial frame of reference, he wanted them—and us—to view things from the inside out, letting God infuse meaning into circumstances.

Mothers likewise have the difficult responsibility of teaching our children to look at things from the inside out. We can equip our children to become a powerful influence in the lives of peers by training them to interpret others through a heart of compassion rather than by observing outward behavior only. For instance, children who remain isolated from others at school might have developmental difficulties or heartache in their private lives that keeps them guarded and withdrawn. Training your children to spot these symptoms, filter them through the heart, and reach out effectively will be a tremendous blessing to children who hurt, not to mention a distinct benefit to your own children.

The high road is the hard road . . . not particularly popular, but fulfilling.

WISDOM WITHIN REACH

These are the proverbs of Solomon, David's son, king of Israel.

Their purpose is to teach people wisdom and discipline, to help them understand the insights of the wise. . . . These proverbs will give insight to the simple, knowledge and discernment to the young.

Let the wise listen to these proverbs and become even wiser. Let those with understanding receive guidance by exploring the meaning in these proverbs and parables, the words of the wise and their riddles.

Fear of the LORD is the foundation of true knowledge, but fools despise wisdom and discipline.

My child, listen when your father corrects you. Don't neglect your mother's instruction. What you learn from them will crown you with grace.

Proverbs 1:1–2, 4–9 NLT

According to the Bible, King Solomon was the wisest person ever . . . until Jesus, that is. Without the immediate access provided by contemporary media and without the convenience of modern transportation, influential men and women from all over the globe traveled long distances by boat or pack-animal caravan in order to listen to the wisdom of Solomon in Israel.

Would people go to such extremes to gain wisdom today? Obviously not, considering that Solomon's wisdom is right at our fingertips yet seldom consulted.

The wise sayings of Solomon were consolidated many years ago into one compilation that resides in the Bible. The book of Proverbs contains hundreds of short, pithy sayings broken down into thirty-one small chapters. As a mother, you will find Proverbs an inexhaustible source of wisdom covering a spectrum of life-related topics.

What would keep a mother from following the admonition to "listen to these proverbs and become even wiser" or from exploring one of these wise sayings with her children daily? Since wisdom is abundantly available to you in the Bible, seize the opportunity to bless your children.

POWER IN DISCERNMENT

Peter and John looked at him intently, and Peter said, "Look at us!" The lame man looked at them eagerly, expecting some money. But Peter said, "I don't have any silver or gold for you. But I'll give you what I have. In the name of Jesus Christ the Nazarene, get up and walk!"

Then Peter took the lame man by the right hand and helped him up. And as he did, the man's feet and ankles were instantly healed and strength-ened. He jumped up, stood on his feet, and began to walk! Then, walking, leaping, and praising God, he went into the Temple with them.

All the people saw him walking and heard him praising God. When they realized he was the lame beggar they had seen so often at the Beautiful Gate, they were absolutely astounded!

Acts 3:4–10 NLT

A miracle! How thrilling it must have been to watch as a man discovered strength and mobility in his legs for the first time. No wonder he was leaping! No doubt he was shouting too.

The first sentence in this critical passage lets us in on an important key to accessing God's perspective and power. Peter and John had lived in close quarters with Jesus for three years. They had witnessed so many of his works of power. One thing they had observed in Jesus was his incredibly intuitive discernment. If his Father was at work in a situation, Jesus knew it. How? He had developed a lens through which he could see the hand of God at work by being intimately involved with him in prayer, observation, and spontaneous obedience. This could be called the lens of love.

As a mom, you can develop a lens through which to determine the will of God and access the power of God similar to what Peter and John did. Develop an intentional habit of prayer, be diligent in observing your children's needs and behavior, and stay actively aligned with God's truth.

Miracles still happen!

SECRETS REVEALED

I will open my mouth in parables, I will utter hidden things, things from of old—what we have heard and known, what our fathers have told us. We will not hide them from their children; we will tell the next generation the praiseworthy deeds of the LORD, his power, and the wonders he has done. He decreed statutes for Jacob and established the law in Israel, which he commanded our forefathers to teach their children, so the next generation would know them, even the children yet to be born, and they in turn would tell their children. Then they would put their trust in God and would not forget his deeds but would keep his commands.

Psalm 78:2–7 NIV

The Israelites understood the importance of leaving a legacy of faith for their children. The nation had entered into a covenant with God after he rescued them from tyranny in Egypt. This covenant of compassion was an understanding and an agreement with God that no other nation possessed. As long as the people were faithful to the covenant, they prospered, both personally and as a nation. Unfortunately, within a generation or two, parents began to neglect the diligent instruction they had received. Throughout the Old Testament of the Bible, the history of Israel is riddled with tragic records of consequential heartache.

What about you? When you were a child, were you taught the truth and power of God? Moreover, are you trying to build a legacy of faith for your own children now? The wisdom contained in the Bible is accessible to anyone anywhere, yet remains a hidden, untapped source of blessing and encouragement unless the Book is read and put into practice. But telling your children about the "praiseworthy deeds" of God and teaching them to obey him will lead them to trust in God and find fulfillment in life.

Simple Success: Love God, Love People

This way, love has the run of the house, becomes at home and mature in us, so that we're free of worry on Judgment Day—our standing in the world is identical with Christ's. There is no room in love for fear. Well-formed love banishes fear. Since fear is crippling, a fearful life—fear of death, fear of judgment—is one not yet fully formed in love.

We, though, are going to love—love and be loved. First we were loved, now we love. He loved us first.

If anyone boasts, "I love God," and goes right on hating his brother or sister, thinking nothing of it, he is a liar. If he won't love the person he can see, how can he love the God he can't see? The command we have from Christ is blunt: Loving God includes loving people.

1 John 4:17–21 MSG

Of all the principles and practices that mothers teach their children, this one ranks the highest. It is of supreme importance. Loving God means loving people. There is no way around it; it is impossible to love God except by demonstrating genuine love for people.

The question is, How do we teach our children this kind of love? It doesn't happen simply by handing down correct information. Love isn't learned in the same way a child learns spelling or American history. Love is learned by living. One of the best ways to teach your children the love of Jesus is to show them what it is to love the way Jesus does.

In this passage John makes it clear that this kind of love isn't motivated by fear or guilt. It is a broad-spectrum type of goodwill that comes from the heart of a person who understands and values other people. It isn't necessarily affection, although it can be affectionate; it is concerned more with the well-being, security, freedom, and sustenance of others.

Finding creative ways together to express goodwill and tend to the needs of others will engage and enlighten your children with surprising effectiveness.

A GOOD NIGHT'S SLEEP

Go ahead and be angry. You do well to be angry—but don't use your anger as fuel for revenge. And don't stay angry. Don't go to bed angry. Don't give the Devil that kind of foothold in your life. . . .

Watch the way you talk. Let nothing foul or dirty come out of your mouth. Say only what helps, each word a gift.

Don't grieve God. Don't break his heart. His Holy Spirit, moving and breathing in you, is the most intimate part of your life, making you fit for himself. Don't take such a gift for granted.

Make a clean break with all cutting, backbiting, profane talk. Be gentle with one another, sensitive. Forgive one another as quickly and thoroughly as God in Christ forgave you.

Ephesians 4:26–32 MSG

The words of Paul in this passage are loaded with wisdom. Paul explains what it means to love someone while in a period of conflict. Whether you implement this passage when in conflict with a child or when teaching a child how to handle anger, you'll find this among the most practical and powerful advice ever written.

Paul begins with an affirmation of the emotion we know as anger. Teach your child that anger isn't wrong; it is inevitable and even necessary at times. But if anger isn't handled responsibly, it can turn into resentment, and that is when our feet could slip off the path. If we train our children to discern the difference between being angry and acting out their anger, they will have a head start in managing relationships effectively.

Most important, learn to watch your own words. Anger slips out of control most frequently in the form of careless words. Teach your children not to let their words run ahead of good judgment. Words are powerful and should be used thoughtfully, not impulsively. If you need to be impulsive about something, let it be forgiveness. You can always rush to reconcile.

Loyally Loved

Your steadfast love, O Lord, extends to the heavens, your faithfulness to the clouds. Your righteousness is like the mountains of God; your judgments are like the great deep; man and beast you save, O Lord.

How precious is your steadfast love, O God! The children of mankind take refuge in the shadow of your wings. They feast on the abundance of your house, and you give them drink from the river of your delights. For with you is the fountain of life; in your light do we see light.

Oh, continue your steadfast love to those who know you, and your righteousness to the upright of heart!

Psalm 36:5–10 ESV

The Psalms are picturesque in expressing God's faithful love. What a wealth of teaching material they provide! As a mom, you can tap into the artful language of the Psalms and let them do the work for you.

Take your children on a field trip with David. Go outside and look up into the highest reaches of the sky and talk about the expanse of God's love. Point out to your children that just as they cannot reach to touch the clouds from where they're standing, neither can they reach the limits of God's loyalty.

Again referencing nature, God's goodness is immovable like a mountain. It is as solid as a rock and towers over the earth in grandeur and in strength. From the heights of God's overarching goodness, he lavishes his blessings on your children's lives like a cool, refreshing stream that flows from a mountainside.

Speaking of streams, God provides rivers of delight to those he loves. A current of joy rushes through the lives of those who drink from the fountain of God's everlasting love, and he sheds the light of wisdom on all who look to him for light.

ATTITUDE IS ALTITUDE

If there is any encouragement in Christ, if there is any consolation of love, if there is any fellowship of the Spirit, if any affection and compassion, make my joy complete by being of the same mind, maintaining the same love, united in spirit, intent on one purpose. Do nothing from selfishness or empty conceit, but with humility of mind regard one another as more important than yourselves; do not merely look out for your own personal interests, but also for the interests of others. Have this attitude in yourselves which was also in Christ Jesus, who, although He existed in the form of God, did not regard equality with God a thing to be grasped, but emptied Himself, taking the form of a bond-servant, and being made in the likeness of men.

Philippians 2:1–7 NASB

You've seen tiny tyrants running rampant in our society—children who ruthlessly dictate their parents' activities and deprive them of their peace. The problem is obvious: they are suffering the effects of self-centeredness gone awry. And if left unchecked, these little overlords might grow up to be insensitive narcissists.

This passage from Paul represents the antithesis of self-centeredness—an attitude of humility. The fluidity of Paul's words reveals something about attitude that can set us free . . . free from the burden of self, that is.

All caring moms want to train their children to have an attitude of humility without negatively affecting a healthy self-image. Paul says the key to a good attitude is learning to value others appropriately. It's critical that you teach your children to value other people in a way that doesn't cause your children to feel devalued. In other words, you train your children not to measure themselves against others—or vice versa—but to learn to appreciate what other people have to offer and to work with others using their own strengths and abilities. This promotes a spirit of unity and cooperation, not to mention a lot more productivity.

LOVE IN ACTION

Simon Peter said to Him, "Lord, not only my feet, but also my hands and my head."

"One who has bathed," Jesus told him, "doesn't need to wash anything except his feet, but he is completely clean. You are clean, but not all of you." For He knew who would betray Him. This is why He said, "You are not all clean."

When Jesus had washed their feet and put on His robe, He reclined again and said to them, "Do you know what I have done for you? You call Me Teacher and Lord. This is well said, for I am. So if I, your Lord and Teacher, have washed your feet, you also ought to wash one another's feet. For I have given you an example that you also should do just as I have done for you."

John 13:9–15 HCSB

Jesus' ministry was coming to an end. He gathered his closest followers one last time to teach them one last thing about love. If you knew you were going to die tomorrow, what last thing would you want to teach your child? It probably wouldn't be a lesson in tennis or fashion design, would it?

Jesus knew that his disciples hadn't understood everything he had taught them, but the one thing he couldn't risk was that they might miss the meaning of love. Love means being loyal to others in spite of conflict, misunderstanding, or difficulty. Love means bending in self-sacrifice to ensure the ultimate good of the one loved.

The most crucial learning your child will ever receive from you is learning in love. And the kind of instruction that love requires is love in action . . . radical, selfless service. Jesus could have said, "I love you so much I could wash your feet." Instead, he wrapped a towel around his waist like a servant and knelt to express to his disciples the most humble demonstration of love they had ever witnessed—and a lesson in love they would never forget.

LETTING THINGS GO

You won't get [what you want] by fighting and arguing. You should pray for it. Yet even when you do pray, your prayers are not answered, because you pray just for selfish reasons.

You people aren't faithful to God! Don't you know that if you love the world, you are God's enemies? And if you decide to be a friend of the world, you make yourself an enemy of God. Do you doubt the Scriptures that say, "God truly cares about the Spirit he has put in us"? In fact, God treats us with even greater kindness, just as the Scriptures say, "God opposes everyone who is proud, but he is kind to everyone who is humble."

Surrender to God! Resist the devil, and he will run from you. Come near to God, and he will come near to you.

James 4:2–8 CEV

Whose purpose is prayer really to serve . . . yours or God's? The answer begs the next question: what then is God's most pressing concern?

Our responsibility to teach our children about true spirituality must go to the root of God's priorities. If our children have the impression that God exists to answer their every request—however selfish or impulsive—they will soon lose faith in prayer. God won't cater to the subjective whims of humans or bend to our pettiness or spite.

Children are naturally self-centered from the beginning. They sulk, hit, and throw tantrums when their peers or parents don't give in to their demands. Unless children receive intentional instruction about how to love others, they won't mature into responsible people.

With a careful selection of your own priorities, teach your children what it means to love God more than you love the "stuff" he has provided. Prove to your child that humility—looking after the welfare and dignity of other people—is more rewarding than pursuing wealth, power, or status. Living close to God means loving people above the things of this world.

No Shortcuts

Would any of you give your hungry child a stone, if the child asked for some bread? Would you give your child a snake if the child asked for a fish? As bad as you are, you still know how to give good gifts to your children. But your heavenly Father is even more ready to give good things to people who ask.

Treat others as you want them to treat you. This is what the Law and the Prophets are all about.

Go in through the narrow gate. The gate to destruction is wide, and the road that leads there is easy to follow. A lot of people go through that gate. But the gate to life is very narrow. The road that leads there is so hard to follow that only a few people find it.

Matthew 7:9–14 CEV

Does this passage cause you to wonder why God would make the road to life so difficult, so hard to find? In truth, it isn't God who makes the way difficult and hard to get to. Jesus said that he is the gate and the light. Considering that the gate is well lit and that he is in full view in the Bible, God has given us everything we need to find true life. If we find ourselves groping for the gate, perhaps it is because we have stayed too long on the wide path—conforming to our culture—which can adversely affect our perspective on the real meaning of being alive.

Mentor your children in the true meaning of life by modeling the words of this passage in your own daily existence. Teach your children what it means to love people the way they themselves long to be loved. Show your children an alternative to prejudice, discrimination, and injustice by practicing mercy. Teach them to treat strangers with respect, to esteem the elderly, and to be gentle with the young. When your children see this teaching in action, they are likely to pass through the gate and into abundant life.

Do Your Part

Encourage each other and build each other up. . . .

Honor those who are your leaders in the Lord's work. They work hard among you and give you spiritual guidance. Show them great respect and whole-hearted love because of their work. And live peacefully with each other.

Brothers and sisters, we urge you to warn those who are lazy. Encourage those who are timid. Take tender care of those who are weak. Be patient with everyone.

See that no one pays back evil for evil, but always try to do good to each other and to all people.

Always be joyful. Never stop praying. Be thankful in all circumstances, for this is God's will for you who belong to Christ Jesus.

Do not stifle the Holy Spirit. . . . Hold on to what is good.

1 Thessalonians 5:11–21 NLT

Have you ever asked the question, What is God's will for my life? Paul answers that question thoroughly in this pragmatic passage. This would be a good place to set up camp and share some important instruction with your child.

The passage teaches that God's will for your child's life boils down to loving others in practical and encouraging ways. The essence of the teaching is this: take responsibility and do your part for the sake of others. For example, Paul says, teach your children to recognize people who work hard at living right. These kinds of people should be treated with respect and appreciation.

Demonstrate what it means to live at peace with others by being patient with people even when it inconveniences you. Welcome interruptions with a joyful spirit. Show your children that taking revenge on others only heaps up more wrongdoing, but being kind and forgiving clears the air and causes celebration. Finally, don't accommodate laziness in others; it isn't in their best interest. Yet strengthen those who are weak-willed or living in fear by encouraging them with your prayers and your praise to God.

FIRST LOVE

This is love: not that we loved God, but that he loved us and sent his Son as an atoning sacrifice for our sins. Dear friends, since God so loved us, we also ought to love one another. No one has ever seen God; but if we love one another, God lives in us and his love is made complete in us.

We know that we live in him and he in us, because he has given us of his Spirit. And we have seen and testify that the Father has sent his Son to be the Savior of the world. If anyone acknowledges that Jesus is the Son of God, God lives in him and he in God. And so we know and rely on the love God has for us.

God is love. Whoever lives in love lives in God, and God in him.

1 John 4:10–16 NIV

If you really want to understand love, you must not start with the human kind but with the love God has for us. His love speaks most profoundly from the cross of Jesus. God loves us so much that he was willing to sacrifice his Son to rescue us. But teaching a child about this kind of love is challenging because children don't understand the need for sacrifice.

Furthermore, John points out another difficulty that moms face—how to love a God you cannot see. So what's the answer? The answer lies in the love of Jesus. We can teach our children to respond to God's love by looking hard at how Jesus loved.

First, Jesus loved without limits. That means there was not a need he wasn't willing to address. His response to people was immediate and generous. Second, Jesus always had time for people who needed him, any time of day. He was never in a hurry or out of patience.

Teach your children to love the same way Jesus loved. If they do, they will be full of the love *of* God, as well as full of love *for* God.

BUTTERFLY FLUTTERS

He took me home with him for a festive meal, but his eyes feasted on *me*!

Oh! Give me something refreshing to eat—and quickly! Apricots, raisins—anything. I'm about to faint with love! His left hand cradles my head, and his right arm encircles my waist! . . .

Don't excite love, don't stir it up, until the time is ripe—and you're ready.

Look! Listen! There's my lover! Do you see him coming? Vaulting the mountains, leaping the hills. My lover is like a gazelle, graceful; like a young stag, virile. Look at him there, on tiptoe at the gate, all ears, all eyes—ready! My lover has arrived and he's speaking to me!

Song of Songs 2:4–10 MSG

The Song of Songs, a love poem written by the great King Solomon, like the rest of the Bible is a God-inspired work. Some believe it is intended to illustrate God's passionate love for his people. Whether this is true, the poetic book from which this passage comes intends at the very least to provide a much-needed sanction of the pure and devoted love between a man and a woman.

In an age in which there is so much confusion about relationships—particularly sexually involved relationships—it is refreshing to find one whole book of the Bible dedicated to this original bond between man and woman that has suffered so much distortion in culture.

For some moms, it can be overwhelming to try to convey these sentiments to a child. The good news is, it isn't necessary to use explicit terms in order to get the point across. The poem moves like a drama, the words fairly dancing off the page in order to invoke emotion. We would do well to let the poetry inspire us to convey its meaning in the way we express our convictions about human love. Since God was concerned enough to include it, we probably should!

Worth the Work, Worth the Wait

Laban had two daughters. The older daughter was named Leah, and the younger one was Rachel. There was no sparkle in Leah's eyes, but Rachel had a beautiful figure and a lovely face. Since Jacob was in love with Rachel, he told her father, "I'll work for you for seven years if you'll give me Rachel, your younger daughter, as my wife."

"Agreed!" Laban replied. "I'd rather give her to you than to anyone else. Stay and work with me." So Jacob worked seven years to pay for Rachel. But his love for her was so strong that it seemed to him but a few days.

Finally, the time came for him to marry her. "I have fulfilled my agreement," Jacob said to Laban. "Now give me my wife so I can marry her."

Genesis 29:16–21 NLT

It might be surprising to some that the Bible contains a few good love stories. This is one of the sweetest. Imagine how different things would be in our world if a man had to work several years to gain a wife! We all tend to place more value on something we have to labor for. Perhaps our culture would place a higher value on marriage if it were available only on the basis of hard work.

How might a mother go about teaching her children to value marriage more within the culture at hand? A critical difference can be made for children by observing how much you value marriage—your own, as well as the marriages of others—in practical terms such as respect, unselfishness, and active support. Your disposition toward marriage will rub off onto your child.

Value can also be communicated through priorities. If you are currently married, that might mean setting aside a special time with your spouse on a regular basis so that the children understand how important the relationship really is. Or it might mean offering to keep someone else's children while they take some time for marriage renewal.

Second Honeymoon

"Come away with me, my fair one! Look, the winter is past, and the rains are over and gone. The flowers are springing up, the season of singing birds has come, and the cooing of turtledoves fills the air. The fig trees are forming young fruit, and the fragrant grapevines are blossoming. Rise up, my darling! Come away with me, my fair one!"

My dove is hiding behind the rocks, behind an outcrop on the cliff. Let me see your face; let me hear your voice. For your voice is pleasant, and your face is lovely. . . .

My lover is mine, and I am his.

Song of Songs 2:10–16 NLT

In this passage King Solomon greets the springtime with deeper appreciation and enthusiasm because of the woman he loves. It seemed to him that the season was more vibrant and alive because love inspired invigoration. As love grows, those in love grow with it, embracing broader horizons and maturing in appreciation for the simple pleasures of living. Just about every aspect of life is enhanced by the joys of being in a mutually satisfying relationship with another person.

After children have come into the family, it is a good idea for moms and dads to get away again to celebrate married love anew. Chances are that you'll discover new depths of the person you've married, because parenting brings out a dimension of personhood that has never been tapped before. Likely you'll also discover common interests that there simply isn't time to pursue together while rearing children. Or you might explore new ones. If nothing else, you will enjoy some much-needed rest and rejuvenation without interruption or constant demands of children—a time to rebuild.

Children benefit from the devoted love of their parents and should learn to respect the priority of marriage.

ANTICIPATION

My lover's left hand is under my head, and his right arm holds me tight. Women of Jerusalem, promise not to awaken or excite my feelings of love until it is ready.

Who is this coming out of the desert, leaning on her lover?

I woke you under the apple tree where you were born; there your mother gave birth to you. Put me like a seal on your heart, like a seal on your arm. Love is as strong as death; jealousy is as strong as the grave. Love bursts into flames and burns like a hot fire. Even much water cannot put out the flame of love; floods cannot drown love.

Song of Songs 8:3–7 NCV

Though children shouldn't be privy to the anticipation of romantic love that married people experience, moms can include them in many aspects of the joy that love brings with it.

Your children need to learn to value not only your motherhood but your womanhood as well. They will discover that your personality reaches deeper than merely being a mom as they observe you in other roles with other people—especially as a woman in love.

Teach your children to appreciate how healthy and productive love is. Let them in on the joy involved in someone else's partnering with you. Share the laughter, the tenderness, and the affection as a family, putting some privacy and time on reserve for your spouse when the children are asleep or otherwise occupied. You will be a much more balanced mom if you give priority to other loving relationships in your life. You'll be a more resourceful mother if you continue to develop fulfilling aspects of your life other than just parenting.

The children will grow up one day, and you'll be glad that you taught them to cherish the people with whom they share themselves and their future.

LOVE AT WORK

Everything in the world is about to be wrapped up, so take nothing for granted. Stay wide-awake in prayer. Most of all, love each other as if your life depended on it. Love makes up for practically anything. Be quick to give a meal to the hungry, a bed to the homeless—cheerfully. Be generous with the different things God gave you, passing them around so all get in on it: if words, let it be God's words; if help, let it be God's hearty help. That way, God's bright presence will be evident in everything through Jesus, and *he'll* get all the credit as the One mighty in everything—encores to the end of time. Oh, yes!

Friends, when life gets really difficult, don't jump to the conclusion that God isn't on the job.

1 Peter 4:7–12 MSG

It is difficult for children to imagine that things won't always be as they are, but in this important passage Peter makes a point of saying that the end of this age is inevitable. However, wrapping it up isn't the only point he wanted to make. The fact is, the end will accomplish two other critical things, as well: it will bring to a fitting conclusion everything that God has been doing to rescue his creation until now, and it will also usher in a new beginning. It is the proven love of God that filled Peter with such anticipation.

What does feeding the hungry and housing the homeless have to do with all of this? More than you might think. The end of this age will include conquering the fiercest enemy—death. In every way that we find ourselves contributing to life—most especially in love—we find ourselves in conflict with God's ultimate enemy, weakening Satan's cause.

Help your children to realize that loving others enough to sustain and nurture life by putting their gifts and talents to work means that they are gaining ground for the kingdom of God.

HUMILITY AND HOSPITALITY

"When you are invited, go and recline in the lowest place, so that when the one who invited you comes, he will say to you, 'Friend, move up higher.' You will then be honored in the presence of all the other guests. For everyone who exalts himself will be humbled, and the one who humbles himself will be exalted."

He also said to the one who had invited Him, "When you give a lunch or a dinner, don't invite your friends, your brothers, your relatives, or your rich neighbors, because they might invite you back, and you would be repaid. On the contrary, when you host a banquet, invite those who are poor, maimed, lame, or blind. And you will be blessed, because they cannot repay you; for you will be repaid at the resurrection of the righteous."

Luke 14:10–14 HCSB

Humility is a tricky thing. Just about the time you think you've got a handle on it, it starts slipping away. Jesus gives us a significant grasp on humility in this clarifying passage.

In the first parable, or story, Jesus is likely making a reference to a great banquet the Jews believed would happen at the end of the age when God's kingdom would be reestablished on the earth. Among the elite there was a great deal of competition for the status that would earn close proximity to God at that banquet table. Jesus' remedy for that competition came in the form of the second parable.

Dignifying the lowliest people in society instead of exalting ourselves is the same as taking the lowest seat at the banquet on that great day. By so doing, we will find the great Host pleased with our love for the underprivileged and the outcasts and responsive to our humble hearts.

Children are blessed when they get to grow up helping their moms take care of those the world ignores or rejects. The kind of love that motivates such behavior comes from an authentic and humble heart.

WATERFALL

Timothy has come back from his visit with you and has told us about your faith and love. He also said that you always have happy memories of us and that you want to see us as much as we want to see you.

My friends, even though we have a lot of trouble and suffering, your faith makes us feel better about you. . . . How can we possibly thank God enough for all the happiness you have brought us? Day and night we sincerely pray that we will see you again and help you to have an even stronger faith.

We pray that God our Father and our Lord Jesus will let us visit you. May the Lord make your love for each other and for everyone else grow by leaps and bounds.

1 Thessalonians 3:6–7, 9–12
CEV

It would be difficult to imagine a more affectionate and expressive outpouring of love than what is reflected in this passage. The apostle Paul had begun this church in Thessalonica while on a mission in Macedonia. Then fierce opposition from those of the Jewish faith who believed that the message of Christ was heresy caused Paul to flee Thessalonica under the cover of night. The Christians there had longed for Paul's return—his teaching, joy, and love in the Spirit—like a child longs for his father. Paul had likewise yearned to continue among them in order to encourage them in their faith. But still at risk of persecution, he sent Timothy to look into their welfare. Paul wrote them this letter after Timothy reported back to him.

Wouldn't you experience the same sentiments Paul did if you were abruptly separated from your children? Paul's words must have rushed over the people's hearts like running water—refreshing words of joy, thanksgiving, hope, yearning, love, and encouragement. Paul gave full vent to the love in his heart for these young Christians. Don't wait for an unexpected disruption in your relationship with your child to give expression to yours.

MULTIPLIED DIVIDENDS

Know therefore that the LORD your God is God, the faithful God who keeps covenant and steadfast love with those who love him and keep his commandments, to a thousand generations. . . . Be careful to do the commandment and the statutes and the rules that I command you today.

And because you listen to these rules and keep and do them, the LORD your God will keep with you the covenant and the steadfast love that he swore to your fathers. He will love you, bless you, and multiply you. He will also bless the fruit of your womb and the fruit of your ground, your grain and your wine and your oil, the increase of your herds and the young of your flock, in the land that he swore to your fathers to give you. You shall be blessed above all peoples.

Deuteronomy 7:9, 11–14 ESV

The words of this passage were originally spoken to the Israelites, who agreed to enter into a specific covenant relationship with the Creator, the One who had delivered them from the cruel tyranny of Egypt. But God had the remainder of the human race in mind when he spoke these words, for his desire was that Israel would become a living illustration of what happens when people accept God as King.

What would happen? Blessings would be heaped on them from heaven in measure difficult to describe. They would have large, happy families and abundant crops. Wine would flow like a fountain and oil like a stream, not to mention the immense increase of their livestock on the land that was theirs to claim forever. In short, the abundance of their existence on the earth would provide overwhelming evidence that they were deeply loved by the Creator of it all, causing the rest of humanity to run to their gates and insist on knowing their God.

Instruct your children that Jesus did keep that covenant—he became that gate. Following him is a sure path to abundant blessing, love, and joy.

JUST MAKE UP YOUR MIND

I know all the things you do, that you are neither hot nor cold. I wish that you were one or the other! But since you are like lukewarm water, neither hot nor cold, I will spit you out of my mouth! You say, "I am rich. I have everything I want. I don't need a thing!" And you don't realize that you are wretched and miserable and poor and blind and naked. So I advise you to buy gold from me—gold that has been purified by fire. Then you will be rich. Also buy white garments from me so you will not be shamed by your nakedness, and ointment for your eyes so you will be able to see. I correct and discipline everyone I love. So be diligent and turn from your indifference.

Revelation 3:15–19 NLT

The geography of the region of Laodicea indicates that ironic contrast: the hot, medicinal waters of one nearby city offered healing for the body; and the cold, pure waters of another nearby town could slake a desperate thirst. The recipients of this letter written by the apostle John were challenged to consider that they were neither hot with healing nor cold with rejuvenating power. They offered neither spiritual refreshment nor spiritual healing to others because they had cultivated a self-centered religion serving selfish goals. Jesus encouraged these Christians to reevaluate their insipid attitudes, repent of their self-serving commitments, and realign their skewed priorities.

Moms need to resist the temptation to compromise genuine love for others in the interest of pursuing personal wealth, security, and comfort. It can be a difficult tightrope to walk sometimes, or at least seem to be. But God generously gives to provide for his children. You can trust him to provide for your family. Keep trusting him. Actively involved in meeting the needs of others, you will teach your children to find real joy in providing the intense warmth of Jesus' grace and the real refreshment of God's Spirit.

CAN YOU HELP ME WITH THE LAUNDRY?

Christ did this, so that he would have a glorious and holy church, without faults or spots or wrinkles or any other flaws.

In the same way, a husband should love his wife as much as he loves himself. A husband who loves his wife shows that he loves himself. None of us hate our own bodies. We provide for them and take good care of them, just as Christ does for the church, because we are each part of his body. As the Scriptures say, "A man leaves his father and mother to get married, and he becomes like one person with his wife." This is a great mystery, but I understand it to mean Christ and his church. So each husband should love his wife as much as he loves himself, and each wife should respect her husband.

Ephesians 5:27–33 CEV

What did Christ do that resulted in this spotless and beautiful church? He completed the human journey flawlessly and then surrendered that perfect life so that his people could take possession of it. That is sacrificial love . . . love carried to the ultimate extreme. The apostle Paul says in this powerful passage that married love should be modeled after this sacrificial love of Jesus for his people. But that isn't "cool" according to current cultural norms. We live in an age that insists on looking out for number one.

How is a mom to get Paul's message across to her children? The best way to convey it is to be simple and practical. That doesn't circumvent the idea of being affectionate and fun-loving too. Being creatively responsive to the need to sacrifice our time, energy, interests, and other resources whenever we can will help our children interpret our sacrifice as an inspiration. On the other hand, if our response is begrudging and insincere, our children could be misled by following our example.

Above all, let love be considerate and kind. Kindness is one of the greatest gifts of a loving heart.

A New Commandment

Jesus said, "Now the Son of Man is glorified, and God is glorified in Him. If God is glorified in Him, God will also glorify Him in Himself and will glorify Him at once.

"Children, I am with you a little while longer. You will look for Me, and just as I told the Jews, 'Where I am going you cannot come,' so now I tell you.

"I give you a new commandment: love one another. Just as I have loved you, you must also love one another. By this all people will know that you are My disciples, if you have love for one another."

"Lord," Simon Peter said to Him, "where are You going?"

Jesus answered, "Where I am going you cannot follow Me now, but you will follow later."

John 13:31–36 HCSB

A new commandment? There was nothing new about the commandment to love one another. What was new was what modified the love his disciples were to have for one another—"Love each other just as I have loved you." Jesus came to show us a new way of loving. Extreme love. Radical love. Scandalous love.

For most, loving others isn't difficult as long as the love is mutual. Loving family and friends and even people with whom we share a common interest is easy. But Jesus' new way of loving includes loving people who aren't like you, who don't like you, and who would even like to do you harm. In fact, Judas—Jesus' betrayer—was in the group whose feet Jesus had just washed. Jesus knew the betrayal was coming, yet he still humbled himself to dignify Judas. That is how radical the love of Jesus really is.

Wise mothers will take these words to heart, teaching their children that love doesn't ask, "What's in it for me?" Genuine love—the new and radical love of Jesus—asks, "Who will love this person if I don't?" For without love there is no hope.

Cozy

He is the lamb who was known long ago before the world existed, but for your good he became publicly known in the last period of time. Through him you believe in God who brought Christ back to life and gave him glory. So your faith and confidence are in God.

Love each other with a warm love that comes from the heart. After all, you have purified yourselves by obeying the truth. As a result you have a sincere love for each other. You have been born again, not from a seed that can be destroyed, but through God's everlasting word that can't be destroyed. That's why Scripture says, "All people are like grass, and all their beauty is like a flower of the field. The grass dries up and the flower drops off, but the word of the Lord lasts forever."

1 Peter 1:20–25 GOD'S WORD

How can a mom inspire her children to love others the way Peter describes in this passage—to love warmly and from the heart—in a world so dominated by hatred and violence?

Peter's instructions in these important verses depend heavily on the context—the return of Jesus: the final state of deliverance, freedom, and joy that is coming to all who are waiting in faith. At that time, all the evil in the world will be wiped out. The point is that those who have put their faith in that promise are empowered to live—and love—as if the deliverance has already come! That is the very expression of faith—a hope that takes hold of what cannot yet be seen.

The key for moms is to help our children adjust their way of seeing. They need to look through the eyes of faith, focusing on what *will* be instead of what currently *is*. It is possible, therefore, to treat an antagonist warmly if you can "see" by faith that the person's deliverance is coming.

Your children will find their place in Christ's mission of deliverance by this very means.

CONVERSATION HEARTS

Listen to the LORD who created you. O Israel, the one who formed you says, "Do not be afraid, for I have ransomed you. I have called you by name; you are mine. When you go through deep waters, I will be with you. When you go through rivers of difficulty, you will not drown. When you walk through the fire of oppression, you will not be burned up; the flames will not consume you. For I am the LORD, your God, the Holy One of Israel, your Savior. I gave Egypt as a ransom for your freedom; . . . because you are precious to me. You are honored, and I love you.

Isaiah 43:1–4 NLT

Isaiah wrote the words of this passage during a very stressful time in Israel. The people had been conquered by foreign powers and taken into captivity because of their unfaithfulness to God. Knowing about their betrayal only adds deeper significance to God's tender words of promise—the promise to restore his people in spite of their unfaithfulness. Our God has relentless mercy and scandalous grace. When most would give up and pull out, God steps in and reminds his wayward people that he hasn't given up on them, nor will he—ever.

There is a crucial principle of parenting in this passage. Children manage to do all sorts of disappointing things—acts that demand a disciplinary response. God's faithfulness in the midst of his own disappointment teaches us not to throw in the towel, not to despair in the face of disheartening behavior. In fact, quite the opposite—in the throes of discipline, it is important for our children to hear us reinstate our love, aspirations, and respect for them. As they realize our love is secure, our children find strength to grasp hold of that love and make the necessary changes in their lives.

ENDURING LOVE

From far away the LORD appeared to his people and said, "I love you people with a love that will last forever. That is why I have continued showing you kindness. People of Israel, I will build you up again, and you will be rebuilt. You will pick up your tambourines again and dance with those who are joyful. You will plant vineyards again on the hills around Samaria. The farmers will plant them and enjoy their fruit. There will be a time when watchmen in the mountains of Ephraim shout this message: 'Come, let's go up to Jerusalem to worship the LORD our God!'"

Jeremiah 31:3–6 NCV

The case for enduring love between a mother and child begins with the evidence of what has already occurred in your life together, continues through the sometimes perilous present, and ends with a promising perspective on what lies ahead. This was how God presented his unfailing love to the children of Israel after a season of necessary discipline. Expressions of enduring love are most needed in times of uncertainty. Children cry out for reassurance, acting out their insecurities in interesting—and oftentimes unpleasant—ways. Fortunately, the fodder for your reassuring expressions of love is close at hand because you share not only your history but also a common vision for the future.

As God's words reaffirmed Israel with hope for the future, you can speak powerfully into your child's heart by first assuring him of what you have been and will continue to be for him, filling in the blanks with real life examples: "I have always been _____ , and I will always be _____ "; then by giving your child a vision of how he will thrive and prosper in this lifelong relationship—"You have already _____ . You will always _____ !"

THE LOVE THAT MATTERS MOST

God loved the world in this way: He gave His One and Only Son, so that everyone who believes in Him will not perish but have eternal life. For God did not send His Son into the world that He might condemn the world, but that the world might be saved through Him. Anyone who believes in Him is not condemned, but anyone who does not believe is already condemned, because he has not believed in the name of the One and Only Son of God.

This, then, is the judgment: the light has come into the world, and people loved darkness rather than the light because their deeds were evil. . . . But anyone who lives by the truth comes to the light, so that his works may be shown to be accomplished by God.

John 3:16–19, 21 HCSB

The love that matters most is an indiscriminate, self-surrendered kind of love, just like the love God has for the world. In conversation one day, Jesus said that God's parental love encompasses all creation. God's concern for his children—every aspect of our lives—also reaches to embrace the more comprehensive context of our existence—the earth, its environs, its nonhuman inhabitants, and its intrinsic beauty.

Mothers likewise bear the immense responsibility of being concerned for their children in a deeply personal dimension as well as in the broadest spectrum of life. Ours is a self-forgetful and innovative kind of love, seeking the good of our children while teaching them to reach responsibly beyond themselves for the sake of others.

Jesus' words reveal God's brilliant strategy to rescue the world by sending him to restore the original significance of being human . . . truly and compassionately human. Jesus shed light on true humanity by imitating the indiscriminate expression of God's love, completely surrendering to its demands. A mother's love is most powerful when she models a lavish and selfless love, teaching her children how to love others as well.

We will not hide these truths from our children; we will tell the next generation about the glorious deeds of the LORD, about his power and his mighty wonders.

—Psalm 78:4 NLT

Rejoice in the LORD and be
glad, you righteous; sing, all
you who are upright in heart!

—Psalm 32:11 NIV